Touch in Child Counseling and Play Therapy

Touch in Child Counseling and Play Therapy explores the professional and legal boundaries around physical contact in therapy and offers best-practice guidelines from a variety of perspectives. Chapters address issues around appropriate and sensitive therapist-initiated touch, therapeutic approaches that use touch as an intervention in child treatment, and both positive and challenging forms of touch that are initiated by children. In these pages, professionals and students alike will find valuable information on ways to address potential ethical dilemmas including defining boundaries, working with parents and guardians, documentation, consent forms, cultural considerations, countertransference, and much more.

Janet A. Courtney, PhD, LCSW, RPT-S, is founder of FirstPlay® Therapy and an adjunct professor at Barry University School of Social Work in Miami Shores, Florida. She is a TEDx speaker and past president of the Florida Association for Play Therapy. She offers certification training to practitioners in FirstPlay® Infant Massage Storytelling and Kinesthetic Storytelling®.

Robert D. Nolan, PhD, is the former executive director of the Institute for Child and Family Health (ICFH) in Miami, Florida. He was a founding member of the Florida Association for Play Therapy and served as its first president. In 2012, he received the lifetime achievement award from the United Way of Miami-Dade.

Touch in Child Counseling and Play Therapy

An Ethical and Clinical Guide

**Edited by Janet A. Courtney
and Robert D. Nolan**

NEW YORK AND LONDON

First published 2017
by Routledge
711 Third Avenue, New York, NY 10017

and by Routledge
2 Park Square, Milton Park, Abingdon, Oxon, OX14 4RN

Routledge is an imprint of the Taylor & Francis Group, an informa business

© 2017 Janet A. Courtney and Robert D. Nolan

The right of Janet A. Courtney and Robert D. Nolan to be identified as the authors of the editorial material, and of the authors for their individual chapters, has been asserted in accordance with sections 77 and 78 of the Copyright, Designs and Patents Act 1988.

All rights reserved. The purchase of this copyright material confers the right on the purchasing institution to photocopy or download pages which bear the eResources icon and a copyright line at the bottom of the page. No other parts of this book may be reprinted or reproduced or utilized in any form or by any electronic, mechanical, or other means, now known or hereafter invented, including photocopying and recording, or in any information storage or retrieval system, without permission in writing from the publishers.

Trademark notice: Product or corporate names may be trademarks or registered trademarks, and are used only for identification and explanation without intent to infringe.

Library of Congress Cataloging in Publication Data
Names: Courtney, Janet A., editor. | Nolan, Robert D., editor.
Title: Touch in child counseling and play therapy: an ethical and clinical guide/edited by Janet A. Courtney and Robert D. Nolan.
Description: New York, NY: Routledge, 2017. |
Includes bibliographical references and index.
Identifiers: LCCN 2016033790| ISBN 9781138638525 (hardback: alk. paper) | ISBN 9781138638532 (pbk.: alk. paper) | ISBN 9781315628752 (ebook)
Subjects: | MESH: Psychotherapeutic Processes | Touch Perception | Child | Counseling | Play Therapy | Professional-Patient Relations–ethics
Classification: LCC RJ505.P6 | NLM WS 350.2 | DDC 618.92/891653–dc23
LC record available at https://lccn.loc.gov/2016033790

ISBN: 978-1-138-63852-5 (hbk)
ISBN: 978-1-138-63853-2 (pbk)
ISBN: 978-1-315-62875-2 (ebk)

Typeset in Times New Roman
by Deanta Global Publishing Services, Chennai, India

To my precious grandchildren, Sophia, Abigail, and Jacob. For the warmhearted hugs and kisses we share and who make my heart melt at just the word, *Mimi*.

JAC

To my children, Sue and Steve, who make me very proud.

RDN

Contents

List of Illustrations	x
List of Child Studies	xii
List of Vignettes	xiii
About the Editors	xiv
About the Contributors	xvi
Foreword by Eliana Gil	xxi
Preface	xxv
Acknowledgments	xxviii

PART I
Overview and the Ethical Implications of Touch   1

1   **Overview of Touch Related to Professional Ethical and Clinical Practice with Children**   3
JANET A. COURTNEY

2   **Ethical and Risk-Management Issues in the Use of Touch**   18
FREDERIC G. REAMER

PART II
Play Therapy Models That Use Touch as an Intervention   33

3   **The Neurobiology of Touch: Developmental Play Therapy with a Child Diagnosed with Sensory Processing Disorder**   35
LYNN STAMMERS

4   **FirstPlay® Infant Massage Storytelling: Facilitating Corrective Touch Experiences with a Teenage Mother and Her Abused Infant**   48
JANET A. COURTNEY, MEYLEEN VELASQUEZ, AND VIKTORIA BAKAI TOTH

5   **Use of Touch in Theraplay® with ADHD Children in a School Setting**   63
ANGELA F. Y. SIU

6 Touching Autism through DIRFloortime® 76
EVA NOWAKOWSKI-SIMS AND AUDREY GREGAN

PART III
Healing Children Traumatized by Touch 89

7 Healing Touch: Working with Children Impacted by Abuse and Neglect 91
JOANNE WHELLEY, ANDREA RAASCH, AND SHAKTI SUTRIASA

8 Hands Are Not for Hitting: Redefining Touch for Children Exposed to Domestic Violence 106
RACHEL SCHARLEPP AND MELISSA RADEY

9 Ethical Use of Touch and Nurturing-Restraint in Play Therapy with Aggressive Young Children, as Illustrated Through a Reflective Supervision Session 120
ROXANNE GROBBEL, KRISTINA COOKE, AND NORMA BONET

10 Healing Adolescent Trauma: Incorporating Ethical Touch in a Movement and Dance Therapy Group 134
CAROL GOLLY, DANIELA RICCELLI, AND MARK S. SMITH

11 The Emotion of Touch: Healing Reactive Attachment Disorder Through Child-Centered Play Therapy 149
JENN PEREIRA AND SONDRA SMITH-ADCOCK

PART IV
Innovations and the Utilization of Touch with Children 163

12 The Role of Touch in Infant Mental Health: Strengthening the Parent–Infant Bond through Child Parent Psychotherapy 165
MAITE SCHENKER, VERONICA CASTRO, AND MONTSERRAT CASADO-KEHOE

13 The Utilization of Touch and StoryPlay® in Preschool Bereavement Groups 178
AMY DAVIS KING AND DANIELLE WOODS

14 The Ethics of Touch with Canines as Co-Therapist with Children 189
BONNIE MARTIN AND JANUS MONCUR

15 Teaching Positive Touch: A Child-to-Child Massage Model for the Classroom 202
DAVID PALMER AND JEAN BARLOW

PART V
Toward the Development of Core Competencies Supporting the Ethics of Touch in Child Counseling and Play Therapy 215

16 Core Competencies and Recommendations Supporting the Ethics of Touch in Child Counseling and Play Therapy 217
SUSAN W. GRAY, JANET A. COURTNEY, AND ROBERT D. NOLAN

Index 231

Illustrations

Figures

1.1	Mediating factors impacting practitioner-initiated and child-initiated touch	9
2.1	Knowing how to establish clear boundaries	20
2.2	Knowing where to draw the line with regard to use of touch	22
3.1	Caring touch promotes healthy interpersonal relationships	38
3.2	"Thank you very much for all your help and support I had lots of fun in a Rainbow Room I am going to miss you"	45
4.1	FirstPlay® builds secure attachment relationships	49
4.2	Happy baby receiving a massage from Mom	50
4.3	Attuning to the cues of the infant.	52
4.4	Legs: Large branches	57
6.1	Holding the therapist's hand enabled Sean to feel safe exploring his new environment	84
7.1	Example of Space Scotch: A Game of Space and Boundaries	102
8.1	The salience of touch in domestic violence	109
8.2	SUN Parent Directions	114
9.1	The therapist helps the child to regulate by using a nurturing-restraint	125
10.1	The group facilitator is connecting through attuned touch	141
10.2	The group members connect with each other through movement and dance	142
11.1	"The most beautiful things in the world cannot be seen or touched, they are felt with the heart." Antoine de Saint-Exupéry, *The Little Prince*	157
12.1	Loving parent touch enhances secure attachment relationships	168
13.1	Nature representations of "Dead" (left) and "Alive" (right) are shown in this collage	185
14.1	Noodle depicted as sexual predator yet very much loved	197

14.2	Therapy canines Jack and Mack	198
15.1	Children practicing child-to-child massage in the classroom	203
15.2	Children start a day of learning with a hand massage	206
15.3	A classroom sharing structured touch activities	210
16.1	The interrelated systems affecting the child	218
16.2	Psychological processes at work in the child's relationships when touch occurs	219

Tables

16.1	Suggested activities to support learning and practice in Touch Competency 1	220
16.2	Suggested activities to support learning and practice in Touch Competency 2	221
16.3	Suggested activities to support learning and practice in Touch Competency 3	222
16.4	Suggested activities to support learning and practice in Touch Competency 4	224
16.5	Suggested activities to support learning and practice in Touch Competency 5	225
16.6	Recommendations supporting the ethics of touch in child counseling and play therapy	227

Child Studies

Chapter 3
Case of Rahim — 42

Chapter 4
Case of Ashley and Her Children — 55

Chapter 5
Case of Andy — 68

Chapter 6
Case of Sean — 81

Chapter 7
Case of John — 99

Chapter 8
Case of Mama P. and Sally — 110

Chapter 9
Case of Amy and Michael — 125

Chapter 10
Movement and Dance Therapy Group Session Example — 139

Chapter 11
Case of Lela — 152

Chapter 12
Case of Rebecca and Katrina — 170

Chapter 13
Case of Suzie — 183
Case of John — 184

Vignettes

Chapter 1

Vignette A: Case of Mary	13
Vignette B: Case of Dillon	13

Chapter 7

Vignette A: Case of Mary	93
Vignette B: Case of Natasha	94
Vignette C: Case of Sarah	96
Vignette D: Case of Brendan	97

Chapter 14

Vignette A: Case of Sally	194
Vignette B: Case of Cara	194
Vignette C: Case of Ben	196
Vignette D: Case of Julie	197

Chapter 15

Vignette A: Case of Jeremy	211
Vignette B: Case of Michael	211

About the Editors

Janet A. Courtney, PhD, LCSW, RPT-S, is founder of FirstPlay® Therapy and an adjunct professor at Barry University School of Social Work, Miami Shores, FL. She is a Registered Play Therapy-Supervisor, TEDx speaker, and a StoryPlay® facilitator. She is past president of the Florida Association for Play Therapy, Chair of the Viola Brody Award Committee, and a member of the Association for Play Therapy Ethics Committee. Dr. Courtney's research into practitioner experiences of training in touch and Developmental Play Therapy is published in the *American Journal of Art Therapy* and the *International Journal of Play Therapy*, and she is a contributing author for the chapter, "Touching Autism through Developmental Play Therapy," in the book, *Play-based Interventions for Children and Adolescents with Autism Spectrum Disorders* (2012, New York: Routledge). She offers a certification in FirstPlay® Therapy (including FirstPlay® Infant Massage Storytelling) and provides training to professionals in the Ethical and Clinical Competencies of Touch, StoryPlay®, Expressive Therapies, and Ecopsychology Play Therapy. She has been invited to speak nationally and internationally including in the Cayman Islands, England, Ireland, Morocco, Russia, and Ukraine. She is a provider through the Florida state boards of Mental Health and Massage Therapy, and an approved provider through the Association for Play Therapy. She specializes in infant mental health, attachment, and trauma-related issues. Dr. Courtney's new form of Kinesthetic Storytelling® can be found in her children's book, *The Magic Rainbow Hug*. Her website is www.FirstPlayTherapy.com

Robert D. Nolan, PhD, was chief psychologist and later executive director of the Institute for Child and Family Health (ICFH), Miami, Florida for more than 50 years, while also maintaining a private practice. He obtained a PhD in psychology from Florida State University, completing his post-doctoral training in child psychology from Judge Baker Children's Center, a Harvard Medical School affiliate. He was a founding member of the Florida Association for Play Therapy (FAPT), and served as its first president, and also served as president of the Florida State Board of Examiners in Psychology. He played a significant role in helping to shape policies pertaining to children's mental health in

Florida at both the state and local level. In 2012, he was awarded the Lifetime Achievement Award through the United Way of Miami-Dade, and, in 2011, he was awarded the David Lawrence Champion of Children's Award through the Children's Trust of Miami-Dade. He has served as an adjunct professor at the University of Miami School of Medicine in the Department of Psychiatry, and in the schools of psychology at Nova Southeastern University and Florida International University. He is constantly looking for healthy, natural ways to benefit children, and is an advocate of yoga and meditation to help children reduce stress and achieve focus. He has provided agency consultations and workshop presentations nationally and internationally including in the Cayman Islands, China, Morocco, Kenya, and England.

About the Contributors

Jean Barlow, BPhil (Education), (Special Education: Emotional and Behaviour Difficulties) University of Birmingham, UK, is founder of a Child2Child Kind and Caring Hands program in the United Kingdom, an international program that teaches a positive touch curriculum to promote healthy peer relationships within schools.

Website: achild2child.co.uk.

Norma Bonet, LCSW, RPT-S, is a clinical manager and supervisor at Family Central in Broward, Florida, and is president of the Florida Association for Play Therapy. She is a state of Florida qualified supervisor to both social work and mental health.

Montserrat Casado-Kehoe, PhD, EdS, MA, RPT-S, is a full Professor of Counseling at Palm Beach Atlantic University, Orlando, Florida, a Licensed Marriage and Family Therapist, and Registered Play Therapist. She trained in Eye Movement Desensitization Reprocessing, and Accelerated Resolution Therapy. She is also a Trust Based Relational Intervention Practitioner and Educator.

Veronica Castro, PsyD, is a clinical supervisor and grant clinician at the Institute for Child and Family Health. She received her PsyD in Clinical Psychology from NOVA Southeastern University at Davie, Florida.

Kristina Cooke, LCSW, RPT-S, Infant Mental Health Specialist, has a private practice, Kids First, Inc., in Marietta, Georgia, where she specializes in working with young children and families. She also offers training and supervision in play therapy.

Carol Golly, LCSW, RPT-S, is a PhD candidate at Barry University School of Social Work in Miami, Florida, and is a Registered Play Therapist Supervisor. Carol's private practice, Naples Center for Child and Family Therapy, is located in Naples, Florida.

Website: carolgolly.com.

About the Contributors xvii

Susan W. Gray, PhD, EdD, Professor Emerita, Barry University School of Social Work, taught masters and doctoral program courses. She served as director of the Doctoral Program and spearheaded a revision of its curriculum. Her numerous publications include articles on touch and the well-received book, *Psychopathology: A Competency-Based Assessment Model for Social Workers*. Dr. Gray was the 2015 recipient of the National Association of Social Workers Lifetime Achievement Award.

Audrey Gregan, Dip Ed Froebel, Dip Special Education, is director of the Garden Play Therapy Centre in Dublin, Ireland. She is a certified Play Therapist/Child Psychotherapist, and a practitioner of DIRFloortime®. She is a member of the British Association of Play Therapy, and the Irish Association of Play Therapists.

Website: thegardenplaytherapy.ie.

Roxanne Grobbel, JD, LCSW, is an Adjunct Professor at Florida Atlantic University and is director of Insight Counseling and Education in Boca Raton, Florida. She has focused her career on trauma-informed care as a Registered Play Therapy Supervisor, Infant Mental Health Specialist, and approved Eye Movement Desensitization Reprocessing consultant and trainer.

Website: insightcounselingandeducation.com.

Amy Davis King, MA, LMFT, certified StoryPlay® practitioner and facilitator, has a private marriage and family therapy practice in Scottsdale, Arizona, working with children and families and specializing in grief and loss issues, and in bereavement groups for children and hospice.

Bonnie Martin, LCSW, RPT-S, specializes in working with children at Lifespan Services, Inc., a group outpatient social services practice, since 1989. She is a Registered Play Therapist Supervisor with more than a decade working with a canine as co-therapist in play therapy with children.

Janus Moncur, LCSW, is owner of Co-Creative Coaching and Counseling, and is a Certified Human Animal Intervention Specialist (CHAIS). She is trained in Eye Movement Desensitization Reprocessing, and Animal-Assisted Therapy. She and her co-therapist canine, Mack, work together as a crisis response team and instructor for National Crisis Response Canines.

Website: janusmoncur.com.

Eva Nowakowski-Sims, PhD, is an Assistant Professor in the School of Social Work at Barry University. She teaches research and human behavior courses in the Bachelor of Social Work and Master of Social Work programs, and Qualitative Inquiry in the PhD program. Her professional and research interests include working with families, assessment, and program evaluation.

David Palmer, CMT, is the founder and director of TouchPro International, which was established in 1986 to introduce the benefits of positive touch through seated massage. He developed the first professional massage chair and a training program for practitioners that has resulted in hundreds of thousands of jobs and millions of massages.

Website: touchpro.com.

Jenn Pereira, PhD, RPT-S, is an Assistant Professor at Arizona State University in the Department of Counseling Psychology and has a PhD in Counseling and Counselor Education from the University of Florida. She is a Licensed Mental Health Counselor, Registered Play Therapist/Supervisor, and Clinical Traumatologist.

Andrea Raasch, LCSW, serves as the Florida State clinical coordinator for Sexual Abuse Treatment Programs through Florida Department of Health Children's Medical Services, where she provides consultation, training, and on-site monitoring to enhance sexual abuse therapy services.

Melissa Radey, MSSW, PhD, is an Associate Professor in the College of Social Work at Florida State University, Tallahassee. Her research examines the intersection of vulnerabilities for low-income, single mothers with weak social support networks, and she is the co-principal investigator for the Florida Study of Professionals for Safe Families.

Frederic G. Reamer, PhD, is Professor in the graduate program of the School of Social Work, Rhode Island College. His recent books include *Risk Management in Social Work: Preventing Professional Malpractice, Liability, and Disciplinary Action*; *Boundary Issues and Dual Relationships in the Human Services*; *Social Work Values and Ethics*; and *Ethical Standards in Social Work*.

Daniela Riccelli, LCSW, CAP, is founder of Startliving Recovery in North Palm Beach, Florida. She is an Adjunct Professor at Barry University, Miami Shores, Florida, and is a board member of the International Association of Social Work with Groups.

Website: startlivingpllc.com.

Rachel Scharlepp, LCSW, RPT-S, is a PhD candidate at Florida State University in the school of counseling and educational psychology. She is clinical director of PlayBig Therapy, a multispecialty center focused on assessing and treating issues associated with trauma, adoption, autism, and behavioral health disorders.

Website: playbigtherapy.com.

Maite Schenker, PhD, is director of Early Childhood Services at the Institute for Child and Family Health. Her PhD in Clinical Psychology is from the University of North Carolina at Greensboro, and she is a member of the

Florida Association for Infant Mental Health and a former co-chair of the Miami Chapter.

Angela F. Y. Siu, PhD, RCP, RPT-S, CPT-S, CTT/T, is an Associate Professor at the Chinese University in Hong Kong, in the Department of Psychology. She is a certified Theraplay® Therapist Trainer, a certified Filial Therapist/Instructor, and a Registered Play Therapy Supervisor with the Association for Play Therapy.

Sondra Smith-Adcock, PhD, is an Assistant Professor at the University of Florida College of Education, Gainesville, Florida, and earned her PhD in Counseling and Counselor Education from the University of North Carolina at Greensboro. She has authored more than 40 publications on counseling-related topics.

Mark S. Smith, PhD, is an Associate Professor at Barry University, Miami Shores, Florida. His MSW is from San Francisco State University. Areas of interest and expertise include trauma-informed and resiliency-focused clinical practice, groups, families, LGBTQ youth and adults, and anti-racist/anti-oppressive social work pedagogy.

Lynn Stammers, MA, is a PhD candidate at the University of Sheffield, UK. She has a Bachelor's degree in Applied Psychology and a Master's degree in Special Education from the University of Leeds, UK. Lynn is founder and director of Dragon Academy in West Yorkshire, England.

Website: dragonacademy.org.uk.

Shakti Sutriasa, LCSW, holds an MA in Education from Michigan State University, an MSW from Barry University and a BA from Boston University. She is an author and runs Decide Differently, a coaching/counseling practice. She spent two decades in education and worked in mental health and hospice.

Viktoria Bakai Toth, LMHC, RPT, is a certified FirstPlay® Therapy assistant instructor, and is a contracted therapist at the Jewish Family and Children's Service of the Suncoast, in Venice, Florida. She has a private psychotherapy practice, providing counseling service and free workshops on mental health related issues.

Website: viktoriabtoth.com.

Meyleen Velasquez, LCSW, RPT-S is Registered Play Therapist Supervisor, certified FirstPlay® Therapy assistant instructor, and Infant Mental Health Specialist. She is currently in a private psychotherapy practice working with individuals, children, and families in Miami, Florida.

Email: meyleen@gmail.com.

Joanne Whelley, PhD, is a Professor at Barry University School of Social Work, Miami, Florida, and was on the faculty of Marywood University School of Social Work. She is a member of Council on Social Work Education's Council on Practice Methods and Specializations, chair of the Values and Ethic track for Council on Social Work Education Annual Program Meeting, and the Advanced Social Work Practice in Trauma.

Danielle Woods, MC, LPC, LISAC, is a StoryPlay® facilitator and director of Faith Works, LLC in Scottsdale, Arizona, where she provides psychotherapy services for children and adults. She is a member of the Association for Play Therapy, Eye Movement Desensitization Reprocessing International Association, and the Arizona Children's Services Network.

Foreword

Eliana Gil

What an honor to be asked by Drs. Courtney and Nolan to write the Foreword to the book they have authored on a highly important topic: the use of touch in psychotherapy. The book is thought-provoking and packed with fascinating ideas and discussions. I found it inspired and inspiring and I don't think it can be reviewed without having a profound effect on the reader. It caused me, in particular, to immediately remember two experiences I had as a graduate student:

Claire was a seven-year-old child who had been exposed to five long years of dramatic and extreme domestic violence—in fact, her mother was finally killed by her relentlessly violent husband. Claire herself was quite paradoxical: Shy, compliant, and soft-spoken at times, and other times impulsive, intense, and physically aggressive in very destructive ways. This child had never been hit directly by her father, but she had witnessed his brutality and his combustible temperament. (Yes, domestic violence is traumatic whether experienced or witnessed.) Later in therapy this little girl was able to tell me that she never felt safe, or like a normal kid. She said she always slept with one eye open, just in case her mother needed her. She specified that when her mother was killed, father had stuffed a towel in mother's mouth so that she couldn't yell. Claire felt guilty to this day that she had not been awake to "save her mother."

I was assigned to work with this child in individual therapy and another therapist worked with the child and her foster parents. The story that came into my mind as I read this book was when the other students and I were watching a family therapy session (with Claire, her foster mother, and their family therapist) through a one-way mirror. My client was behaving very differently than she behaved with me and the focus of the session was the foster mother providing a litany of "bad behaviors" in Claire. I remember feeling bad for Claire, especially because I could see the look of disappointment, frustration, and embarrassment on her face. To me it was bad enough that the foster parent only focused on negative behaviors and the family therapist could not get a word in edgewise, but to add to Claire's humiliation the foster mother was going on and on in front of a group of strangers who were watching through the window. I remember wishing I could go in the room and take Claire with me somewhere more kind and accepting of her. But I was there as a young student and hadn't yet learned to trust my clinical intuition. The therapy session went from bad to worse as Claire refused to answer a barrage of questions about "why" she was acting in such an uncooperative way. Finally, Claire went over and slapped her foster mother and kicked the therapist in the legs!

Everyone behind the one-way mirror, including my teacher, burst into laughter and continued to laugh for what seemed like a very long time. I just had eyes for my colleague, the family therapist, who seemed uncertain and scared, and kept looking to the mirror for some kind of guidance. None was available.

The session came to an end shortly after Claire became violent, and when we all processed the session, I was amazed at everyone's reluctance to step in with a clear directive that violence was not acceptable. I offered a few words, with great hesitation since I felt in the minority, but no one listened and the teaching (and learning) moment passed.

The other case was of a youngster, Ken, who had been neglected and deprived of attention, affection, or consistent care. He had non-organic failure to thrive and he looked fragile and full of fear. His most common stance was to withdraw from human interactions. It was so hard for me to know what to do. I didn't want to scare him by approaching too quickly but I felt that the work ahead was about Ken having a reparative experience guided by me. I had very little guidance on this case because my supervisor didn't work with children, so I relied heavily on the tenets of Child-Centered Play Therapy.

About nine months later, my supervisor asked why I had not terminated the case. I was in an agency where it was not customary to see children long-term. I told her that Ken was making great progress. When she asked for a specific example of progress (she stated she had not seen any signs in my progress notes, not quite understanding or valuing play therapy), I told her that, in the last month, he had started climbing into my lap for a few moments, seemingly to check out if proximity was safe. He had also started bringing a little blanket with him and pretending to sleep, waking up suddenly and going to play with something else.

My supervisor was stern and clear. I was to stop allowing the child to crawl into my lap immediately, and I was to discourage his attachment to me. She told me that I had one more month with him and after that, his treatment would be terminated. I cannot tell you how ecstatic I was when this supervisor was promoted and transferred to another department quite quickly, and I was able to see Ken for another six months before termination of treatment was again forced. During our sessions, Ken became more and more comfortable with proximity, with safety, and began to trust. He would often ask for a hug "hello" and "goodbye" and I reciprocated. In an act of secret defiance, I kept allowing him to crawl in my lap, and sometimes rocked him in place and sang a song to him. (I did not put that in my progress notes!)

Luckily, he had a wonderful foster parent who eventually adopted him. I insisted on some play sessions between Ken and his foster mother, trusting my instincts that dyadic work was also necessary even if I didn't have appropriate supervision. To be fair, I had some absolutely priceless (substantive, inspiring) supervision experiences as well. These two experiences just came to mind in reading this book.

The issue of touch in psychotherapy has been widely discussed among mental health professionals for years, and the polarization of yesteryear appears to be relaxing with some of the emerging research on child development, attachment, and neuroscience that emphasizes the potential benefits and necessity of using appropriate touch in clinical work with children (and their families). As I read assertions about the resistance to using clinical touch in psychotherapy, I envision that much individual and collective work remains to be done. Nonetheless, this book is a wonderful compilation of valuable and much-needed scientific and clinical data.

This book identifies why the clinical use of touch has been viewed as complex, and at the same time provides clear direction for how to begin to make individual and collective (policy) changes that ensure child clients receive optimal care and encounter attachment opportunities necessary for developing self-esteem and self-efficacy, and crafting skilled social interactions even when their past experiences have been impoverished, violent, or lacking in empathy and physical affection.

Each chapter in this book is unique and each author, armed with a solid foundation in child development, neuroscience, and attachment theory, outlines truly remarkable approaches that come to life in the clinical case examples. To me, when I can read about clinical perceptions of a topic, and then "see" how that perception leads to specific clinical behaviors that inform and promote specific goals, I know that I have a book I can learn from, and indeed I did. The chapters are full of innovative ideas about how to promote safe and appropriate touch with children and youth, and the creativity of approach is congruent with the depth and foundation of theories. There is a consistent tapestry of interwoven theories and approaches that make this book a stand-out. The recognition that there are multiple ways of working that can be effective and valuable—as long as there is a strong grounding in theory, research, and clinical experience—is quite refreshing, and many of the discussions and interventions lend themselves to clinical creativity by example.

It's impossible for me to pick out a favorite chapter, and maybe that's not even an appropriate exercise, because they are so diverse. I do recognize that the authors are uniquely suited to offer their guidance since they have focused on the topic of the clinical applications of touch for decades. The chapters are thus credible, inventive, and accessible to the reader. There is a discussion of some of the well-known play therapy models of Developmental Play Therapy (Brody) and Theraplay® (Booth & Jernberg), as well as some new and exciting approaches (FirstPlay® Infant Massage Storytelling, StoryPlay®, Child-2-Child Kind and Caring Hands), and the proficient integration of touch with DIRFloortime®, dance and movement therapy, Child–Parent Psychotherapy, and Animal-Assisted Therapy. These approaches are demonstrated with children with Reactive Attachment Disorder, witnesses of domestic violence, and abused children, to name a few. The persistent question of whether the therapist or the parent provides touch is also examined, and the specifics of "how" and "when" are also deliberated, making this a usable treatise on the subject. The topic of trauma and its impact is also woven throughout this text, as well as the research findings that currently guide trauma-informed practice.

Too often we hear about boundaries in reference to touching that should *not* occur. This book offers a new perspective, and that is: teaching children about appropriate touch in as many ways as possible, even including another original school-based program in which children provide gentle massage to each other! Imagine that—calming touch incorporated into the classroom. Ah, hope springs eternal! One interesting chapter also addresses the issue of restraint and the authors suggest that nurturing restraint is an appropriate and overlooked intervention when working with aggressive children.

As many of you know, my professional career concentrated on working with physically and sexually traumatized children, as well as those traumatized by chronic neglect. The discussion about touching abused kids (especially in the context of cultural, age, and gender differences) has been persistent and fraught with polarized emotions. I recently did a workshop at the International Theraplay® conference where the topic was touching sexually abused children. Obviously, there is a lot to consider and clinical touch must be, as stipulated in the book, carefully integrated into treatment. However, the book asserts the many benefits of clinical touch that is respectful, that prioritizes children's full consent, and that is attuned to the distinctive needs of each child and parent. This book provides clinical guidance by articulating core competencies for clinicians and offering comprehensive, simple, and clear recommendations for developing a well-informed approach to clinical touch. Needless to say, countertransference and person-of-the-therapist issues are handled with sensitivity and insight. The subject of ethics is also discoursed and incorporated into most of the chapters.

By the end, the reader is fully satisfied and inspired to embrace the possibilities of clinical touch more fully. In fact, a roadmap becomes more clear about the level of preparation a clinician must undertake in order to provide harmonious and trustworthy touch that optimizes global assistance to children's growth and development, possibly altering negative world views, biological and brain reactions, and casting the potential of rewarding relationships in a novel, necessary way. This book is critical in psychotherapist development, both for new clinicians facing these issues under supervision, and for veterans who have witnessed the polarization of this issue for years. Bravo to Drs. Courtney and Nolan for bringing this critical issue, central in their professional lives, to an audience eager for insight and guidance.

Preface

Touch is a natural and essential component of human growth and development. In fact, without sufficient amounts of nurturing touch, even if our basic needs such as food and hygiene are met, we will not thrive and may even die. Practitioners who provide counseling services to children are often presented with a multitude of situations that may involve some form of touch, from a child spontaneously hugging the therapist, to a therapist reaching out to hold a crying child's hand, to the dilemma of a child inappropriately touching a therapist. However, the topic of touch with children in therapy has seldom been addressed in the literature, with the vast majority of the literature focused primarily on adult client populations—a repeated observation stressed by the chapter authors. Moreover, the multifaceted issues surrounding touch in practice with children are arguably far more complicated (and also very different) than factors related to touch with adults. Unfortunately, there are few ethical and clinical practice guidelines, research studies, clinical case examples, competency standards, or resources available that can help guide practitioners in this regard. This may leave some practitioners—student interns and those new to the field—feeling unprepared and uncertain about how to handle challenging situations that may arise in child therapy sessions.

The purpose of this book, therefore, endeavors to address that gap in the literature to provide students, supervisors, graduate and undergraduate university professors, marriage and family counselors, mental health counselors, psychologists, child psychiatrists, expressive arts therapists, child welfare social workers, play therapists, school counselors *and* teachers, agency and school administrators, pediatricians, pediatric nurses, occupational therapists, and other professionals who work with children a resource specifically targeted to address treatment and ethical considerations related to child practice. The case examples and vignettes throughout this book represent a range of childhood developmental stages from infancy to adolescents and a diversity of therapy settings, theoretical approaches, and child problems—accordingly, all case identifying information has been changed to protect confidentiality. The clinical case studies provide a beginning foundation of qualitative research and a springboard for further examination of the mediating factors that influence non-erotic physical contact within therapy sessions. As such, all of the chapter authors have applied their own ethical and clinical perspectives regarding touch in practice with children based upon a compilation of expertise in the realms of: (a) child development and welfare; (b) years of clinical practice experience in child counseling and play therapy; (c) teaching graduate and undergraduate level curriculums related to children in marriage and family, social work, play therapy, psychology, and school counseling; (d) providing supervision in multidisciplinary settings; and (e) extensive research of the literature and other resources on the subject of touch.

The book is divided into five parts. Part I is titled "Overview and the Ethical Implications of Touch." The first chapter (Janet A. Courtney) provides a broad overview of the topic of touch related to children in clinical practice and sets the stage for the chapters that follow. The ethical and risk management considerations related to touch are examined in Chapter 2 (Frederic G. Reamer).

Part II, titled "Play Therapy Models that Use Touch as an Intervention," provides four different play therapy models demonstrating how touch has been successfully utilized to enhance attachment relationships, including Developmental Play Therapy in Chapter 3 (Lynn Stammers). Note, this chapter also provides a comprehensive discussion on the neurobiology of touch. Chapters 4, 5, and 6 include FirstPlay® Therapy—a parent–infant massage and storytelling program (Janet A. Courtney, Meyleen Velasquez, and Viktoria Bakai Toth); Theraplay®—including a discussion on ADHD (Angela F. Y. Siu); and DIRFloortime®, treating children diagnosed with autism (Eva Nowakowski-Sims and Audrey Gregan).

Part III, titled "Healing Children Traumatized by Touch," describes child counseling and play therapy treatment methods that help children who have experienced some type of trauma in their lives related to touch, including children harmed through physical or sexual abuse or neglect, discussed in Chapter 7 (Joanne Whelley, Andrea Raasch, and Shakti Sutriasa); children traumatized through domestic violence in Chapter 8 (Rachel Scharlepp and Melissa Radey); child aggression toward the therapist and a nurturing restraint protocol is presented in Chapter 9 (Roxanne Grobbel, Kristina Cooke, and Norma Bonet); traumatized adolescents and a group dance/movement intervention is presented in Chapter 10 (Carol Golly, Daniela Riccelli, and Mark S. Smith); and Reactive Attachment Disorder and Child-Centered Play Therapy are addressed in Chapter 11 (Jenn Pereira and Sondra Smith-Adcock).

Part IV, titled "Innovations and the Utilization of Touch with Children," provides interventions that utilize touch as a responsive measure to the child's needs in therapy, as well as innovative models related to touch. Chapter 12 (Maite Schenker, Veronica Castro, and Montserrat Casado-Kehoe) discusses how touch is utilized in Infant Mental Health treatment with parents; Chapter 13 (Amy Davis King and Danielle Woods) demonstrates how touch was utilized within a StoryPlay® based children's grief support group; Chapter 14 (Bonnie Martin and Janus Moncur) discusses how touch is facilitated in canine-assisted therapy with children; and Chapter 15 (David Palmer and Jean Barlow) presents a novel school-based peer-to-peer touch-focused program that strengthens peer relationships.

The final chapter of the book (Susan W. Gray, Janet A. Courtney, and Robert D. Nolan) comprises Part V, titled "Toward the Development of Core Competencies Supporting the Ethics of Touch in Child Counseling and Play Therapy." This chapter proposes recommendations toward the development of five clinical competencies in touch, as well as a summary of recommendations supporting the ethics of touch in child counseling and play therapy.

As you read through this book, note that the authors have shared their expertise and experiences with a deep respect for the sensitive, and sometimes controversial, perceptions pertaining to touch in therapy with children. In doing so, they have dedicated many hours of thoughtful reflection—mulling over the multifaceted clinical and ethical challenges that impact this topic, exploring the neurobiology of touch, taking risks of vulnerability in presenting their case examples, seeking consultations from peers, and thinking out of the box to offer some new ethical and practice standard recommendations—all this in hope to promote emotionally healthy interpersonal touch awareness for the children and families that we work with. And to that end, we, the editors of this book, "take our hats off to them" for committing themselves in service of the topics presented.

Janet A. Courtney, PhD
Robert D. Nolan, PhD

Acknowledgments

Janet A. Courtney

This book is dedicated, in part, to the late Viola Brody, PhD, author of *The Dialogue of Touch*, who sparked my desire to research and understand more about touch in child therapy and touch experiences of practitioners in training. I cherish her visits to my home to present weekend-long workshops—even at the age of 95. I am especially thankful to Dr. Susan W. Gray, my former Barry University Dissertation Chair, for her unwavering support and the honor of being her co-author on significant publications. I am sincerely grateful to Dr. Nancy Boyd Webb, a valuable member of my dissertation committee, and an inspiring role model to me. I am greatly appreciative to Dr. Phyllis Scott, Dean of the School of Social Work at Barry University, and to *all* the Barry faculty who share my commitment to improving the lives of children. The groundbreaking work of Tiffany Field at the Touch Research Institute, and its training program, enhanced my knowledge and provided the inspiration to write this book. I am thankful to Kathy Lebby, CEO of the Association for Play Therapy (APT), who has supported my research efforts on the topic of touch, and to Dr. Dee Ray, Chair of the APT Research Committee, who provided valuable feedback. And a heart full of gratitude to Dr. Joyce Mills for all her encouragement and for teaching me about the power of *story* in the healing process. A warm hug to Dr. Eliana Gil for all her supportive feedback and care to the outstanding foreword in this book.

To my dear husband, Bob Nolan, my best friend, and co-editor on this book, thank you for sharing this journey—and for reminding me of the importance of balance in my life. I am thankful to my late father, Richard C. Courtney, who instilled my desire to learn, and didn't answer my questions, instead prodding me to "Look it up in the encyclopedia"! Much love to my mother—a natural-born play therapist; my brother, Allen, and sister, Carol; my sons, Jesse and Austin; and daughter-in-law, Stephanie—for their love and support and being my cheerleaders through this process. My deepest heartfelt gratitude to Prem Rawat, founder of the Prem Rawat Foundation, for his vital humanitarian and peace education efforts throughout the world.

I want to thank Anna Moore at Routledge, who immediately recognized the importance of this book, and a huge thank you to Deanta Global's Lara Silva

McDonnell and copy editor, Margaret McDonell, for all their excellent attention to detail and careful editing of this book. To my colleagues and dear friends, too many to mention, I give a heartfelt hug for your support and heartening words. My deep gratitude goes to all the authors of this book who had the resolution and fortitude to address this topic. Finally, I am indebted to all the courageous children and families I have had the honor to work with and who helped grow my understanding about the intricacies and genuine value of caring touch encounters within the therapeutic relationship.

Acknowledgments

Robert D. Nolan

First of all, I want to thank my co-editor, Janet—that bundle of constructive energy who was so determined that our shared vision on the importance of the nature of touch in the lives of children be shared with others in the child mental health field. Thanks also to all of the staff at the Institute for Child and Family Health where I spent 50 years of my life, first as chief of psychology and eventually as executive director, who have dedicated their lives to helping children and who have shared so many incredible stories with me, adding considerably to my education. I also want to recognize and thank those organizations who, through their financial support, contributed to the welfare of many thousands of children. They include the Miami-Dade County Commission, the Florida Department of Children and Families, the Children's Trust, and the United Way of Dade County. A big thanks to Anna Moore at Routledge Publishing who recognized the significance of this subject to the professional community, and to all of the chapter authors who so diligently shared their knowledge and clinical experiences with all of us in the wonderful adventure of working with children. Most of all I want to express my love and appreciation to the many children who contributed immeasurably to my understanding of the healing process and the essential value of touch as an important and sometimes critical element of that process.

Part I
Overview and the Ethical Implications of Touch

1 Overview of Touch Related to Professional Ethical and Clinical Practice with Children

Janet A. Courtney

> The healing capacity of touch has been latent in our species all along, awaiting only the right culture and intellectual climate.
> Renée Weber, PhD, "A Philosophical Perspective on Touch"

- A young boy you are meeting for the first therapy session runs toward you and wraps his arms around your waist giving you a hug. How do you respond?
- In later stages of therapy, a therapist reaches out and touches a child's hand when she begins to cry. How do you think the child might respond?
- A school-aged girl wants to sit in your lap as you read a story. Do you let her?
- A young boy who was sexually abused abruptly grabs the breast of his female therapist. How should she respond?

The Professional Context of the Problem of Touch Related to Children

Child counselors and play therapists are challenged daily with ethical and clinical decisions related to touch, such as the ones listed above. Knowing how to best respond or intervene is not easy. What adds to the difficulty is that the topic of touch with children has seldom been addressed in the literature and there are few best-practice guidelines or competency standards available for handling touch-related boundary dilemmas. Lynch & Garrett (2010) advised that touch in practice with children appears to "occupy an unsure space and has tended to remain an ambiguous area for many" (p. 393). As well, many practitioners are understandably concerned about professional liability regarding touch issues that arise in sessions. In fact, the quandary about touch and children is not limited to the psychological field but is relevant for teachers in the classroom, medical personnel, religious institutions, and to the general consciousness of our society (Carlson, 2006; Field, 2014).

Prior to the 1980s there was only moderate concern over the issue of touching children within our schools and mental health systems—in fact, touch as treatment with children and families was promulgated, for example, Virginia Satir (Haber, 2002). However, the pendulum swung swiftly during the eighties as high-profile child sexual abuse cases came to the forefront (Carlson, 2006). The sobering reality of abuse by those who were placed in trusted positions to care for children had an enormous impact on policy changes that reverberated through many different institutions and systems that involved children. The vital need to create policies to protect children from abuse resulted in new and more rigorous procedures including the implementation of "no-touch" rules by many school systems and agencies; stricter hiring standards and background checks; increased education about the signs and symptoms of abuse; increased reporting mandates of suspected abuse; and more child-oriented programs that taught children about body ownership and appropriate and inappropriate touch (Carlson, 2006; NASW, 2012). However, as Carlson (2006) stated, "No-touch rules, however, do little to solve the larger society-wide problem of sexual abuse of children" (p. 61).

Some professionals have advocated that the unintended effect of no-touch policies has resulted in a negative impact on children as a consequence of caregivers withholding affection and nurturing necessary to the basic needs of young children (Brody, 1997; Carlson, 2006; Field, 2014). McNeil-Haber (2004) cautioned that no-touch policies with young children could have a "detrimental affect on the therapeutic process" and further reminded that children "may have difficulty understanding that a no-touch policy is not about their personal relationship with the therapist" (p. 132). In view of that, Field (2003) raised the question: "Can you imagine a therapist counseling a hospice patient without being able to touch him or her?" (p. 4).

Nonetheless, the apprehension related to touch with children (and the potential consequences associated with it) has infused itself into the therapy playroom—as well as other settings such as client's homes, schools, hospitals, and even therapy held in outdoor environments. When this author has spoken to mental health professionals about their perspectives on touch in therapy, they often provided a brief case description where touch generated a pivotal point of positive change for a child in therapy. However, these conversations are quickly trailed by a cautionary look and statement of concern. Many clinicians fear the potential of being falsely accused of inappropriately touching a child. Consequently, they may try to remove any such predicament by refraining from touch (McNeil-Haber, 2004; Zur & Nordmarken, 2016)—even when they may consider it to be therapeutically appropriate. This could be especially true for male therapists who, much like male teachers (Cushman, 2009), may feel uncomfortable with touch when working with young children, or who may feel they are at a higher risk for allegations.

Clinicians train for many years to obtain their hard-earned credentials and the risk of a potential lawsuit due to a false allegation is a reality, albeit a rare one (Zur & Nordmarken, 2016). What compounds these trepidations is that touch is highly inevitable in a playroom environment (Courtney & Siu, 2017). Meaning: intended or not, touch can happen—whether it's a child tapping a therapist on the shoulder, or hands touch while passing a crayon—touch happens! The wide range of dynamics of touch in providing counseling services to children are complicated, and policies, laws, regulations, and guidelines *are* needed to protect children from abuse (see Association for Play Therapy, 2015). Beyond that, the question arises: How best can practitioners walk the tightrope between providing child clients with attuned, empathetic, and responsive touch, and the same time protect themselves from a professional liability standpoint, while also proficiently managing the myriad of instances when touch happens—including acts of physical aggression by a child? It is these considerations and others that this book will be addressing.

Historical Context of Touch

Although touch has been used as a healing art since ancient times, attention to the topic historically is scant, as Weber noted, "touch as an interactional modality has been neglected" (1990, p. 13). In China around 2760 BCE, healing touch was described in an acupuncture manuscript, and around 400 BCE the Greek physician, Hippocrates advocated that a physician must be skilled in *rubbing* the body for health. And Greek philosopher Aristotle, who lived between 384–322 BCE, in trying to figure out exactly what *organ* touch is related to (such as the organ of seeing is the eyes), finally surmised that it must be the *heart* and that touch is so crucial to living that, "its absence spells doom to man and all animals" (as summarized by Weber, 1990, p. 18).

In the New Testament people wanted to be close to Jesus because they were miraculously healed through his touch. Many religions heal through laying-on-of-hands while Buddhist monks are often trained in the healing touch therapy, Reiki, founded in the 1800s. For centuries, we have known that children will not thrive, or may even die, without caring touch. In the thirteenth century the Holy Roman Emperor Fredrick II wanted to see if children would develop a natural language without human interaction. Fifty children were taken from their mothers and given to foster mothers who were instructed not to speak to or engage with the children, just to feed and bathe them. All the children died because they could not live without the "clapping of hands, and gestures, and gladness of countenance, and blandishments" (Davidson, 2011, p. 50).

The *Feeling* Dialogue of Touch

Montagu (1986, p. 128) informed us that the word "touch" is derived from the Old French word *touche*, of which the definition included the act of feeling something—the emphasis being on the operative word "feeling." Thus touch, as Montagu enlightened us, was originally connected to emotion and we use the word touch in our common daily usage to denote different types of feeling states such as "That really *touched* my heart," or "She is so *touchy*." Fascinatingly, emerging research may support the notion that certain kinds of light touch may indeed be connected to emotion and may also play a part in attachment and bonding. Denworth (2015) advised, "This newly recognized system, known as affective or emotional touch, consists of nerve fibers triggered by exactly the kind of loving caress a mother gives to a child" (p. 32). Touch, therefore, is a powerful form of emotional communication and, unlike the other sensory systems, it is inherently reciprocal. Weber (1990) distinguished between them thus: "I can see but not be seen, and hear without being heard, but I cannot touch without being touched" (p. 24).

A very intriguing and moving conversation highlighting the reciprocity of touch took place between play therapy pioneers Gary Landreth and Viola Brody, when Dr. Landreth interviewed Dr. Brody about the role of touch in therapy with children in Developmental Play Therapy—a touch-based model of play therapy (see Center for Play Therapy, 1995, for the interview). In order to demonstrate the impact of touch in the therapeutic relationship, Dr. Brody initiated a sustained hand-holding experience with Dr. Landreth and asked him to comment on what he experienced. She listened as he stated that he could feel warmth and strength emanating from her, but she was also interested in what he felt and experienced for himself, with the emphasis on the touch-dialogue that was happening between them. The intention of the exercise being: what do children experience, assimilate, learn, and *feel* for themselves when touched in a caring way by a caretaker or practitioner who can be fully present with them? Thus interpersonal touch creates an emotional dialogue between the one touched and the one touching, and as Linden (2015) pointed out, "the sense of touch is intrinsically emotional (feelings!) and that social warmth and physical warmth are interrelated" (p. 173). (Developmental Play Therapy is elaborated on in Chapters 3 and 4; see also Theraplay in Chapter 5.)

> Amazing personal stories demonstrating the power of touch for infants can be found on Youtube: View a mother and father's astounding account of providing skin-to-skin contact to their non-breathing infant, *Loving Touch and Mom's Intuition: Kate Ogg and Jamie's Story*, retrieved: http://fb-232.dailymegabyte.com/doctors-say-theyve-lost-the-baby/. And watch a twin-sister story that actually changed medical protocols, *The Rescue Hug*, retrieved: https://www.youtube.com/watch?v=0YwT_Gx49os

The Relevance of Advances in Neuroscience to Touch in Clinical Practice

Although the skin is our largest and oldest sensory organ, it has been the least researched of all our senses (Field, 2014). The rise in neuroscience research over the past 20 years has led to a deeper understanding of how the circuits of the mind are connected to memory, touch sensations, emotions, and trauma (Field, 2014; Linden, 2015; Schore, 2012; van der Kolk, 2014). Understanding of neurobiological processes and "getting comfortable with the brain" (p. 191), as Badenoch (2008) puts it, must now be an essential component of a therapist's educational understanding. Schore (2012) advised that "no theory of human functioning can be restricted to only a description of psychological processes; it must also be consonant with what we now know about biological structural brain development" (p. 1).

Through the field of interpersonal neurobiology we now know as *fact*—through neuroimaging, what Bowlby (1953) early on only intuited as *theory*—that the quality of early human attachment relationships (including *how* infants and children were touched) directly impacts on lifelong physical, emotional, relational, and brain development—both positively and negatively (Badenoch, 2008; Kestly, 2014; Schore, 2012; Siegel, 2012). The advances in brain research since the mid-1990s have generated a broader understanding of the (brain)-*mind-body* connection as the psychological field moves to embrace a bio-psycho-social-cultural (and spiritual) paradigm shift of healing with clients (Schore, 2012). The following viewpoint from van der Kolk (2014) may speak collectively to our changing mental health field perspective: "I discovered that my professional training, with its focus on understanding and insight, had largely ignored the relevance of the living, breathing body, the foundation of our selves" (p. 89).

This deeper comprehension of neurobiology has added new insight into touch, empathy, and interpersonal relationships. The discovery of mirror neurons—nerve cells that fire when you watch another person perform an action (Ramachandran, 2011), are also connected to a network of "resonance circuits" (Badenoch, 2008, p. 31) which stimulates our ability to have empathy for another person—one of the most important attributes a practitioner brings to the healing process. What is relevant to touch, as neuroscientist Ramachandran (2011) explained, is that there are also *sensory* mirror neurons in the brain that are activated when we watch another person being touched, even though we do not actually physically feel the sensation ourselves, our body reacts as if the touch was indeed happening to us. Because of this phenomenon, Ramachandran has fondly labeled these cells "Gandhi neurons" (p. 124). This knowledge can better assist practitioners in understanding vicarious witnessing of trauma, such as children who witness domestic violence, as well as grasping the impact of trauma related to differences in right and left brain processing (Schore, 2012; van der Kolk, 2014).

The Role of Oxytocin and Caring Touch

When caring touch is provided it releases the essential "feel good" neurotransmitters including oxytocin, serotonin, and dopamine. Oxytocin, coined the "love" hormone (Field, 2014), is also considered the calming and connectivity hormone, which when released simultaneously lowers the stress hormone, cortisol—resulting in helping children relax. Uvnäs-Moberg (2003) wrote, "Pleasant touch and warmth activate the calm and connection system, bringing on a feeling of well-being" (p. 108). Thus, as van der Kolk (2014) advised, "We have an ability to regulate our own physiology ... through such basic activities as breathing, moving, and *touching* [emphasis added]" (p. 38). Armed with this knowledge, practitioners can then educate parents about the physical and emotional changes that can occur when parents provide the right kind of attuned touch to their children.

The Role of Cortisol and Hurtful Touch

Equally relevant, parents need to be educated that the stress hormone, cortisol, is released when physical punishment is applied and that repeated episodes of a fear response related to slaps, smacks, and hitting where a child must submit without an ability to fight back or flee can damage a child's brain and lead to diseased neural networks (Durrant & Ensom, 2012). Furthermore, long-term research on the effects of physical punishment, sometimes the only form of touch that kids receive, has been shown to have negative effects on children, including higher levels of depression, anxiety, and drug and alcohol abuse; aggression toward parents, siblings, peers, and later, spouses; and they are more likely to develop antisocial behavior, among other problems (Durrant & Ensom, 2012; Gershoff & Grogan-Kaylor, 2016). Mental health professions, overall, do not sanction the use of corporal punishment (Gharabaghi, 2008).

Practitioners who develop knowledge about neurobiology are better equipped to educate parents about the impact for their children of interpersonal touch experiences related to emotional and physical processes. (Note, the neurobiology of touch is further discussed in Chapter 3.)

The Relevance of Touch in Clinical Practice

The remaining sections in this chapter address the multiple and interrelated factors concerning touch that impact on the therapeutic encounter with children in therapy sessions.

Mediating Factors and the Context of Touch Related to Ethical Practice

There are no absolute answers about how to handle touch situations that arise in therapy. For example, a hug given to a grieving child may produce positive therapeutic outcomes, while a hug given to a child who was harmed through touch could be frightening; rejecting a sobbing child's reach for a hug could be deeply hurtful or even traumatizing to a child, and to withhold caring nurturance in times of need could be arguably unethical (Aquino & Lee, 2000; McNeil-Haber, 2004; Zur & Nordmarken, 2016). As well, Linden (2015) advised, "touch sensation can convey very different emotional meaning, depending on gender, power dynamic, personal history, and cultural context of the touch initiator and

Figure 1.1 Mediating factors impacting practitioner-initiated and child-initiated touch.

receiver" (p. 31). Therefore, how touch is *perceived* by the child or parents and the clinical considerations involved in the touch must be considered within the *context* of the presenting situation and can be influenced by a variety of factors (refer to Figure 1.1). Aristotle conceptualized that ethical Virtue is about doing the right thing, at the right time, toward the right person, with the right intention, and in the right manner (Aristotle, 1998, adapted, pp. 32–33). And that often the *right* course of action depended upon the need to examine the particular details of each individual situation. He called this "Practical Wisdom" (Aristotle, 1998). In adopting Aristotle's concept of Practical Wisdom, the following is a list of some of the common mediating factors that can assist in the examination of therapeutic encounters comprising touch, using a hypothetical child named Annie:

1 **Child-Initiated Touch:** Annie might excitedly run to *greet* the therapist at the beginning of a session and give a hug. She might want to teach the therapist a patterned *playful hand game* learned at school, or Annie could tap the therapist's arm to get her *attention* to show an injury on her body. Annie might naturally lean against the therapist while playing a game, a *normative* type of touch, or she may become angry and *aggressively kick or hit* the therapist. (McNeil-Haber, 2004; Zur & Nordmarken, 2016).
2 **Practitioner-Initiated Touch:** The therapist may touch Annie's hand in order to *refocus* or *anchor* her to the moment, or to get her *attention*. *Nurturing*

touch may be provided to Annie by holding her hand for comfort. The therapist could provide a *buffered* type of touch to count Annie's fingers playfully with a puppet, or the therapist could provide *assistance* to Annie in tying her shoe. A *celebratory* high-five might be initiated by the therapist if Annie stated she made an A on a test. The therapist may need to provide *safety* by holding Annie's hand if she tries to abruptly run out of the office, or she may need to be *restrained* by the therapist if an out-of-control behavior is not contained through limit setting (see Chapter 9) (McNeil-Haber, 2004; Zur & Nordmarken, 2016).

3 **Practitioner–Child Unintended Touch:** The therapist's arm could *accidentally* bump Annie's arm when passing in the playroom, or hands could touch when completing a *task* such as placing an item in or out of the sandtray.

4 **Child's Diagnosis:** Children's diagnoses must also be taken into consideration regarding touch. For example, many children diagnosed with Sensory Processing Disorder (SPD) or Autism Spectrum Disorder (ASD), have touch sensitivities such as being oversensitive or undersensitive to touch. Children diagnosed with ASD have difficulty in discerning social interactions, and if Annie was on the autism spectrum, she might *misinterpret* the nuances of a touch in therapy sessions and could perceive that an accidentally bumped arm could have been purposely intended by the therapist, thus producing a range of reactions including anger. An attuned therapist could then use the encounter to start a conversation about accidental touch which could then be bridged as a therapeutic teaching moment to discuss how this can happen in peer-to-peer social interactions. (Touch issues related to ASD are addressed further in Chapter 6, and a case example of a child diagnosed with SPD is presented in Chapter 3.)

Touch reactions are also related to children's early life attachment experiences. If Annie had a diagnosis of Reactive Attachment Disorder (RAD), we would understand that her turning away from physical contact that the therapist might initiate is in one way a self-protective attachment-based response; and that this protective behavior is a reflection of Annie's previous abortive attempts to become attached to someone (Brody, 1997). (A case example of a child diagnosed with RAD is presented in Chapter 11.) If Annie was diagnosed with Attention Deficit Hyperactivity Disorder (ADHD) the therapist might initiate touch to help refocus and/or calm her. (Refer to Chapter 5 for a discussion and case example on ADHD.)

5 **Child and Family Problems:** Children's life circumstances of trauma such as neglect, physical abuse, sexual abuse, and domestic violence will significantly impact on touch situations that may arise within sessions—including any child *transference reactions* toward the therapist. Children who were physically abused are primarily harmed through *hands*—the same means that deliver a caring touch. Thus, if Annie had been physically abused and the therapist raised a hand in close proximity to scratch an ear, Annie might flinch or shrink away for safety—an automatic response to a perceived threat related to trauma. It is therefore important for therapists to recognize

that children who resist contact or seem uncomfortable with touch may be reacting to a traumatic past or current experience where their trust through touch has been violated. Additionally, inappropriate touching of the therapist by a child and sexualized behaviors need to be sensitively addressed (Gil & Shaw, 2014). (Note, issues related to sexual and physical abuse and neglect are discussed in Chapter 7; and domestic violence in Chapter 8. Boundary issues are discussed in Chapter 2.)

6 *Child's Developmental Stage:* Children's needs regarding touch change at different developmental ages and the younger the child the more touch that potentially can occur within sessions. If Annie was four years old, she may want to crawl in the therapist's lap if reading a story. However, if Annie was a teenager that would be highly inappropriate and therapists usually interact with similar boundaries with adolescents as they do with their adult clients. If Annie was an infant, the focus primarily would be to facilitate bonding and attachment by nurturing touch experiences between the parent (caregiver) and infant. (See Chapter 10 regarding touch and adolescents; and Chapters 4 and 12 for touch related to infants.)

7 *The Type of Therapy Session:* The type of session such as individual, family, or group is another consideration. If Annie wanted a hug, the context would be different if the therapist was alone with her or if the hug happened within a family session when others were present.

8 *The Developmental Phase of Therapy:* A hug would take on different meaning if it was the first appointment with Annie verses the termination phase of therapy.

9 *Type of Therapeutic Modality:* Most child therapies that utilize touch as an intervention focus primarily on healing attachment-related issues including the play therapy models presented in Part II of this book: Developmental Play Therapy, Theraplay®, DIR Floortime, and FirstPlay® Therapy. In other modalities, such as Client Centered Play Therapy or StoryPlay® (see Chapters 11 and 13), touch may be used minimally or only as a responsive measure to what might be happening in the moment based upon the needs of the child. As well, some touch-based modalities were designed to specifically enhance peer-to-peer relationships, as demonstrated in the Child-2-Child Kind and Caring Hands School program (see Chapter 15). And, some therapists include animals in play therapy sessions where touch between a child and canine (for example) is therapeutically facilitated (see Chapter 14).

10 *The Practitioner's Experience Level:* The practitioner's years of clinical experience will also affect their ability to respond during sessions. If Annie became aggressive during the therapy session, the seasoned therapist might know of several alternatives of how to handle the problem.

11 *The Practitioner's Gender:* The therapist's gender in relationship to the child's gender may influence the touch experience. If Annie was a teenager and she hugged her male therapist, that hug may be perceived differently than if the therapist was female.

12. **Child and Family Cultural Norms:** How children and families give, receive, and perceive touch is highly influenced by their cultural background. Those from Hispanic, Mediterranean (including Jewish) societies, and some African backgrounds are noted as higher-touch cultures—meaning closer body proximity, hugging, patting, and kissing (Schneider & Patterson, 2010). The cultures of America, Great Britain, and Holland, in general, are considered more lower-contact cultures (Field, 2014). In American culture, high- and low-touch differences can vary by region, as Californians have been noted to touch more than New Englanders, and those from southern states are known to touch more. Regional differences are also found in Europe, where Northern Europeans are noted as displaying less physical contact than those in higher-contact Southern European countries including Spain, France, Italy, and Greece (Field, 2014). People can also acculturate to the touch norms of a new country. However, as Montagu (1986) pointed out, even though every culture may have certain norms about touching, every family system within a culture has its own differences regarding touch in relationships.

13. **Child and Family Religious Norms:** Children's religious family background will also influence a child's experience of touch. Some religious practices indicate norms regarding acceptable or unacceptable touch in relationships. For instance, Orthodox Jews and Muslims may prohibit men and women from touching (Schneider & Patterson, 2010), and in some Buddhist backgrounds the head is considered sacred and touching it is taboo (Carlson, 2006). Many Christian congregations encourage contact among parishioners (male and female) as part of the church service where members might shake hands or give hugs.

14. **The Practitioner's Examination of Countertransferences:** The therapist's own history related to touch experiences will highly influence the therapeutic encounter (Gil & Johnson, 1993). Indeed, perhaps more than any other area of professional countertransference inquiry, it should be considered a priority that practitioners explore how their own life experiences related to touch can potentially affect their behaviors and actions in their work with children. Schore (2012) advised that countertransference reactions represent unconscious "nonverbal right brain–mind–body communications" (p. 41). Thus, to touch another or to be touched by another can immediately trigger emotional and physiological memory reactions that a practitioner may not consciously register within the moment (van der Kolk, 2014). And these unconscious processes may instigate reactions toward a client in ways that could potentially cause harm or retraumatize a child. Training experiences in touch can give practitioners an opportunity to examine their own personal relationship to touch in order to build self-awareness to effectively work with clients (Courtney & Gray, 2014). Clinical supervision can also play a role in helping practitioners understand feelings of comfort surrounding

touch (VanFleet *et al.*, 2010), and identify potential countertransferences. (See also Chapter 9.)

Mediating Factors in Action: Two Different Responses Related to Physical Aggression toward the Therapist

The following vignettes demonstrate how a therapist adapted her therapeutic interventions in response to physical aggression in consideration of the presenting mediating factors.

Vignette A: Case of Mary

Empathetic Response: Individual Session: Agency Play Therapy Room

> Mary, age 10, was in a temporary shelter after being removed from her parent's home due to severe physical abuse. During a play therapy session, Mary assigned the role of "child" to the therapist and she was role-playing the "mother." Mary (playing mother) directed the therapist to "play with the toys." The therapist began playing as directed. Soon after, Mary grabbed the therapist's arm and stated, "Get up, go to the corner!" When the therapist [playing the child] was placed in the corner, the child slapped the therapist in the face and screamed, "Shut up!" The therapist quickly took control and stepped out of the role-play and provided empathy. In a calm and caring tone, the therapist stated, "Mary, you are showing me what has happened to you, how you have been treated. I am so, so sorry that you were hurt in that way." The therapist saw Mary's facial expression change from anger to tears. She nodded her head "yes" and leaned into the therapist for comfort, and the therapist responded with a comforting hug. The therapist told her, "In here, even during play, no one hurts or hits anyone. I want you to know that you are safe." In this situation, the therapist understood the severe trauma related to Mary's experiences and had to connect with the emotional right-brain processes of empathetic resonance before attending to the cognitive left-brain functioning. This provided a safe, corrective, emotional and physical experience for Mary.

Vignette B: Case of Dillon

Psychoeducational, Modeling, and Refocusing Response:
Family Session: Home Visit

> The therapist was seeing a parent–child dyad for home visit sessions. The mother was struggling with her 6-year-old son, Dillon's, behavior. The mother stated that the father had been physically "harsh" in his discipline methods with the children; however, Dillon had no contact with his father after the divorce. Dillon, who was diagnosed with ADHD, was having

problems with impulsive aggressive acting out—hitting kids at school. During one session, Dillon became irritated and impulsively punched the therapist in the nose. At that moment, the therapist took Dillon's hand in hers, looked him in the eye and stated, "Hitting is not safe. It's my job to keep us safe. If you feel angry, let me show you how you can get those mad feelings out in a safe way."

Realizing that Dillon lacked the understanding and skills to manage his impulses, the therapist showed Dillon and his mother how Dillon could punch the couch cushion with a deep outward breath. The therapist then asked the mother if she would be willing to try the activity. After watching his mother, the therapist observed that Dillon was anxious and his attention was diverted. She then calmly touched Dillon's shoulder lightly, and said, "Dillon, it's okay. I'm here to help you keep safe." This relieved some of his anxiety and helped him refocus. He then practiced hitting the cushion and breathing out with a loud "roar." The therapist advised his mother that this redirection helped Dillon express his anger in a safe way, but she had to carefully monitor the activity. Dillon was given other alternatives to release his frustration and self-regulate at school and home. The therapist was also able to therapeutically work with the aggressive themes that emerged in Dillon's play, relieving his underlying hurt regarding his father's abandonment.

Case Vignettes Commentary

Even though both cases presented in-the-moment problems of physical aggression toward a therapist, the *context* of the mediating factors involved—the Practical Wisdom—called for two very different interventions. During both sessions the therapist was able to maintain protection and safety for the children. At the same time, the therapist maintained her professionalism and remained calm. Note how the therapist responded and initiated touch following the incidents to provide a nurturing corrective experience for Mary, and to provide an anchoring and re-orienting experience for Dillon. Following the sessions, the therapist was able to process any countertransferences that emerged related to the physical aggression, and she also created ways to rebalance herself (a startling slap and punch, even from a young child, can sting). She documented the circumstances and also evaluated what she could have done or said differently before, during, and after the incidents.

Concluding Comments

Touch is essential to children's healthy development and the intricacies of touch between practitioners and children in counseling and play therapy, and for other professionals who work with children, are complex. Many practitioners may feel uncertain about clinical and ethical best practices, or insufficiently prepared to handle issues that may arise related to touch with children. The ultimate goal of this book, therefore, is for practitioners to increase professional awareness about touch and to enhance clinical knowledge and skills to ethically, sensitively, and appropriately deal with the varied mediating factors that impact on touch within therapy sessions with children. We now turn to Chapter 2, which explores in detail the risk management and ethical considerations of touch in clinical practice.

Discussion Questions

1 Reflect back to the four questions that were asked on the opening page in this chapter and, with a colleague, discuss how you would handle the situations described.
2 With a colleague, review the list of mediating factors and discuss your thoughts on each one as it relates to practice.
3 Reflecting on your own cultural norms related to touch, discuss with a colleague the following questions:
 - Would you consider your cultural background as high, medium, or low touch?
 - What were your cultural or religious norms regarding touch and physical contact?
 - How did your family members give and receive affection?
 - Were there differences in touch between genders in the family?
 - What were the norms regarding touch with non-family members?
 - How do your cultural norms related to touch influence your practice decision making with children and families from different cultural backgrounds?

References

Aquino, A.T., & Lee, S.S. (2000). The use of nonerotic touch with children: Ethical and developmental considerations. *Journal of Psychotherapy in Independent Practice, 1(3)*, 17–30. DOI:10.1300/J288v01n03_02

Aristotle. (1998). *Nicomachean ethics* (unabridged). Mineola, NY: Dover Publications (Dover Thrift Editions).

Association for Play Therapy. (2015). *Paper on touch: Clinical, professional, & ethical issues*. Retrieved on 1 November, 2016 from: http://c.ymcdn.com/sites/www.a4pt.org/resource/resmgr/Publications/Paper_On_Touch_2015.pdf

Badenoch, B. (2008). *Being a brain-wise therapist: A practical guide to interpersonal neurobiology*. New York: Norton.

Bowlby, J. (1953). *Child care and the growth of love*. London: Penguin Books.

Brody, V.A. (1997). *The dialogue of touch: Developmental play therapy* (2nd ed.). Northvale, NJ: Jason Aronson.

Carlson, F. (2006). *Essential touch: Meeting the needs of young children*. Washington, DC: National Association for the Education of Young Children.

Center for Play Therapy (Producer). (1995). *Developmental play therapy: A clinical session and interview with Viola Brody*. [DVD]. Available from Center for Play Therapy, University of North Texas, P.O. Box 13857, Denton, Tx 76203-6857.

Courtney, J.A. (2012). Touching autism through developmental play therapy. In L. Gallo-Lopez & L.C. Rubin (Eds.), *Play-based interventions for children and adolescents with autism spectrum disorders* (pp. 137–157). New York: Routledge.

Courtney, J.A., & Gray, S.W. (2014). A phenomenological inquiry into practitioner experiences of developmental play therapy: Implications for training in touch. *International Journal of Play Therapy, 23(2)*, 114–129. DOI:10.1080/07421656.2011.599719

Courtney, J.A., & Siu, A.Y. (2017). *Practitioner experiences of touch with children in child counseling and play therapy*. Manuscript submitted for publication.

Cushman, P. (2009). Three men teachers, three countries and three responses to the physical contact dilemma. *International Journal of Education, 1(1)*. Retrieved on 1 November, 2016 from: http://www.macrothink.org/journal/index.php/ije/article/view/210/144

Davidson, J.P. (2011). *Planet word*. New York: Penguin Group.

Denworth, L. (2015, July/August). The social power of touch: A long overlooked system of nerves that respond to gentle strokes may be crucial to our ability to form connections with one another. *Scientific American Mind*, 30–39.

Durrant, J., & Ensom, R. (2012). Physical punishment of children: lessons from 20 years of research. *Canadian Medical Association Journal, 184(12)*, 1373–1377. DOI: 10.1503/cmaj.101314

Field, T. (2003). *Touch*. Cambridge, MA: MIT Press.

Field, T. (2014). *Touch* (2nd ed.). Cambridge, MA: MIT Press.

Gershoff, E.T., & Grogan-Kaylor, A. (2016, April 7). Spanking and child outcomes: Old controversies and new meta-analyses. *Journal of Family Psychology, 30(3)*. DOI:10.1037/fam0000191

Gharabaghi, K. (2008). Values and ethics in child and youth care practice. *Child & Youth Services, 30(3/4)*, 185–209. DOI:10.1080/01459350903107350

Gil, E., & Johnson, T.C. (1993). *Sexualized children: Assessment and treatment of sexualized children and children who molest*. Rockville, MD: Launch Press.

Gil, E., & Shaw, J.A. (2014). *Working with children with sexual behavior problems*. New York: Guilford Press.

Haber, R. (2002). Virginia Satir: An integrated, humanistic approach. *Contemporary Family Therapy, 24(1)*, 23–34. Retrieved on from: http://link.springer.com/article/10.1023/A:1014317420921

Kestly, T.A. (2014). *The interpersonal neurobiology of play: Brain-building interventions for emotional well-being*. New York: W.W. Norton.

Linden, D. J. (2015). *Touch: The science of hand, heart, and mind*. New York: Penguin.

Lynch, R., & Garrett, P.M. (2010). More than words: Touch practices in child and family social work. *Child & Family Social Work, 15*, 389–398. DOI:10.1111/j.1365-2206.2010.00686.x

McNeil-Haber, F.M. (2004). Ethical considerations in the use of nonerotic touch with children. *Ethics and Behavior, 14*, 123–140. DOI:10.1207/s15327019eb1402_3

Montagu, A. (1986). *Touching: The human significance of the skin* (3rd ed.). New York: Harper & Row.

National Association for Social Workers (NASW). (2012). *Social workers and child abuse reporting: A review of state mandatory reporting requirements.* Washington, DC: NASW Press.

Ramachandran, V. S. (2011). *The tell-tale brain: A neuroscientist's quest for what makes us human.* New York: Norton.

Schneider, E.F., & Patterson, P.P. (2010, December). You've got that magic touch: Integrating the sense of touch into early childhood services. *Young Exceptional Children, 13(5)*, 17–27. DOI:10.1177/1096250610384706

Schore, A.N. (2012). *The science of the art of psychotherapy.* New York: Norton.

Siegel, D.J. (2012). *The developing mind: How relationships and the brain interact to shape who we are* (2nd ed.). New York: Guilford Press.

Uvnäs-Moberg, K. (2003). *The oxytocin factor: Tapping the hormone of calm, love, and healing.* Cambridge, MA: Da Capo Press.

van der Kolk, B. (2014). *The body keeps the score.* New York: Penguin.

VanFleet, R., Sywulak, A.E., & Sniscak, C.C. (2010). *Child-centered play therapy.* New York: Guilford Press.

Weber, R. (1990). A philosophical perspective on touch. In K.E. Barnard & T. Brazelton (Eds.), *Touch: The foundation of experience* (pp. 11–43). Madison, CT: International Universities Press.

Zur, O., & Nordmarken, N. (2016). *To touch or not to touch: Exploring the myth of prohibition on touch in psychotherapy and counseling.* Retrieved on 1 November, 2016 from: http://www.zurinstitute.com/touchintherapy.html

2 Ethical and Risk-Management Issues in the Use of Touch

Frederic G. Reamer

> Touch has a memory.
> John Keats, *What Can I Do to Drive Away*

Debate about the clinical use of touch is an ethics-related lightning rod. For decades, clinicians have jousted in their efforts to defend the appropriate use of touch or denounce its potential and actual perils. This controversy is a quintessential example of an ambidextrous ethical dilemma. On one hand, proponents claim that clinicians' judicious use of touch can promote therapeutic progress, strengthen the therapeutic alliance, communicate acceptance and caring, and enhance clients' self-esteem (Bonitz, 2008; Calmes *et al.*, 2013; Cornell, 1997; Cowen *et al.*, 1983; Dunne *et al.*, 1982; Durana, 1998; Eiden, 1998; Field, 2003; Field *et al.*, 1997; Goodman & Teicher, 1988; Horton *et al.*, 1995; Levitan & Johnson, 1986; Phelan, 2009; Smith *et al.*, 1998; Willison & Masson, 1986). On the other hand, critics argue that clinicians' use of touch places their feet on a slippery slope that can cause considerable harm for both clients and practitioners. From this perspective, physical contact between clinician and client can exacerbate clients' confusion about boundaries in relationships, lead to exploitation of clients, and serve as a prelude to sexual misconduct (Bonitz, 2008; Eyckmans, 2009; Holroyd & Brodsky, 1977, 1980; Holub & Lee, 1990; Karbelnig, 2000; Kertay & Riviere, 1993; McNeil-Haber, 2004; Phelan, 2009; Pinson, 2002; Redleaf, 1998; Stenzel & Rupert, 2004; Stockwell & Dye, 1980).

This protracted controversy exemplifies the key feature of an ethical dilemma: questions about moral right and wrong, and duty and obligation. Thus, it behooves contemporary clinicians to fully grasp pertinent ethical and risk-management issues when they consider the possible use of touch for clinical purposes in their work with children and adolescents.

The Concept of Boundaries in Clinical Work

At the center of debate about clinicians' use of touch is the concept of boundaries. To fully appreciate the complex boundary issues related to the clinical use of touch, it is important for practitioners to distinguish between boundary violations and boundary crossings (Gutheil & Gabbard, 1993; Reamer, 2012; Smith & Fitzpatrick, 1995). A boundary violation occurs when a clinician engages in a dual relationship with a client or colleague that is exploitive, manipulative, deceptive, or coercive. Examples include practitioners who touch clients for sexual gratification or other self-serving purposes. Boundary violations are inherently unethical because they are likely to harm clients (Celenza, 2007; Epstein, 1994; Kitchener, 1988; Pope, 1988, 1991; Zur, 2007).

Sexualized touch between practitioners and clients has been prohibited as far back as the time of Hippocrates, in the late fifth century BCE, whose prominent oath proclaims that "Whatever houses I may visit, I will come for the benefit of the sick, remaining free of all intentional injustice, of all mischief and in particular of sexual relations with both female and male persons, be they free or slaves" (Celenza, 2007, p. xiii). Unethical touch between clinicians and clients can take two principal forms (Simon, 1999). First, overt sexual touch includes sexual intercourse, oral sex, fondling the genital area, touching the breasts, genital exposure, and passionate kissing. Second, touching behavior entails sexualized touching of body parts, such as clients' shoulders, arms, legs, knees, face, hair, or neck; sexualized hugging; and holding the client on one's lap.

A number of empirical studies demonstrate the seriousness and magnitude of sexualized touch between clinicians and clients (Bouhoutsos, 1985; Bouhoutsos et al., 1983; Coleman & Schaefer, 1986; Feldman-Summers & Jones, 1984; Gabbard, 1989; Pope, 1991; Pope & Bouhoutsos, 1986; Reamer, 2015). Research to date has focused nearly exclusively on adult clients; however, the compelling results highlight the various ways in which sexual contact between clinicians and clients can occur and cause harm. In a classic study, Pope (1986) reports on the frequency of successful malpractice claims filed against psychologists during a ten-year period. The most frequent claims category involved sexual contact; approximately 45 percent of dollars spent in response to claims against psychologists resulted from claims of sexual contact. Gartrell and colleagues (1986) reported in their groundbreaking survey of psychiatrists that 6.4 percent acknowledged sexual contact with their adult patients, and this may be an underestimate in light of the stigma associated with such behavior.

During a twenty-year period, nearly one in five lawsuits (18.5 percent) against social workers insured through the malpractice insurance program sponsored by the National Association of Social Workers (NASW) Insurance Trust alleged some form of sexual impropriety, and more than two-fifths (41.3 percent) of insurance payments were the result of claims concerning sexual misconduct (Reamer, 2015). (These results do not report the age of the clients.) Clearly, sexualized touch and contact between clinicians and clients is a significant problem. The best available national data suggest that between 8.0 percent and 12.0 percent of male counselors or psychotherapists and between 1.7 percent and 3.0 percent of female counselors or psychotherapists admit having had sexual relationships with current or former clients (Olarte, 1997).

In contrast to such clear boundary violations, a boundary crossing occurs when a clinician is involved in a dual relationship with a client in a manner that is not

Figure 2.1 Knowing how to establish clear boundaries.
Source: ©iStock.com/Murielselsis

intentionally exploitive, manipulative, deceptive, or coercive. Boundary crossings related to touch are not inherently unethical. In principle, the consequences of boundary crossings may be harmful, salutary, or neutral (Gutheil & Gabbard, 1993). Boundary crossings involving touch are harmful when the touch has negative consequences for the client or practitioner. For example, a clinician who touches a client in what the practitioner considers to be in the form of a benign and nurturing physical gesture may confuse the client and compromise the client's mental health because of complicated transference issues triggered by the touch.

Alternatively, some boundary crossings, including touch, may be helpful to clients. Zur (2007) and a number of other clinicians (Calmes *et al.*, 2013; Downey, 2001; Durana, 1998; Hunter & Struve, 1998) summarize the ways in which, handled judiciously, touch may prove, in some special circumstances, to be therapeutically useful to a client. The literature suggests that potentially helpful touch in a clinical context may be viewed as:

1. Ritualistic or socially accepted gestures for greeting and good-bye on arrival and departure (such as handshakes, a greeting or farewell embrace, and other culturally accepted gestures).
2. Conversational marker (such as a light touch on the arm, hand, back, or shoulder that is intended to make or highlight a point, or convey attention).
3. Consoling touch (such as touching the hand or shoulder of the client or providing a comforting hug).
4. Reassuring touch (generally geared to encouraging and reassuring clients and usually involves a pat on the back or shoulder).
5. Playful touch (such as touching the hand, shoulder, or head while playing a game with a child or adolescent client).
6. Grounding or reorienting touch (for example, when touch is intended to help clients reduce anxiety or dissociation by using touch to the hand or arm or by leading clients to touch their own hands or arms).
7. Task-oriented touch (such as touch that is merely ancillary to the task at hand, for example, offering a hand to help a child stand up or bracing an arm around a client's shoulders to keep the client from falling).
8. Corrective experience (for example, when a therapist who practices forms of therapy that emphasize the importance of corrective emotional experiences rocks a child).
9. Instructional or modeling touch (when therapists model how to touch or respond to touch by demonstrating a firm handshake, holding an agitated child, or responding to unwanted touch).
10. Celebratory or congratulatory touch (for example, when a therapist gives a child a pat on the back or congratulatory hug when the client has achieved a goal).
11. Experiential touch (for example, touch that takes place when a clinician conducts an experiential exercise, such as teaching gestures during assertiveness training, or asking family members participating in family sculpting to assume certain positions in relationship to each other).
12. Referential touch (for example, when the clinician lightly taps the arm or shoulder of a client, indicating that he or she can take a turn or be silent).
13. Inadvertent touch (when touch is unintentional, involuntary, and unpremeditated, such as an inadvertent brush against a client by the clinician).
14. Touch intended to prevent someone from hurting another (for example, when a clinician must stop or restrain a child who threatens to harm an acquaintance or family member during a clinical session).
15. Touch in a clinician's self-defense (for example, when a clinician feels the need to use touch to physically defend against an assault by a client).
16. Therapeutic touch in body psychotherapies (for example, touch used by somatic and body psychotherapists who regularly use touch as part of their theoretically prescribed clinical intervention).

Some boundary crossings involving touch can produce mixed results (see Figure 2.2). A clinician's touch may be both helpful and harmful to the same client, perhaps

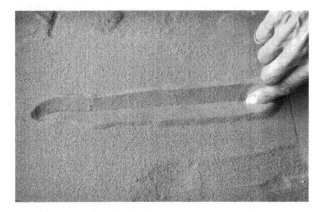

Figure 2.2 Knowing where to draw the line with regard to use of touch. (Photo used with permission from Robert D. Nolan.)

at different times in the clinical relationship—helpful in that the client feels cared for and valued by the clinician and harmful in that the touch exacerbates the client's confusion about boundaries in the professional-client relationship.

Ethical and Legal Risks

Given the lack of consensus among practitioners about the appropriateness of touch in the clinical relationship, clinicians would do well to consider current standards pertaining to the use of controversial, albeit innovative, interventions. Innovations are critically important to every profession. Advances in knowledge, based on creative conceptualization and the results of evaluative research, are essential elements in professionals' efforts to refine and enhance their ability to help people. Innovations in the form of alternative and nontraditional treatments, such as therapeutic touch, however, also carry risk. Although some innovations clearly improve professionals' ability to assist people in need, and are supported by research and evaluation data, others can be destructive and dangerous.

Problems potentially associated with clinicians' creative use of touch take two forms. The first involves practitioners who have difficulty using touch skillfully—issues of competence. For instance, clinicians who have not obtained formal training, certification, or supervision in the therapeutic use of touch may exacerbate clients' emotional condition because of their unskilled application of these approaches. The second form of high-risk interventions involves clinicians' creative use of touch in ways that are not widely endorsed by seasoned colleagues, are not based on solid empirically based or other research evidence, and which may pose significant risks to clients.

In extraordinary cases, clients who believe that clinicians have touched them inappropriately may file lawsuits that allege practitioner negligence or licensing board complaints (angry clients may also file ethics complaints with a professional association to which the clinician belongs, such as the National Association of Social Workers, American Psychological Association, American Counseling Association, or American Association for Marriage and Family Therapy). Occasionally, clinicians who touch clients sexually have criminal charges filed against them. In a case in Virginia, a licensed therapist was sentenced to ten years in prison for engaging in sexual contact with a minor client (Smythe, 2015).

Disgruntled clients and third parties (for example, a minor child's parents or guardian) who file a formal complaint with a state licensing board typically allege that a clinician engaged in an incompetent, unorthodox, or nontraditional intervention or behavior, such as some forms of touch, that was unethical and significantly harmed the complainant. In one case, parents of a thirteen-year-old client filed a complaint with the state licensing board alleging that the therapist fondled their daughter during a clinical session that the therapist referred to as "holding therapy."

State licensing boards have the authority to conduct formal investigations and hearings in response to complaints filed against licensees. Licensing boards have a number of options when they find sufficient evidence to indicate that a practitioner who engaged in unethical touch violated standards contained in state licensing statutes or regulations (such as reprimanding the clinician; requiring specialized education, consultation or supervision; and suspending or revoking the clinician's license). Some clients who believe they have been harmed by clinicians who allegedly touched them inappropriately file lawsuits in civil court (Reamer, 2015). These lawsuits usually claim that the clinician engaged in professional malpractice, a form of negligence, either by delivering services, such as therapeutic touch, in harmful ways (an act of commission) or by failing to provide clients with the services they needed (an act of omission). The concept of negligence applies to professionals who are required to perform in a manner consistent with the legal concept of the standard of care in the profession, that is, the way an ordinary, reasonable, and prudent professional would act under the same or similar circumstances (Austin *et al.*, 1990; Madden, 2003).

In general, malpractice occurs when there is evidence that

1 At the time of the alleged malpractice, a legal duty existed between the clinician and the client. Clinicians establish a duty once they enter into a professional-client relationship.
2 The clinician was derelict in that duty (that is, touched a client inappropriately). Clinicians who touch clients may be charged with misfeasance or malfeasance. This is an important distinction. Misfeasance is customarily defined as the commission of a proper act in a wrongful or injurious manner, or the improper performance of an act that might have been performed lawfully (Gifis, 1991). Thus, a clinician who uses an acceptable form of therapeutic touch negligently—either because of inadequate training or lack of skill—might be accused of misfeasance; these forms of touch, which are based on solid research and theoretical foundations, should only be used by

practitioners who have sufficient training, knowledge, and competence. In contrast, malfeasance is ordinarily defined as the commission of a wrongful or unlawful act (Bernstein & Hartsell, 2008; Gifis, 2010). Thus, a clinician who touches a client sexually after convincing her that this would be therapeutic might be accused of malfeasance.

3   The client suffered some harm or injury (e.g., a client who was touched by a clinician inappropriately may suffer severe emotional distress and require additional mental health services, lose time at school, and have difficulty sustaining intimate relationships).

4   The clinician's dereliction of duty was the direct and proximate cause of the harm or injury (the client's emotional injuries and losses were the result of the clinician's inappropriate or incompetent touch).

Ordinarily, civil suits filed against practitioners are based on tort or contract law, with plaintiffs (the individuals bringing the suit) seeking some form of redress for injuries that they claim to have incurred. Such injuries may be economic (the costs associated with mental health services for a child who has been harmed by a clinician's touch), physical (resulting from a suicide attempt committed by a client who is despondent about the consequences of her clinician's use of controversial treatment techniques that include touch), or emotional (depression or anxiety brought about by a clinician's injurious use of nontraditional or unorthodox interventions involving touch). As with criminal trials, defendants in civil suits are presumed blameless until proven otherwise. In ordinary civil suits, the standard of proof required to find clinicians liable for their use of nontraditional and unorthodox interventions involving touch is based on the notion of preponderance of the evidence (in contrast to the stricter standard of proof beyond a reasonable doubt used in criminal proceedings).

Ethical and Risk-Management Guidelines

There is legitimate debate about whether some forms of therapy with children should be allowed to incorporate physical touch as a component of the therapeutic approach (Austin *et al.*, 1990; Bonitz, 2008; Epstein, 1994; Reamer, 2012, 2015). According to Syme (2003, p. 67),

> The decision of whether to offer touch or not will depend on both theoretical and ethical considerations. Orthodox psychoanalysts do not touch their clients for theoretical reasons, though there is little research to support this. The relational theory of some psychotherapists supports the use of touch in certain instances, as do most regressive and some humanistic theories. Here again there is little research but some of the research and some subjective accounts of clients do suggest that there are positive effects of touch. It is also clear that non-erotic touch can have negative effects. The ethical considerations are firstly whether the therapist has adequate training both

theoretically and technically in the use of touch. Secondly therapists must not use touch if it is in any way alien to themselves. Thirdly touch should be offered only if it is really in the service of the client's needs.

Clinicians should also be particularly sensitive to cultural, ethnic, and religious norms pertaining to physical touch. For example, it would be inappropriate for a male clinician to shake the hand of an adolescent female client who is a strictly observant Jew because Orthodox rules (known as *negiah*) prohibit physical contact between unmarried members of the opposite sex. Similarly, a clinician should not touch the head of a Cambodian (Khmer) child, because some believe that the soul resides in the head and should not be disturbed.

Clinicians who use touch can and should take a number of practical steps to protect clients from harm and to prevent ethics complaints, malpractice claims, and criminal charges. Sexualized touch is clearly unethical and should always be avoided. Mental health professionals should never use clinical techniques involving touch that, on their face, expose clients to serious risk. These are the easy cases, in that a cross section of clinicians would readily agree that colleagues who use such clinical techniques and interventions violate the substantive standards of care in the profession.

However, in some instances, significant numbers of clinicians may endorse the use of touch in the treatment of children, even when the intervention may expose clients and themselves to some degree of risk (Bonitz, 2008). Thus, a cross section of experienced, reasonable, and prudent colleagues can disagree about whether certain novel or controversial interventions involving touch are unethical, negligent, or ineffective. For example, some clinicians argue vigorously that holding therapy is a helpful, constructive approach when working with some clients. Others, however, argue that this approach is filled with clinical and legal risk and that practitioners should avoid its use (Miller, 1997; Welch, 1989). In this and many other instances, thoughtful and principled clinicians may examine the known facts about the relative advantages and disadvantages of touch and disagree about the appropriateness of its use.

Clinicians can best protect clients and themselves by following the *procedural standard of care* (Reamer, 2015)—the steps that an ordinary, reasonable, and prudent practitioner should and would take in deciding whether to use a nontraditional, experimental, unorthodox, or controversial clinical intervention or technique such as touch. The procedural standard of care includes seven key elements: consulting colleagues and supervisors; obtaining proper informed consent; reviewing relevant ethical standards; reviewing relevant regulations, laws, and policies; reviewing relevant literature; obtaining legal consultation when necessary; and documenting and evaluating decision-making steps.

Consulting Colleagues and Supervisors

Clinicians who are considering the use of touch should consult colleagues and supervisors who have specialized knowledge or expertise related to this clinical approach. Clinicians in private or independent practice should broach these issues in peer consultation groups. Clinicians employed in agencies that sponsor institutional ethics committees (committees that provide staff with a forum for consultation on difficult cases) should take advantage of this form of consultation when they face complicated ethical and treatment issues involving touch.

Obtaining Proper Informed Consent

Clinicians have always recognized the critical importance of a client's consent to treatment and intervention. Informed consent is especially important when clinicians plan to use touch, given the diversity of professional opinion about its appropriateness.

In general, for consent to be considered valid, six standards must be met: coercion and undue influence must not have played a role in the client's decision; clients must be capable of providing consent (when treating minors, clinicians should obtain their clients' *assent*, in addition to parental or guardian consent); clients must consent to specific procedures and intervention approaches; the forms of consent must be valid; clients must have the right to refuse or withdraw consent; and clients' decisions must be based on adequate information (Rozovsky, 2000). Clinicians should use clear and understandable language to inform clients of the purpose of the services, risks related to the services, limits to services because of the requirements of a third-party payer, relevant costs, reasonable alternatives, clients' right to refuse or withdraw consent, and the time frame covered by the consent. Practitioners should provide clients with an opportunity to ask questions.

Reviewing Relevant Ethical Standards

It is critically important that clinicians become familiar with and consult standards in their respective codes of ethics (for example, in social work, psychology, counseling, marriage and family therapy, and nursing). Generally, relevant codes of ethics do not prohibit all forms of touch, but prohibit inappropriate touch. For example, the National Association of Social Workers *Code of Ethics* states: "Social workers should not engage in physical contact with clients when there is a possibility of psychological harm to the client as a result of the contact (such as cradling or caressing clients). Social workers who engage in appropriate physical contact with clients are responsible for setting clear, appropriate and culturally sensitive boundaries that govern such physical contact" (p. 13).

Reviewing Regulations, Laws, Standards of Practice, and Policies

Clinicians who are considering the use of touch should always review relevant regulations, laws, standards of practice, and policies (both public policies and agency policies). For example, several states have adopted laws explicitly prohibiting exploitative dual relationships, which can be a by-product of some nontraditional and unorthodox interventions that include touch (Bullis, 1995; Reamer, 2015).

Reviewing Appropriate Literature

Practitioners should always stay current with relevant professional literature on the use of touch in clinical contexts. Ideally, clinicians should base their use of touch on recognized knowledge, including empirically based knowledge. When contemplating the use of touch, practitioners should always take time to gather and study pertinent publications, especially those that are likely to be viewed as authoritative (Association for Play Therapy, 2015). Courts and licensing boards may consider relevant literature as evidence of prevailing standards of care (along with expert testimony and national practice standards).

Obtaining Legal Consultation

Clinicians who consider using touch should anticipate possible, even if not probable, legal ramifications. Practitioners who use nontraditional and unorthodox interventions involving touch increase their risk for legal exposure. Thus, it behooves those who consider using touch to obtain a legal opinion about relevant risks from a lawyer who specializes in professional malpractice and negligence. Clinicians who seek legal advice may enhance their ability to argue that they made a good-faith effort to practice ethically.

Documenting and Evaluating

Careful and thorough documentation and evaluation enhance the quality of the services that clinicians provide to clients. Comprehensive records are necessary to assess clients' clinical circumstances; plan and deliver services appropriately; facilitate supervision; provide proper accountability to clients, other service providers, funding agencies, insurers, utilization review staff, and the courts; evaluate services provided; and to ensure continuity in the delivery of future services (Reamer, 2001, 2005; Sidell, 2011). Thorough documentation also helps to ensure quality care in the event that a client's primary clinician is unavailable. In addition, thorough documentation can help protect practitioners who are named in ethics complaints and lawsuits (e.g., documentation can provide evidence that a clinician obtained timely consultation and supervision concerning the use of touch; obtained a client's informed consent [or assent, in the case of a minor] prior to the delivery of services; reviewed relevant practice and ethical standards, literature, standards of practice, statutes, and regulations; and, when necessary, sought legal consultation).

The extent to which clinicians follow these steps when making a decision may become a key issue during the adjudication of an ethics complaint or a lawsuit. For example, licensing board members or attorneys might ask which supervisors the clinician consulted and when; which professional literature, ethical and practice standards, and regulations she reviewed and when; and what training she received related to the use of a particular intervention. The quality of the practitioner's adherence to the procedural standard of care may have a direct bearing on the outcome of the case. More important, adhering to these procedural steps when contemplating the use of touch is likely to enhance the quality and effectiveness of the clinician's practice. After all, practitioners who routinely obtain consultation and supervision; review ethical and practice standards, policies, regulations, laws, and literature; document and evaluate their interventions; and obtain legal consultation when necessary are thorough, conscientious practitioners who are more likely to serve their clients well.

Conclusion

Clinicians should think creatively about interventions that may be helpful when they serve children and adolescents. Clinical innovations are important to the profession and its clients. Clinicians who consider using touch with minor clients should be vigilant in their efforts to ensure that their approaches are ethical and protect clients. It also behooves practitioners to take practical steps to prevent ethics complaints and malpractice claims alleging that they used touch in a way that was unethical and harmful. Some forms of touch are clearly unethical and should be avoided at all costs. Unfortunately, a relatively small number of unscrupulous, unethical, and impaired clinicians may use touch to exploit clients for self-serving purposes.

At times, however, there is a much finer, and more ambiguous, line between clinicians' ethical and unethical use of touch. In some instances, practitioners may find that a cross section of thoughtful, principled, and earnest colleagues disagree about the appropriateness of touch in the clinical context. In such circumstances, clinicians can best protect clients, and themselves, by conscientiously implementing the procedural standard of care and taking assertive steps to obtain proper consultation and supervision; reviewing relevant and practice standards, regulations, laws, policies, and literature; obtaining legal consultation when necessary; and documenting and evaluating their decision-making steps and interventions. In the final analysis, this comprehensive strategy is the very best way to protect both clients and practitioners.

Discussion Questions

1 Summarize your understanding of the distinction between boundary *violations* and boundary *crossings* in relation to clinicians' use of touch to provide services to children and adolescents. Describe three clinical scenarios that illustrate boundary *violations* involving the use of touch. Describe three clinical scenarios that illustrate boundary *crossings* involving the use of touch.
2 Under what clinical circumstances do you think the use of touch is appropriate in work with children and adolescents? Why?
3 Imagine that you have been appointed clinical director of a therapy program that provides services to abused and neglected children and adolescents. Develop guidelines that clinicians on your staff will be expected to follow concerning their use of touch in their work with clients.

References

Association for Play Therapy (2015). Paper on touch: Clinical, professional, and ethical issues. Retrieved on 10 October, 2016 from: http://c.ymcdn.com/sites/www.a4pt.org/resource/resmgr/Publications/Paper_On_Touch_2015.pdf

Austin, K., Moline, M., & Williams, G. (1990). *Confronting malpractice: Legal and ethical dilemmas in psychotherapy.* Newbury Park, CA: Sage.

Bernstein, T., & Hartsell, B. (2008). *The portable lawyer for mental health professionals* (2nd ed.). New York: Wiley.

Bonitz, V. (2008). Use of physical touch in the "talking cure": A journey to the outskirts of psychotherapy. *Psychotherapy: Theory, Research, Practice, Training, 45*, 391–404. DOI:10.1037/a0013311

Bouhoutsos, J. (1985). Therapist-client sexual involvement: A challenge for mental health professionals. *Professional Psychology: Research and Practice, 14*, 185–196.

Bouthousos, J., Holroyd, J., Lerman, H., Forer, B., & Greenberg, M. (1983). Sexual intimacy between psychotherapists and patients. *Professional Psychology: Research and Practice, 14*, 185–196. DOI:10.1037/0735-7028.14.2.185

Bullis, R. (1995). *Clinical social worker misconduct.* Chicago: Nelson-Hall.

Calmes, S., Piazza, N., and Laux, J. (2013). The use of touch in counseling: An ethical decision-making model. *Counseling and Values, 58*, 59–68. DOI:10.1002/j.2161-007x.2013.00025.x

Celenza, A. (2007). *Sexual boundary violations: Therapeutic, supervisory, and academic contexts.* Lanham, MD: Aronson.

Coleman, E., & Schaefer, S. (1986). Boundaries of sex and intimacy between client and counselor. *Journal of Counseling and Development, 64*, 341–344. DOI:10.1002/j.1556-6676.1986.tb01128.x

Cornell, W. (1997). Touch and boundaries in Transactional Analysis: Ethical and transferential considerations. *Transactional Analysis Journal, 37*, 30–77.

Cowen, E., Weissberg, R., & Lotyczeuski, B. (1983). Physical contact in helping interactions with young children. *Journal of Consulting and Clinical Psychology, 51*, 132–138. DOI:10.1037/0022-006x.51.1.132

Downey, D. (2001). Therapeutic touch in psychotherapy. *Psychotherapy, 36*, 35–38. DOI:10.1037/e565592006-009

Dunne, C., Bruggen, P., & O'Brien, C. (1982). Touch and action in group therapy of younger adolescents. *Journal of Adolescents, 5*, 31–38. DOI:10.1016/s0140-1971(82)80016-x

Durana, C. (1998). The use of touch in psychotherapy: Ethical and clinical guidelines. *Psychotherapy: Theory, Research, Practice, Training, 35*, 269–280. DOI:10.1037/h0087817

Eiden, B. (1998). The use of touch in psychotherapy. *Self and Society, 26*, 3–8.

Epstein, R. (1994). *Keeping boundaries: Maintaining safety and integrity in the psychotherapeutic process.* Washington, DC: American Psychiatric Press.

Eyckmans, S. (2009). Handle with care: Touch as a therapeutic tool. *Gestalt Journal of Australia and New Zealand, 6*, 40–53.

Feldman-Summers, S., & Jones, G. (1984). Psychological impacts of sexual contact between therapists or other health care practitioners and their clients. *Journal of Consulting and Clinical Psychology, 52*, 1054–1061. DOI:10.1037/0022-006x.52.6.1054

Field, T. (2003). *Touch.* Cambridge, MA: MIT Press.

Field, T., Shanberg, S., Kuhn, C., Fierro, K., Henteleff, T., Mueller, C., Yando, R., & Burman, I. (1997). Bulimic adolescents benefit from massage therapy. *Adolescence, 131*, 555–563.
Gabbard, G. (Ed.). (1989). *Sexual exploitation in professional relationships.* Washington, DC: American Psychiatric Press.
Gartrell, N., Herman, S., Olarte, S., Feldstein, M., & Localio, R. (1986). Psychiatrist-patient sexual contact: Results of a national survey. *American Journal of Psychiatry, 143*, 1126–1131. DOI:10.1176/ajp.143.9.1126
Gifis, S. (1991). *Law dictionary* (3rd ed.). Hauppauge, NY: Barron's.
Gifis, S. (2010). *Law dictionary* (6th ed.). Hauppauge, NY: Barron's.
Goodman, M., & Teicher, A. (1988). To touch or not to touch. *Psychotherapy: Theory, Research, Practice, Training, 25*, 492–500. DOI:10.1037/h0085374
Gutheil, T., & Gabbard, G. (1993). The concept of boundaries in clinical practice: Theoretical and risk-management dimensions. *American Journal of Psychiatry, 150*, 188–196. DOI:10.1176/ajp.150.2.188
Holroyd, J., & Brodsky, A. (1977). Psychologists' attitudes and practices regarding erotic and nonerotic physical contact with patients. *American Psychologist, 32*, 843–849.
Holroyd, J., & Brodsky, A. (1980). Does touching patients lead to sexual intercourse? *Professional Psychology, 11*, 807–811. DOI:10.1037/0735-7028.11.5.807
Holub E., & Lee S. (1990). Therapists' use of nonerotic physical contact: Ethical concerns. *Professional Psychology: Research and Practice, 21*, 115–117. DOI:10.1037//0735-7028.21.2.115
Horton, J.A., Clance, P., Sterk-Elifson, C., & Emshoff, J. (1995). Touch in psychotherapy: A survey of patients' experiences. *Psychotherapy: Theory, Research, Practice, Training, 32*, 443–457. DOI:10.1037/0033-3204.32.3.443
Hunter, M., & Struve, J. (1998). *The ethical use of touch in psychotherapy.* Thousand Oaks, CA: Sage.
Keats, J. (1973). *John Keats: The complete poems.* New York: Penguin.
Karbelnig, A. (2000). Physical contact between psychotherapist and patient: Ethical, legal, and psychoanalytical considerations. *The California Psychologist, 33*, 32–34.
Kertay, L., & Riviere, S.L. (1993). The use of touch in psychotherapy: Theoretical and ethical considerations. *Psychotherapy: Theory, Research, Practice, Training, 30*, 32–40. DOI:10.1037/0033-3204.30.1.32
Kitchener, K. (1988). Dual role relationships: What makes them so problematic? *Journal of Counseling and Development, 67*, 217–221. DOI:10.1002/j.1556-6676.1988.tb02586.x
Levitan, A., & Johnson, J. (1986). The role of touch in healing and hypnotherapy. *American Journal of Clinical Hypnosis, 28*, 218–223. DOI:10.1080/00029157.1986.10402657
McNeil-Haber, F.M. (2004). Ethical considerations in the use of nonerotic touch in psychotherapy with children. *Ethics & Behavior, 14*, 123–140. DOI:10.1207/s15327019eb1402_3
Madden, R. (2003). *Essential law for social workers.* New York: Columbia University Press.
Miller, L. (1997). An explanation of therapeutic touch using the science of unitary man. *Nursing Forum, 18*, 278–287. DOI:10.1111/j.1744-6198.1979.tb00680.x
Olarte, S. (1997). Sexual boundary violations. In *The Hatherleigh guide to ethics in therapy* (pp. 195–209). New York: Hatherleigh.
Phelan, J.E. (2009). Exploring the use of touch in the psychotherapeutic setting: A phenomenological review. *Psychotherapy: Theory, Research, Practice, Training, 46*, 97–111. DOI:10.1037/a0014751

Pinson, B. (2002). Touch in therapy: An effort to make the unknown known. *Journal of Contemporary Psychotherapy, 32*, 179–196. DOI:10.1023/a:1020545010081

Pope, K. (1986). New trends in malpractice cases and changes in APA's liability insurance. *Independent Practitioner, 6*, 23–26.

Pope, K. (1988). How clients are harmed by sexual contact with mental health professionals: The syndrome and its prevalence. *Journal of Counseling and Development, 67*, 222–226. DOI:10.1002/j.1556-6676.1988.tb02587.x

Pope, K. (1991). Dual relationships in psychotherapy. *Ethics and Behavior, 1*, 21–34. DOI:10.1207/s15327019eb0101_3

Pope, K., & Bouhoutsos, J. (1986). *Sexual intimacy between therapists and patients.* New York: Praeger.

Reamer, F. (2001). *The social work ethics audit: A risk management tool.* Washington, DC: NASW Press.

Reamer, F. (2005). Documentation in social work: Evolving ethical and risk management standards. *Social Work, 50*, 325–334. DOI:10.1093/sw/50.4.325

Reamer, F. (2012). *Boundary issues and dual relationships in the human services.* New York: Columbia University Press.

Reamer, F. (2015). *Risk management in social work: Preventing professional malpractice, liability, and disciplinary action.* New York: Columbia University Press.

Redleaf, A., (1998). *Behind closed doors: Gender, sexuality, and touch in the doctor/patient relationship.* Westport, CT: Auburn House.

Sidell, N. (2011). *Social work documentation: A guide to strengthening your case recording.* Washington, DC: NASW Press.

Simon, R. (1999). Therapist-patient sex: From boundary violations to sexual misconduct. *Forensic Psychiatry, 22*, 31–47.

Smith, D., & Fitzpatrick, M. (1995). Patient-therapist boundary issues: An integrative review of theory and research. *Professional Psychology: Research and Practice, 26*, 499–506. DOI:10.1037/0735-7028.26.5.499

Smith, E., Clance, P., & Imes, S. (Eds.). (1998). *Touch in psychotherapy: Theory, research, and practice.* New York: Guilford Press.

Smythe, K. (2015). Alexandria therapist sentenced to ten years in prison. Retrieved on 25 October, 2016 from: https://www.alexandrianews.org/2015/alexandria-therapist-sentenced-to-ten-years-in-prison/

Stenzel, C.L., & Rupert, P.A. (2004). Psychologists' use of touch in individual psychotherapy. *Psychotherapy: Theory, Research, Practice, Training, 41*, 332–345. DOI:10.1037/0033-3204.41.3.332

Stockwell, S., & Dye, A. (1980). Effects of counselor touch on counseling outcome. *Journal of Counseling Psychology, 27*, 443–446. DOI:http://dx.doi.org/10.1037/0022-0167.27.5.443

Syme, G. (2003). *Dual relationships in counselling and psychotherapy.* London: Sage.

Welch, M. (1989). *Holding time.* New York: Simon & Schuster.

Willison, B., & Masson, R. (1986). The role of touch in psychotherapy: An adjunct to communication. *Journal of Counseling and Development, 64*, 497–500. DOI:10.1002/j.1556-6676.1986.tb01180.x

Zur, O. (2007). *Boundaries in psychotherapy: Ethical and clinical explorations.* Washington, DC: American Psychological Association.

Part II
Play Therapy Models That Use Touch as an Intervention

3 The Neurobiology of Touch
Developmental Play Therapy with a Child Diagnosed with Sensory Processing Disorder

Lynn Stammers

The basic principle of Developmental Play Therapy is that a child who experiences touch from a capable toucher will grow toward a healthy maturity and will heal from earlier trauma and neglect.

Viola Brody, *The Dialogue of Touch*

The Brain Science of Nurturing Touch

Our bodies and brains are inextricably interwoven and dependent on each other for interacting with and interpreting—not only our physical—but also our social environment (Barnard & Brazelton, 1990; Cozolino, 2013; Linden, 2015). An accumulating research base informs us of the complexity of the skin as a sensory organ (McGlone, Wessberg, & Olausson, 2014). Our bodies are covered by and protected with skin, and, as the first sense to develop prenatally, it is identified as the most sensitive sense organ in the body (Field, 2014; Gallace & Spence, 2010). Sensory experience in the body is the means by which we come to develop a sense of self, learn to regulate our emotional response to stressful incidents, and understand the feelings of others, providing our "most fundamental means of contact with the outside world" (Gallace & Spence, 2010, p. 246).

Placing touch within the context of an attuned relationship, an important element in the therapeutic dyad, is seen to be supportive of the neurological process examined by neuroscience research (McGlone, Wessberg, & Olausson, 2014; Field, 2014; Schore, 2012). The core qualities of healthy social interaction are attunement, empathy, and self-regulation (Wilkinson, 2010), which are mediated by touch (Szalavitz & Perry, 2010; Porges, 2011). We cannot function socially without some measure of each of these qualities, and affective and developmental neuroscience research suggests that these qualities are rooted in our earliest experiences that influence brain structure and development (Cozolino, 2013; Perry & Szalavitz, 2006; Badenoch, 2008; Schore, 2012; Siegel, 2012). The processing of sensory stimuli increases the brain's capacity to function in an integrative way. Harlow's (1958) research with baby monkeys raised the profile of touch by demonstrating an association between touch and social development, placing touch at the center of early developmental experience (Barnard & Brazelton, 1990; Linden, 2015).

Emotional Touch

Touch is mediated by a number of different sensors in the skin, each one highly specialized in the tactile function it provides, for example proprioception, pain, temperature, and the sensory experience of texture (Barnard & Brazelton, 1990; Field, 2014; Cozolino, 2013; Linden, 2015). The skin has two distinct sets of receptors: one in hairy skin and one in hairless, both with specialized touch sensors to facilitate a broad spectrum of kinesthetic experience (Linden, 2015). Recent developments in understanding a separate and specific mechanism for emotional touch suggests that particular fibers respond explicitly to gentle touch on the hairy parts of the skin. These areas have specific C-fibers, known as C-tactile fibers, that have been found to be responsible for the conveying of tactile information related to interpersonal touch (Linden, 2015). The C-tactile fibers are purposely tuned for interpersonal touch and connect with areas of the brain known to be related to social perception and social cognition.

The neurological connection to the prefrontal cortex via the amygdala is considered particularly relevant in the brain's evaluation of the context that affective touch is being experienced and contextual aspects of the touch being experienced are identified as significant in the quality of the touch experience (McGlone, Wessberg, & Olausson, 2014). For example, the process of neuroception, that is, the intrapersonal capacity to evaluate the environment for threats of danger from either people or situations, occurs below the level of awareness and can inhibit the effects of the bonding chemical oxytocin if a situation or person is perceived as unsafe (Porges, 2011; van der Kolk, 2014). The importance of contextual factors in the dynamics of the touch experience (McGlone, Wessberg, & Olausson, 2014; Linden, 2015) demonstrates clear clinical implications particularly relevant within the therapeutic setting (Porges, 2011).

The Role of Oxytocin in Relationships

Close interpersonal relationships are linked with regular and consistent touch (Szalavitz & Perry, 2010; Gallace & Spence, 2010). Research suggests that oxytocin, a protein produced in the brain, enables us to feel connected with others, and affectionate touch releases this chemical of well-being into the brain (Szalavitz & Perry, 2010; Porges, 2011; Uvnäs-Moberg, 2003). This neuropeptide has been implicated in maternal bonding between mother and child and correlated with decreasing stress levels (Field, 2014). The soothing effect of mothers or other caregivers responding sensitively and quickly to their infants crying by picking them up and holding them close to their body releases oxytocin, the benefits of which become associated with the person administering the touch. The regulation of stress hormones has been associated with the tactile responses between mother and child and identified as a factor in resilience (Linden, 2015), making the sensory experience of touch of particular significance in our ability to respond to stressful situations. Oxytocin inhibits harmful stress hormones in the brain, acting as a buffer to the stress response (a protective mechanism of the neural system); however, in situations which feel unsafe, although the oxytocin may be released, Porges (2011) suggested that "we may struggle against the attempted embrace" (p. 14).

Neural Systems

An evolutionary imperative prioritizing lower brain development optimizes survival, but in order to take the necessary steps toward becoming social and cognitive human beings, development is dependent upon the early context of human interaction. It is this process of connection that enables the higher brain structures to develop more sophisticated interactions between the mother and child initially, and eventually others within the family and further afield (Badenoch, 2008; Cozolino, 2013; Porges, 2011; Schore, 2012; Siegel, 2012). An important component of social, emotional development is the process of understanding another. A critical aspect of brain structure, identified in the brain as *mirror neurons*, is thought to be critical in the development of empathy (Szalavitz & Perry, 2010) and to facilitate our sense of self in relation to others (Cozolino, 2006). Aspects of infant care are "felt" by a young child, for example, a wet diaper, hunger, or discomfort, via the skin's sensory system; mirror neurons create opportunities for resonance between the main caregiver and the baby, allowing the development of empathy: an appreciation of what another might be "feeling" (Badenoch, 2008; Siegel, 2012; Cozolino, 2006, 2013).

Interoception

Everything we do relies on touch (Field, 2014) and all interpersonal experiences impact on neurological development. Van der Kolk (2014) described interoception as "our awareness of our subtle sensory, body based feelings: the greater that awareness, the greater our potential to control our lives" (pp. 95–96). Sensations *create* our earliest implicit memories, influencing long-lasting expectations about the world we live in and the people we will meet. The influence of incoming visual, auditory, olfactory, and kinesthetic signals, particularly in relation to the responses of significant others, on limbic structures of the right hemisphere are responsible for, as Badenoch (2008) poetically wrote, "the graceful dance between mother and child" (pp. 52–53). Siegel (2012) suggested that this process allows the development of interoception, a means to understand ourselves in relation to others.

At the heart of development in newborns is the attachment relationship with the main caregiver. The work of Bowlby (1969) is significant in understanding the concept of the internal working model and attachment theory as a way of understanding the influence of this early interpersonal stimulus on the emotional and social development of the child. A significant aspect of attachment is the motivational process it initiates, producing proximity-seeking behavior of the child toward adults. A mother's attunement to her child therefore promotes integration and self-regulation (Porges, 2011).

Neuroplasticity

The significance of early environmental influences on the course of brain growth might appear initially to infer that patterns of social interaction are set and fixed early in development, remaining constant throughout life. Fortunately, neuroscience informs us of the possibility of altered trajectories through the mechanism of neuroplasticity. Neuroplasticity allows the brain to be adaptable to a variety of individualized experiences in response to the environment (Perry & Szalavitz, 2006; Siegel, 2012). All interpersonal experiences, including touch, impact on neurological development with the brain pruning and growing neurons in response to sensory stimulation; "neurons that fire together wire together," states Hebb (1949, as cited in LeDoux, 1998, p. 214). This process ensures that any unnecessary neurological connections are discarded, allowing for greater adaptation and capacity for survival in the individual environment. Brain networks that are supportive of safe social interaction can overlay and replace early neural networks wired in an environment of poor attunement and care (Cozolino, 2013).

The significance of touch as a sensory pathway and its effect on neuroplasticity is understandable given the importance of the role of the skin in supporting

Figure 3.1 Caring touch promotes healthy interpersonal relationships.
Source: ©123rf.com/CathyYeulet

the earliest learning of the infant (Field, 2014). Research shows that the skin and nervous system arise out of the same embryonic layer. Therefore, not only is the skin important as a means of communication between individuals (see Figure 3.1) but additionally is able to help regulate arousal (Field, 2014). Since children's positive development is dependent upon effective emotional regulation (Porges, 2011) safe, nurturing touch in a therapeutic setting is a useful means of working with children who have reduced sensory integration and who struggle with emotional dysregulation.

The Therapeutic Relationship and the Brain–Mind–Body Connection

In a plenary address at the American Psychological Association, Schore (2009) reported a shift in emphasis away from the cognitive practice of psychotherapeutic interventions, placing greater emphasis on interpersonal neuroscience. Schore (2012) stressed the importance of the role of the relational unconscious identified with right-brain function, which is reflected in the focus now being taken by both clinicians and researchers. This right-brain credibility moves the emphasis in therapy away from the verbal, cognitive operation, where the therapeutic liaison is based on a one-sided conversation by the client and "heard" by the therapist, to a more dynamic understanding about the healing power of this dyadic relationship. Although this view is now becoming more widely accepted, the trend toward understanding the influences of relationship in psychotherapy has been evolving for many years. Schore (2012) advised that it is the more recent ventures in interpersonal neurobiology and the cross pollination between fields that have yielded valuable insights into the relational discourse of therapy.

Understanding the intersubjectivity of the therapeutic experience brings to the fore early theories and understanding of the construct of attachment (Porges, 2011). Bowlby (1969) made the connection between the necessary consistent care of an infant by a significant adult and the child's ability to thrive. Nurturing adult attachments provide children with protective, safe havens and secure bases from which to explore and engage with others and their environment. Studies of children growing up in institutions or other isolated situations revealed the impact on brain architecture of a deficit in human interaction in the early stages of development (Perry & Szalavitz, 2006).

It is suggested that a developing brain requires another brain in relationship to itself (Schore, 2012). The reciprocal influence on the brains of both mother and child by a whole symphony of brain chemicals working together to regulate the brain structure of both, appears to be one aspect of brain regulation that is activated through this significant relationship (Cozolino, 2006). Likewise, implicit within this relational interaction is the brain–mind–body connection (Schore, 2012) and how this impacts our understanding about the important role that touch can potentially play within the therapeutic relationship.

Implications for the Use of Therapeutic Touch in Therapy with Children

As the foregoing sections highlighted, touch is an essential element in the healthy development of the brain. If for any reason a child did not receive an experience of healthy touch in early life due to abuse or neglect, opportunities for a reparative touch experience are not lost. Fortunately, neuroscience confirms that the brain is plastic and capable of change, thereby providing the opportunity to revisit early developmental experiences that include the important element of touch, so that we can alter the brain's trajectory of development in a positive way. This suggests that there is hope for a child who has difficulty in developing social relationships, isolated and locked away, and unable to engage with others who live around him. Social and affective neuroscience suggests that children can heal from early life experiences that were developmentally missed (Perry & Szalavitz, 2006).

The use of *nurturing touch* offers therapists the opportunity to provide an optimal therapeutic environment to promote emotional growth with the children who come into our sphere of influence. In no way does this diminish concerns within our society of the difficulties posed by some individuals who abuse the positive role that touch is intended to give to children (Aquino & Lee, 2000). The ethical and clinical considerations intended to ensure the appropriate and safe implementation of touch in the therapeutic environment are addressed in the next section.

Affective and developmental neuroscience research suggests that touch as part of an attuned response provides a nurturing therapeutic environment to facilitate cognitive and social/emotional development. Therapeutic approaches that use touch as an intervention are becoming increasingly acknowledged in the field as valuable tools of healing (van der Kolk, 2014). According to the Association for Play Therapy's *Paper on Touch: Clinical, Professional, and Ethical Issues* (2015), "When a child experiences touch from a caring and safe caregiver, many things happen to promote healthy growth. Children develop a sense of self and the ability to relate to others; they learn to modulate affect; and develop a belief in his or her own self-worth and ability to master their environment" (p. 1).

The Ethical and Clinical Considerations of Nurturing Touch

Physical contact is a normal part of human experience and touch is often provided particularly at times of distress as it contributes to a general sense of well-being (Field, 2014). However, the topic of touch in child treatment is controversial and there appears to be much confusion and fear that surrounds this topic (Aquino & Lee, 2000; Zur & Nordmarken, 2016). The controversies surrounding touch in therapy have created touch as a taboo subject that brings with it implications of not only ethical but also legal ramifications (Aquino & Lee, 2000;

Zur & Nordmarken, 2016). The climate of a no-touching policy can also be understood as arising out of a desire to protect children from the unhealthy approaches of sexual predators.

The client's safety brings a heightened sense of responsibility for the therapist, and the necessary principles of self-awareness, congruence, and understanding of the *client's needs* are imperative when utilizing touch in sessions (Aquino & Lee, 2000). When working with children who are identified as having sensory integration issues, touch can be a significant barrier due to their resistance to close physical contact (Garland, 2014). However, there is evidence that they can overcome this difficulty and interpersonal neuroscience research, as reviewed in this chapter, suggests that touch has important biological, emotional, and social benefits.

Aquino and Lee (2000) provided recommendations for ensuring appropriate and safe touch in the therapeutic environment. Of paramount importance is that the clinical framework is based upon "sound developmental and clinical principles" (p. 28), understanding that the goal of all therapeutic work is the *meeting of the child's needs*. Actions involving touch should be free from any element of secrecy in order to ensure an ethically safe environment. In my work with children, professional safeguards include: The school administrators are able to walk past my room and see what is happening at any time through a small, high window. I share the playroom with another colleague and this ensures another adult is present throughout my sessions. Touch activities are limited to hands, arms, shoulders, back, and feet (Courtney, 2012), and all sessions are reviewed with a clinical supervisor. I also offer opportunities for parents to join sessions with their child so they can witness and engage in the Developmental Play Therapy (DPT) activities and hopefully transfer them to home.

Developmental Play Therapy

The replication of early developmental experiences is at the heart of DPT, with the therapeutic interactions primarily taking place between therapist and child. In DPT, touch is understood to be vital to facilitate the necessary changes needed in the child for onward growth to take place (Brody, 1997; Courtney & Gray, 2014). Metaphorically, touch becomes the bridge of healing between therapist and child when either the bridge has never been built or some catastrophe has washed the bridge away. Although the techniques involved in DPT are important, it is the therapeutic relationship that creates an environment to facilitate the emergence of what Brody (1997) describes as a child's felt sense of self, a key ingredient to a healthy understanding of inner-self, necessary for normal human growth and development (Bowlby, 1969; Barnard & Brazelton, 1990; Courtney & Gray, 2014). For Brody (1997), touch is a precursor to other forms of communication and social and emotional growth.

The process of DPT is therefore representative of the necessary stages of neurological development and in effect is mirrored in Perry's Neurosequential Model (Perry, 2006). The use of first-play is based upon the inter-relational activities that frequently occur between parents and baby, for example, singing games, "patty cake," and hide and seek (Courtney, 2013). It is the pleasurable element that is an indicator of a basic developmental need being met, and can be measured in the smiles and laughter of the child. Brody advocated that touch experienced in an attuned way with an adult who is fully present promoted healing and growth. During the process the child experiences themselves as felt; "recognizing themselves as an *I* and recognizing the Toucher as an *Other*" (Brody, 1997, p. 7).

Case of Rahim

The following DPT case presentation was conducted by the author of this chapter who had prior extensive training in DPT interventions. All identifying information in this case has been changed to protect confidentiality.

Some children have challenged my expectations more than others and this case stripped away any resistance that I had to using touch as a therapeutic intervention. The positive outcomes that the role of touch played in the treatment process exceeded my expectations.

Case Background and Presenting Problem

Rahim, age six, was diagnosed with Sensory Processing Disorder (SPD) and was referred for counseling services due to behavioral difficulties at school. The teaching staff reported Rahim as being socially disengaged, avoidant of eye contact and any type of touch, and limited in his verbal communication. He displayed outbursts of dangerous behaviors that were directed at other children, and were perceived by the teachers to be expressions of frustration. Additionally, Rahim did not engage in play with other children, appearing to lack empathy, and he was happiest when seated in front of a computer screen. An intake assessment with his mother suggested that there were definitely two sides to him. At times he could be kind and lovable, but often inexplicably rejected parental affection. Additionally, he exhibited fierce and frightening behavior directed toward his younger sister. Issues of frustration arose around bedtime settling and the ringing of the phone, which would cause him to pick it up and throw it. There seemed to be no sense of playfulness or of that communicative dance that forms the basis of healthy emotional relationships.

Sensory Processing Disorder and Treatment Plan

Sensory problems encompass a broad spectrum of behavior, such as verbal and non verbal communication, social interaction, oversensitivity and undersensitivity to touch, and deficit in imaginative play and problem solving. Rahim's symptoms were observed to include a number of these behaviors. Garland (2014) recommended incorporating kinesthetic opportunities into work with children diagnosed with SPD in order to address sensory integrative issues. One of the overriding challenges for treatment was Rahim's oversensitivity to touch. Garland (2014) emphasized that being oversensitive to touch is one of the most difficult types of sensory modulation issues (p. 65). The underlying principle for the treatment plan was to offer opportunities for sensory engagement within a safe and attuned environment providing the developmental experiences to build Rahim's neurobiological circuitry for social connections (Badenoch, 2008; Perry, 2006). Therefore, the DPT sensory touch interventions were assessed as the most appropriate treatment approach and the treatment plan was reviewed with his mother, who signed the informed consent.

The Process

Below is an excerpt of the first session where I engaged Rahim in a DPT singing "Hello" game, and also deliberately chose an activity with a scarf to get a sense of how he felt about light touch on his face. Surprisingly, this was not a problem for him.

DPT Session 1

THERAPIST: *Making eye contact, I reached out and took one of Rahim's hands in mine and in an animated voice sang,* "Hello Rahim, Hello Rahim, how are you, how are you? I can see your brown twinkling eyes and your brown hair."
RAHIM: *He responded by putting both hands together.*
THERAPIST: "Look at how long your fingers are." *I then counted his fingers on one hand with a gentle squeeze.* "One, two, three ... and you're looking at me."
RAHIM: *He accepted the touch and gave me his other hand.*
THERAPIST: "Ah, let's see the other hand, what a smooth hand this is and look, what have we here? Oh, it goes up, up, up and down the other side, down, down, down ...' Being attuned to Rahim's behavioral responses to the touch, I monitored this intervention closely.*
RAHIM: *He maintained eye contact and sat still across from me on the floor during this activity.*
THERAPIST: *I picked up a scarf and tossed it in the air.* "Look Rahim." *I put the scarf on my head, waited briefly, and then pulled the scarf off and said,* "Peek a boo!"
RAHIM: *He looked a bit startled but didn't move away.*
THERAPIST: *Repeated* "Peek a boo" *but with a quieter voice.*
RAHIM: *He began to smile a little.*

THERAPIST: "Do you want to pull it off my head Rahim?" *I place the scarf on my head and gently guide his hands to the corners of the scarf. He pulls immediately and I say,* "Peek a boo." *We repeat this activity and then I stated,* "Do you want to try, Rahim?"

RAHIM: *He was quiet and looking directly at me.*

THERAPIST: "Shall we put the scarf over Rahim's head?" *I observed no resistance to this idea as I placed the scarf on his head. Then in a soft voice, I said,* "Peek a boo," *while pulling the scarf off.*

RAHIM: *He smiled at me.*

THERAPIST: *His smile indicted that he enjoyed the game and I repeated the activity by adding increased levels of sensory experience.*

Reflections

Over time, Rahim became more accepting of different tactile textures. Initially he rejected anything messy (e.g., touching clay on his hands), becoming upset and rushing around trying to shake the mess off. Gradually he accepted the soothing effect of washing hands that appeared to calm him. The early therapy sessions focused mostly on kinesthetic experiences. By the twelfth session he had moved beyond his need for the activities to be initiated by me, and our relational dance was becoming more attuned as Rahim began to find a sense of self and become more self-directed. He also demonstrated an increased neurological capacity for comfort around social interactions and his attachment relationship with me became more secure. One aspect that had been missing in his play had been symbolism and imagination, and over time his imaginary play increased to play with puppets and creative pictures expressing his thoughts and feelings.

Conclusion of the Process

During the early sessions there were times of resistance and discomfort for Rahim where he would attempt to withdraw. By careful, sensitive attunement, I was able to engage him through relationship-based activities. The therapeutic process continued over two years and ended when the time came for Rahim to move on to another school. The treatment plan changed to accommodate his social and emotional development, gradually introducing opportunities to play with family members and his peers. Significantly, Rahim's mother continued to use her understanding of the need for the first-play games and strategies shared with her to address Rahim's frustration at home. After our final session Rahim was able to write a beautiful "thank you" note to me that was very readable and expressive of his *feelings* about his experience with me in the Rainbow Room (see Figure 3.2).

The Neurobiology of Touch 45

Figure 3.2 "Thank you very much for all your help and support I had lots of fun in a Rainbow Room I am going to miss you." (Drawing used with permission.)

Chapter Summary

Somewhere in Rahim's developmental journey the usual neural networks that enable individuals to connect in satisfying ways with significant others had not developed. The child study illustrates how Rahim gained a felt sense of self that came into being through the joyful use of touch in the first-play activities, as provided by the attuned presence of the therapist. Brain plasticity allowed for a new subjective response to social interaction to develop. In the end, Rahim became more vocal in his interactions, increasing his potential for thought, imagination, and understanding that bridged outside of the therapeutic setting into his relational world with others.

Interpersonal neurobiology places relationship at the center of healthy social interaction. The therapeutic relationship offers the opportunity for children with communication difficulties, resulting from a sensory integration deficit, to heal. DPT centers upon the relationship between therapist and child, using touch as the mode of engagement leading to a physical felt-sense of the self. The DPT activities helped to desensitize Rahim's response to touch while maintaining a sense of safety (Porges, 2011). Attunement gives access to experiences necessary to build structures essential for the development of a social brain. Caring touch releases vital hormones, such as oxytocin and other neuropeptides, that can help to calm children, decrease stress, and facilitate bonding. The development of mirror neurons creates a sense of self in relationship with another, as well as affective C-tactile fibers in the skin that connect to the areas of the brain related to social perception and cognition (Linden, 2015). The neuroplasticity of the brain encourages the possibility of change in interpersonal relationships such as those provided by DPT.

Discussion Questions

1 Discuss with a colleague your thoughts about the advances in neuroscience of touch and how this new emerging knowledge impacts practice with child clients and families.
2 Reflecting on the case presentation, discuss with a colleague your thoughts, feelings and reactions about the therapist's use of touch with Rahim. How did the therapist's assessment and understanding of Rahim's diagnosis affect her decision to use DPT as an intervention? In what ways did the therapist carefully monitor Rahim's responses to the touch? What role, in your judgment, did the therapist's training in DPT play in helping her to ethically implement the touch interventions within sessions?

References

Aquino, A.T., & Lee S.S. (2000). The use of nonerotic touch with children. *Journal of Psychotherapy in Independent Practice, 1(3)*, 17–30. DOI:10.1300/J288v01n03_02

Association for Play Therapy. (2015). *Paper on touch: Clinical, professional, & ethical issues*. Retrieved on 25 October, 2016 from: http://c.ymcdn.com/sites/www.a4pt.org/resource/resmgr/Publications/Paper_On_Touch_2015.pdf

Badenoch, B. (2008). *Being a brain-wise therapist: A practical guide to interpersonal neurobiology*. New York: Norton.

Barnard, K.E., & Brazelton, T.B. (1990). *Touch: The foundation of experience*. Madison, CT: International Universities Press.

Bowlby, J. (1969). *Attachment and loss. Vol. 1: Attachment*. New York: Basic Books.

Brody, V.A. (1997). *The dialogue of touch: Developmental play therapy* (2nd ed.). Northvale, NJ: Jason Aronson.

Courtney, J.A. (2012). Touching autism through developmental play therapy. In L. Gallo-Lopez & L.C. Rubin (Eds.), *Play-based interventions for children and adolescents with autism spectrum disorders* (pp. 137–157). New York: Routledge.

Courtney, J.A. (2013). *The curative touch of a Magic Rainbow Hug*, video recording, TEDx Talk. Retrieved on 25 October, 2016 from: https://www.youtube.com/watch?v=kYZqyjzuaOw

Courtney, J.A., & Gray, S.W. (2014). A phenomenological inquiry into practitioner experiences of developmental play therapy: Implications for training in touch. *International Journal of Play Therapy, 23(2)*, 114–129. DOI:0.1037/a0036366

Cozolino, L. (2006) *The neuroscience of human relationships: Attachment and the developing brain*. New York: Norton.

Cozolino, L. (2013). *The social neuroscience of education*. New York: Norton.

Field, T. (2014). *Touch* (2nd ed.). Cambridge, MA: MIT Press.

Gallace, A., & Spence, C. (2010). The science of interpersonal touch: An overview. *Neuroscience and Biobehavioral Reviews, 34*, 246–259. DOI:10.1016/j.neubiorev.2008.10.004

Garland, T. (2014). *Self-regulation interventions and strategies: Keeping the body, mind and emotions on task in children with autism, ADHD or sensory disorders*. Eau Claire, WI: PESI.

Harlow, H. (1958). The nature of love. *The American Psychologist, 3*, 673–685. Retrieved on 25 October, 2016 from: http://psychclassics.yorku.ca/Harlow/love.htm

LeDoux, J. (1998). *The emotional brain: The mysterious underpinnings of emotional life.* New York: Touchstone.

Linden, D.J. (2015). *Touch: The science of hand, heart, and mind.* New York: Penguin.

McGlone, F., Wessberg, J., & Olausson, H. (2014, May, 21). Discriminative and affective touch: Sensing and feeling. *Neuron, 82*, 737–755. Retrieved 12 January, 2106 from: http://dx.doi.org/10.1016/j.neuron.2014.05.001

Perry, B., & Szalavitz, M. (2006). *The boy who was raised as a dog: And other stories from a child psychiatrist's notebook—What traumatized children can teach us about loss, love and healing.* New York: Basic Books.

Perry, B.D. (2006). Applying principles of neurodevelopment to clinical work with maltreated and traumatized children: The neurosequential model of therapeutics. In N.B. Webb (Ed.), *Working with traumatized youth in child welfare* (pp. 27–52). New York: Guilford Press.

Porges, S.W. (2011). *The Polyvagal theory: Neurophysiological foundations of emotions, attachment, communication, self-regulation.* New York: Norton.

Schore, A.N. (2009). Paradigm shift; the right brain and the relational unconscious. Plenary address. *American Psychological Association Convention.* Toronto Canada.

Schore, A.N. (2012). *The science of the art of psychotherapy.* New York: Norton.

Siegel, D.J. (2012). *Pocket guide to interpersonal biology: An integrative handbook of the mind.* New York: Norton.

Szalavitz, M., & Perry, B.D. (2010). *Born for love: Why empathy is essential—and endangered.* New York: Harper Collins.

Uvnäs-Moberg, K. (2003). *The oxytocin factor: Tapping the hormone of calm, love, and healing.* Cambridge, MA: Da Capo Press.

van der Kolk, B. (2014). *The body keeps the score.* New York: Penguin Group.

Wilkinson, M. (2006). *Coming into mind.* New York: Routledge.

Wilkinson, M. (2010). *Changing minds in therapy.* New York: Norton.

Zur, O., & Nordmarken, N. (2016). *To touch or not to touch: Exploring the myth of prohibition on touch in psychotherapy and counseling.* Retrieved on 25 October, 2016 from: http://www.zurinstitute.com/touchintherapy.html

4 FirstPlay® Infant Massage Storytelling
Facilitating Corrective Touch Experiences with a Teenage Mother and Her Abused Infant

Janet A. Courtney, Meyleen Velasquez, and Viktoria Bakai Toth

> The earliest self-experience is recognition of the body. This body awareness comes about through the physical contact and playful and loving attitudes the mother [parent] provides.
>
> Viola Brody, *The Dialogue of Touch*

I (Courtney) watched in fascination at what was unfolding at a table near me at a restaurant: A baby was sitting on his mother's lap, their eyes joined in a gaze of playful anticipation. The mother held the baby's hands together, and then in an animated high-pitched voice she said, "How big is Jesse?" She then paused. At the same time, I observed the baby lean in with a look of curious expectation, one eyebrow raised and a hint of a smile. Then the mother's face lit up and she sang: "Soooo big," as she opened the baby's arms. At that moment, the baby let out a long belly laugh, and the mother responded with laughter and kisses, her family laughed, the waitress laughed, I laughed, and people at surrounding tables began to giggle. The joy of the moment was contagious. And what happened next? The mother repeated the activity. "Soooo Big" is a whole complete STORY in and of itself. Ahhhhh, attunement in action, my analytical mind nodded—the building block of a healthy secure attachment relationship.

Introduction

Stuart Brown, the well-known psychiatrist and researcher of play, wrote that this type of joyful union between a parent and child is "synchronizing the neural activity in the right cortex of the brain." In fact, he advised that if one were to wire up both mother and baby to an electroencephalogram (EEG), we would see that "their brain currents are actually in sync" (Brown, 2010, p. 82). This form of play is often referred to as *first-play*, or *pre-symbolic* play (Courtney, 2013), or the "first relationship" as Stern (2002) labeled it; because it is the *first* type of play that humans experience in life. And unlike symbolic play, which a child can engage in independently, first-play requires an interactive experience with an

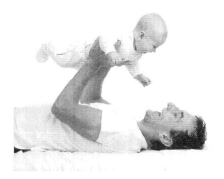

Figure 4.1 FirstPlay® builds secure attachment relationships.

Source: ©123rf.com/Photobac

attuned and sensitive caregiver and is a vital precursor to higher forms of social, emotional, and cognitive development.

As illustrated in Figure 4.1, a tremendous amount of sensory input is happening in this first-play moment of enjoyment—eye contact, visual stimulation, auditory variation, and smell, but the most important sensory element of all is touch—without which a child may die (Spitz & Wolf, 1946). Through these early experiences the infant's brain is being wired to engage in a lifetime of healthy interpersonal relationships (Badenoch, 2008; Kestly, 2014; Schore, 2012). It is within this awareness of the critical role that positive touch experiences play in the development of healthy children—psychologically, emotionally, socially, and physically, and the detrimental impact of negative or inappropriate touch or neglect that FirstPlay® therapy was created as a preventative and intervention-based treatment approach.

FirstPlay Therapy®

FirstPlay Therapy® is an attachment-based, parent-child model that combines first-play activities with therapeutic storytelling implemented by trained practitioners who model, guide, facilitate, and supervise parents to provide attuned touch to their infants and children to build healthy attachment relationships. Founded by Courtney (Courtney, 2014, 2015), FirstPlay Therapy® is an alchemy of several theoretical and research underpinnings, including Developmental Play Therapy, Modern Attachment Theory (Schore, 2012), Filial Therapy, Family Play Therapy (including intergenerational systems theory), Ericksonian-based storytelling (StoryPlay®), mindfulness practice, and the literature and research pertaining to neurobiology, touch, infant massage, and infant mental health. Formulated as a resiliency and strength-based model, FirstPlay® Infant Massage Storytelling is a parent–infant program for ages birth to two years. In this model the therapist demonstrates the first-play activities on a baby doll while the parents simultaneously practice the storytelling techniques with their own infant.

The Role of Touch in Developmental Play Therapy

FirstPlay® is an adapted Developmental Play Therapy (DPT) model. Supported by the constructs of attachment theory (Bowlby, 1988), DPT was developed by play therapy pioneer Viola Brody in the late 1960s, and is considered a "close cousin" to Theraplay[8] (Myrow, 2000, p. 3). Central to DPT was its emphasis on touch (responsive, attuned, and nurturing). Brody claimed that touch is our first communication—hence the name of her book, *The Dialogue of Touch* (Brody, 1997)—and stressed that the nurturing and joyful touch component between an adult and child, including rocking, singing, first-play activities, and physical holding (gentle) was intrinsically healing (Courtney & Gray, 2014). Brody (1997) advised that children who missed those crucial first-play stages (through neglect, for example) can be helped by a practitioner to experience those joyful touch interactions by creating, in DPT sessions, the first-play opportunities necessary for them to return to an earlier stage of development and "pick up what they need and bring it forward to the present" (p. 9).

Modern Attachment Theory

Attachment theory has evolved significantly since its introduction by John Bowlby (1988) in the 1950s, who advocated that the quality of parent–infant bonds sets the stage for healthy emotional and psychological development. Schore (2012) proposed an expansion of Bowlby's attachment theory constructs to go beyond how attachments are formed (safety, internal working models, a secure base) to include the research into brain development. This is achieved by the sensitivity of the caretaker to cultivate "synchronous, reciprocal, and jointly satisfying mother-infant interactions" (Schore & Schore, 2012, p. 43). Thus, *modern* attachment theory is informed by neuroscience and, from this perspective, Schore and Schore described secure attachment relationships as "the essential matrix for creating a right brain self that can regulate its own internal states and external relationships" (2012, p. 44).

Infant Massage Promotes Infant Mental Health and Attachment

Infant massage techniques (Field, 2011, 2014; McClure, 2000; Schneider & Patterson, 2010) have also been adapted into the FirstPlay® model to promote infant mental health and parent-child attachment. Perry (2006) lists "therapeutic massage" as a developmentally appropriate intervention for ages birth to two years as infants need "rhythmic movement" and "patterned sensory input (auditory, tactile, motor)," "simple narrative," and "attuned responsive caregiving and emotional and physical warmth"

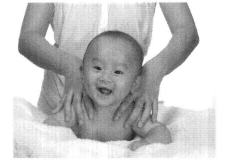

Figure 4.2 Happy baby receiving a massage from Mom.

Source: ©Shutterstock.com/Aseph

(p. 41). Field (2014) advocated that massage not only benefits the baby, but also the caregivers giving the massage, and recommended that it should be included in the daily routine for *all* babies (see Figure 4.2). Research has revealed the qualitative and quantitative positive benefits of infant massage and parent–infant touch interactions (Drehobl & Fuhr, 2000; Field, 2011, 2104; Linden, 2015; McClure, 2000; O'Brien & Lynch, 2011; refer also to Touch Research Institute at the University of Miami, n.d., and Center on the Developing Child, 2016).

> Note: Although parents are taught simple techniques of infant massage through a metaphoric story and other first-play activities, the overriding guiding principles are for FirstPlay® practitioners to facilitate parent-infant bonding and attachment, and to focus on the *strengths* of the family and encourage new ways for parents to provide sensitive and caring touch.

Family Play Therapy and Intergenerational Family Systems Theory

Because FirstPlay® is a play therapy parent-child model, it is supported by the foundations of Family Play Therapy, Intergenerational Family Systems Theory, and Filial Therapy (Gil, 2014; Webb, 2011). Psychiatrist Murray Bowen conceptualized the family as an emotional network of interlocking relationships, and his concept of *multigenerational transmission process* claimed that certain patterns of interrelating, such as how attachments are formed, how intimacy is managed, how conflicts are handled, and so forth, can persist from generation to generation (Goldenberg & Goldenberg, 2013). In FirstPlay®, parents may be exposed to first-play nurturing-touch activities that they had never experienced as an infant and will therefore be learning new ways of interrelating with their infants that will have a positive impact on generations to come. Thus, the more self-awareness that parents can develop about their own early life relationships the better able they are to develop empathy and enhanced connection with their own children.

Filial Therapy—Parents as "Change Agent"

Filial Therapy was developed in the 1960s by Louise and Bernard Guerney (Bratton *et al.*, 2015; Guerney, 2015). However, instead of the Filial model, where parents receive training in Client Centered Play Therapy techniques, FirstPlay® practitioners provide direct training to parents in the infant-massage storytelling techniques as outlined in the *FirstPlay Parent Manual*© (Courtney, 2015). This is accomplished by practitioners demonstrating the *Baby Tree Hug*© story and the touch-based activities on a baby doll (a common parent-training method used in infant mental health and infant massage programs). At the same time, practitioners also model, instruct, facilitate, and supervise parents to use the techniques with their infant. Parents are thus empowered to confidently provide attuned and caring touch to their baby as taught by the FirstPlay® practitioner (O'Brien & Lynch, 2011). As in Filial Therapy, the key factor in FirstPlay® is that the "parent-child [infant] relationship is the essential and curative factor for children's well-being" (Bratton et al., 2015, p. 129). Guerney (2015), who advocated toward parents as vital "change agents" wrote,

> The advantage to assigning a therapeutic role to the parents is that they become temporarily removed from the entanglements of the family dynamics. They learn new ways of relating to the child. They execute new concepts and perceptions of family relationships … parents become part of the solution instead of part of the problem. (p. x)

Ericksonian-Based Storytelling and StoryPlay®

FirstPlay® is unique in that the application of the first-play activities includes an Ericksonian-based therapeutic story. Joyce Mills, PhD, adapted Milton Erickson's work to a play therapy model she founded, titled StoryPlay® (Mills & Crowley, 2014). In Ericksonian storytelling, indirect positive messages are embedded within the story to "activate inherent healing processes that can reach a child [and parent] at a deeper level of consciousness" (Courtney & Mills, 2016, p. 19). In FirstPlay®, a therapeutic story, the *Baby Tree Hug©*, is told in combination with the first-play and infant massage activities as provided in the *FirstPlay Parent Manual©* (Courtney, 2015).

Mindfulness: Calming Aids Parental Attunement in FirstPlay®

Infants can sense the mood of their parents—especially when parents are anxious, upset, and stressed. It is therefore imperative that parents learn strategies to help themselves focus, calm, and self-regulate, and in FirstPlay® this is the first step in teaching parent-infant attunement. Badenoch (2008) advised that there is a growing body of research that supports the notion that sustained attention "produces not only momentary functional changes in neural connections, but enduring structural changes as well" (p. 133). Prem Rawat, known worldwide for his global peace initiatives, advised, "The first step [to rid conflict] is for individuals to nurture and practice peace within

Figure 4.3 Attuning to the cues of the infant.
Source: ©Shutterstock.com/Anneka

their own hearts" (2016, p. 13). In FirstPlay®, prior to giving the story-massage to their infant (see Figure 4.3), parents are guided to find a peaceful place within themselves by learning a brief method to "calm and relax" using a *Rainbow Hug©* imagery (Courtney, 2015).

Harmful Effects of Touch in Infancy

Infants are the most vulnerable population when it comes to touch. Unlike children, adolescents, adults, or the elderly, if someone is touching them and they do not want to be touched, they have no ability say "Stop it," or "Leave me alone." Nor are they able to run or move away, or block a slap or punch, and they certainly are not able to tell someone else if they have been hurt through touch. According to Perry (2006), developmental trauma alters the brain and results in enduring emotional, behavioral, cognitive, social, and physical problems. Van der Kolk (2014) further advised, "whatever happens to a baby contributes to the emotional and perceptual map of the world that its developing brain creates" (p. 56). Fortunately, as Linden (2015) stated, in situations where infants have been neglected and deprived of touch, gentle massage can "reverse the deleterious effects of touch deprivation on infants" (p. 27). Practitioners who work with high-risk populations can intervene to provide education and parent-training in responsive and nurturing touch to prevent abuse and neglect, or to even teach parents corrective forms of touch (as in the case with the teenage mother and her abused infant presented later in this chapter).

FirstPlay Therapy® Training and the Ethics of Touch

Central to the success of FirstPlay® as an intervention is the therapist receiving comprehensive training and supervision leading to a certification. FirstPlay® encompasses 37 hours of training that includes parent–infant volunteers who join the training on day four. As in DPT training (Brody, 1997; Courtney & Gray, 2011, 2014), a portion of the training in FirstPlay® focuses on providing experiential activities that afford opportunities for practitioners to examine their own experiences of touch to increase professional self-awareness and to examine any countertransferences that may emerge (Courtney & Gray, 2014). Young (2005) addressed the importance of ethics of training in touch, "One significant aspect of training in this area is to ensure that the therapist's own needs and issues about touch have been either brought to awareness or preferably dealt with effectively" (p. 42).

Another ethical consideration of touch in FirstPlay® is that the application of the touch-based activities is carried out by the parents, not by the practitioner. The goal of FirstPlay® is for the practitioner to facilitate the parents or caregivers (such as foster parents or grandparents), and the infant to bond. Accordingly, this removes any concerns of liability (Aquino & Lee, 2000) about practitioners touching an infant or child. Finally, the FirstPlay® program is ethically commenced through an informed consent that is reviewed with the parents, as well as a separate Health Care Provider Consultation form that parents can show to their infant's health care provider to discuss any possible physical health concerns that may be contraindicated against the massage activities found in the FirstPlay® *Baby Tree Hug*© story.

Implementing Ethical Touch in FirstPlay® Infant Massage Storytelling

Practitioners are trained to ethically implement FirstPlay® activities by teaching parents how to engage in respectful touch with their infant. This is accomplished in the following four ways:

1. By modeling and guiding parents to ask their infant's *permission* prior to beginning a FirstPlay® baby massage storytelling session—completed by parents using a playful voice inviting their infant for story-massage while simultaneously showing their hands and making eye contact.
2. By teaching parents to be conscious of their own body movements when touching.
3. By guiding parents in a quick calming relaxation imagery to help them center and be present for the interaction.
4. By educating parents how to read their infant's cues for engagement readiness and for supervising ongoing interaction (Benjamin & Sohnen-Moe, 2014; Brazelton & Sparrow, 2006; McClure, 2000)—as detailed in this next paragraph.

Infant Cues for Engagement & Touch:	**Infant Cues for Not Ready for Engagement:**
• Smiling and/or relaxed face	• Turns head and gazes away
• Face brightens	• Moves eyes around
• May wiggle legs and arms in excited motion	• Flails arms or closes arms
• Body is relaxed	• Kicks legs
• Offers direct eye contact	• Begins to hiccup
• Reaches out arms	• Fusses, spits up, chokes
• Happy cooing, giggling, vocalizations	• Continues to be fussy or cries
	• Arches back, or pulls away
	• Begins intense crying, not able to be comforted

In addition to the above, Drehobl and Fuhr (2000) warn practitioners to avoid abrupt hand movements near an abused infant as this could be perceived as threatening. Instead, practitioners are directed to hold their hands still at the sides of an infant's peripheral view and in a soft voice and tender manner ask the infant for permission to touch.

Case of Ashley and Her Children

Corrective Touch with a Teenage Mother and Her Abused Infant

Perry (2006) advocated that therapeutic interventions must be congruent with a child's developing mind and FirstPlay® Infant Massage Storytelling is a developmentally appropriate model for infants. New pathways of connecting emerged in the following case where FirstPlay® was implemented with a teenage mother to facilitate a corrective experience of attuned nurturing touch to her physically abused infant residing in supervised dependency care with the maternal grandmother. Gil (1991) advised that a corrective approach "provides the child with the experience of safe and appropriate interactions that engender a sense of safety, trust and well-being. In other words, there is an attempt to demonstrate to the child through therapeutic intervention the potentially rewarding nature of human interaction" (p. 52). (All the identifying information presented in this case study has been changed to protect confidentiality.)

Presenting Problem and Family Background

The family entered the child welfare system following allegations of physical abuse on the infant (one month old at the time) by the teenage mother and the baby's father. The mother, Ashley, was a 19-year-old African American female with three children, 5-month-old female named Chris and 3-year-old twin boys. The allegations were verified by severe bruising on the infant's arm and leg areas. All the children were removed from the mother's home and placed in foster care, and eventually placed in the care of the maternal grandmother (Ms. Smith). Ashley then moved in with her mother (Ms. Smith) with court-mandated supervised contact for all the children. The father was not involved in the children's lives.

Assessment Phase

The following assessments were conducted: an interview with Ashley, an interview with Ms. Smith, observations of the mother-infant interactions, and a completion of a family systems genogram. The genogram revealed an intergenerational pattern of physical abuse and emotional distancing of relationships. As well, Ashley stated she could not recall any positive touch experiences growing up. Observations of the mother-infant dyad revealed that Ashley experienced difficulty bonding with Baby Chris and in reading her cues, as evidenced by minimal caring touch and no use of words when engaging with her. Her patience level with her children was low and she became quickly frustrated. For example, when Baby Chris cried, Ashley would roll her eyes mumbling, "What now!" in an angry tone. This initially raised clinical concerns regarding the mother's ability to parent independently considering the allegations of abuse to the infant.

Initial Treatment Plan

The following goals were established for the family:

1 Build Ashley's awareness of her own attachment and first-play experiences related to touch.
2 Increase Ashley's ability to appropriately read and respond to her infant's cues.
3 Teach Ashley skills of self-regulation and to recognize her triggers of frustration and anger.
4 Educate Ashley on how to provide sensitive and attuned caring touch, and provide a corrective experience of touch for the infant–mother dyad.
5 Implement FirstPlay® Infant Massage Storytelling instruction.

Case Ethical Considerations Regarding Touch and the Abused Infant

The FirstPlay® practitioner in this case was sensitive to the knowledge that this infant had been abused by the mother and therefore took extra care to provide safety and security for the infant *and* mother. Schore (2012) noted that "the right brain imprints not only regulated but also dysregulated attachment experiences, and therefore relational trauma" (p. 124). Knowing that the touch activities could potentially be frightening and retraumatizing to Baby Chris due to the past violence and thus activating the major fear center of her brain (the amygdala), as an instinctual protective mechanism (Schore, 2012), the practitioner was sensitive to include the following security enhancing measures: (1) created a therapeutic alliance with the mother and grandmother first to establish safety within the adult relationships, (2) modeled to Ashley how to be aware of her body movements and hand placements, (3) facilitated Ashley to ask for her infant's *permission* for touch and to be attuned to her ongoing cues for engagement, and (4) taught Ashley how to *calm and relax* herself prior to beginning the sessions—the first step in attunement.

FirstPlay® Case Implementation

Step One: FirstPlay® Infant-Massage Storytelling Planning Session

Ashley and Ms. Smith were educated about the benefits of nurturing touch and first-play activities to an infant's emotional and psychological health, and how

FirstPlay® Infant Massage Storytelling   57

creating healthy attachments and bonds can positively influence brain development and lifelong interpersonal relationships. The FirstPlay® Infant Massage Storytelling model was explained, noting that the therapist would be demonstrating the techniques on a doll while Ashley would simultaneously practice the activities with Baby Chris. Ashley was provided with the informed consent and the Health Care Practitioner Consultation form to discuss with her pediatrician.

Step Two: Reviewing the FirstPlay® Parent Handbook

Ashley, Ms. Smith, and the children were present during all FirstPlay® sessions. An area was set up for the massage with blankets and a large pillow for Baby Chris to rest for the activity. This practitioner set up in a similar manner, sitting next to the mother with the baby doll. The *FirstPlay® Parent Handbook* was then reviewed with Ashley and Ms. Smith and they were then guided in the *Rainbow Hug©* imagery as a way to calm, focus, and relax, and as a first step in the attunement process. Next, the *Baby Tree Hug©* story was introduced and Ashley was advised that in the story we pretend the baby is a tree—the feet are the roots, the arms and legs the branches, the hands the leaves, and so forth. She was also asked to choose the type of tree (flower/fruit/nut) to tell the story. Ashley chose a mango tree!

The FirstPlay® practitioner demonstrated to Ashley (Ms. Smith was observing too) how to *ask for permission* from Baby Chris for the massage, which sets the stage for respectful body boundaries and to develop attunement in their

Legs: Large branches

Story: "The mango tree has long, strong branches. The first branch begins here at the very top and ends all the way at the bottom. We can even climb those branches going up, up, up, and then again down, down, down."

Branch Leg Glide Instructions: With one hand supporting the baby's foot and leg, use the other hand to glide down the leg from the top of the thigh to the ankle.

(Excerpt from *The Baby Tree Hug©*, in *The FirstPlay Parent Handbook©*. Photo used with permission from Developmental Play & Attachment Therapies, Inc.)

Figure 4.4

relationship. The therapist then modeled this task by asking the doll, "Would you like a *story-massage?*" in a playful voice while showing the hands in a sensitive way. Being mindful that Baby Chris had been abused by hands, the practitioner guided and supervised Ashley to then do the same actions and voice prompts by asking Baby Chris for *permission.*

Step Three: Demonstrating the Techniques and Facilitating Attunement (Selected Excerpts)

The FirstPlay® story-massage begins the touch activities provided to the legs and feet; the therapist first reads a portion of the *Baby Tree Hug©* story and then demonstrates on the doll how the techniques are actually performed. (Refer to Figure 4.4 for an example of the story and instructions.) This process is followed throughout the whole session by telling the next sentence of the story and then demonstrating the activities, and so forth. While Ashley was massaging the baby's toes, the practitioner noticed that Ashley *smiled for the first time* and highlighted that in the following interaction:

FP-THERAPIST: *Seeing mother's smile.* "Look how you smile when you touched her toes!" *Therapist observed both Baby Chris and Ashley gazing at each other—the mother is quiet and smiling. Baby Chris also smiles while looking at Mom.*

FP-THERAPIST: "And look how she is looking at you smiling, she likes it when you smile and play with her." *As the story continued, it was observed that Baby Chris turned her head away and kept pulling her arm away while Ashley continued the massage. The therapist then stated,* "I wonder what Baby Chris is trying to tell us right now?"

ASHLEY: *Looking at the therapist, the mother stopped the massage.*

FP-THERAPIST: "Remember when I was telling you earlier that Chris will let us know what she is comfortable with and when she needs a break?"

ASHLEY: "Yes," *nodding.*

FP-THERAPIST: "I noticed that she was pulling her arm away. What do you think she was trying to tell us?"

ASHLEY: "She didn't like it."

FP-THERAPIST: *Being mindful and sensitive of mother's feelings:* "You know, even when they are that little, they will find a way to communicate with us. As parents, we have to listen and watch closely since they can't use words yet."

ASHLEY: "Do we stop?"

FP-THERAPIST: "Well, since you noticed that she did not want the massage on her arm, then we move to the next step. Maybe next time you do it, she will want it on her arm but if not, then we do like today, respect her wish and move on. The same rules apply for any other part of the massage. It is so important for her to know that Mom understands her."

ASHLEY: *Holds baby's foot and gives it a gentle squeeze.*
BABY CHRIS: *Looks at mother and is observed as calm and relaxed.*
FP-THERAPIST: "I see that you really know what she likes." *When the story was finished, one of the twins laid down where the baby had been as if ready for his turn.*
ASHLEY: *Begins tickling her son as he bursts into laughter.*
FP-THERAPIST: "He is really enjoying playing with you and I noticed that you are laughing too. You both like playing together. I can teach you another game to play with him too."
ASHLEY: "Okay"
FP-THERAPIST: *Showing her in the parent handbook:* "See, here you will find some song and game ideas to play with the kids. We can try 'This Little Piggy'; do you know it?"
ASHLEY: "No," *shaking her head.*
FP-THERAPIST: *The therapist remembered that Ashley stated she could not recall any positive touch experiences as a young child.* "Here, I will show you on the doll and you can practice it on your little one." (*Therapist demonstrates "This Little Piggy" on the doll while Ashley watches.*)
ASHLEY: *Smiling and practicing the first-play "Piggy" activity with the child, she ends the play with a big tickle.*
CHILD: *Laughing and enjoying the interaction—looking at Mom.*
FP-THERAPIST: "Look how much fun you are both having! Let's try that again!"

At the end of the visit, Ashley was encouraged to practice the FirstPlay® story with Baby Chris, even if it was only the calming "Birdie Resting Nest" activity ("birdie" flying through the air and then the hands rest gently on the baby's chest) it was enough to achieve a good benefit. And Ashley was encouraged to also do the "Piggy" activity with the twins. A session was set for the next week.

Next Week Follow-Up Session

Ashley stated that she had practiced some of the activities on the baby's legs and arms. Ms. Smith reached for the *FirstPlay Parent Handbook©* and stated that she had also practiced the *Baby Tree Hug©* during the week.

FP-THERAPIST: "It's so great that you were able to practice with her this week. Can you show me what you both worked on?"
ASHLEY: "Okay." *Ashley began to massage the infant's legs.*
BABY CHRIS: *The therapist observed that Baby Chris was initially looking away from Ashley; however, as soon as Ashley began the massage, she intently made eye contact with Ashley.*
FP-THERAPIST: "Wow, as soon as you started massaging her, she started looking into your eyes. She is feeling really connected with you and I see you are looking at her too."

ASHLEY: *Smiling and focusing on Baby Chris, she continues massaging.*
FP-THERAPIST: "I can see that you are really doing the massage steps. One of the important things to remember before starting is making sure that we ask for *permission*. Remember how we did it last time? Let's try it." *The Therapist demonstrated again on the doll, and observed that although the mother smiled and looked at Baby Chris, there was minimal verbal communication. The therapist then modeled parts of the story on the doll while creating an animated, fun, verbal tone, which Ashley then practiced with Baby Chris.*

Summary

This case study demonstrated the initial steps and methods of FirstPlay® Infant Massage Storytelling in action, and underscored the importance of touch to attachment, regulation, bonding, trauma, and infant mental health. The FirstPlay® practitioner's therapeutic skills of empathetic listening, attunement, non-judgmental presence, and insight created a therapeutic alliance with the mother and grandmother of safety and trust. The creation of safety in the relationships and teaching techniques of mindfulness-calming allowed for the therapist to then facilitate the caregivers to sensitively read the cues and provide caring touch to Baby Chris.

When empathy and attunement are present in the parent–infant relationship the foundations for a healthy and secure attachment are created. As the mother in the case study learned to provide touch in an attuned, caring, and gentle manner, we know through neuroscience that the baby's brain is being wired for healthy interpersonal relating through the corrective experience of seeing her mother as a secure base (Schore, 2012). In this manner, the infant can develop a healthy and secure attachment and an intergenerational cycle of violence can be broken.

Discussion Questions

1. Discuss with a colleague the role of touch in FirstPlay® Infant Massage Storytelling and how this may differ in approach to other child-oriented therapeutic modalities that use touch as an intervention.
2. Reflecting back on the table of infant cues for contact readiness and not readiness, role play with a colleague a case scenario similar to the one presented in this chapter. Role play a therapist who is facilitating attuned touch awareness to a parent engaged with his or her infant. Process the experience and then reverse roles.
3. Discuss in a group or with a colleague the potential feelings and countertransferences that could possibly emerge for a therapist when working with parents who have abused or neglected their infant.

References

Aquino, A.T., & Lee, S.S. (2000). The use of nonerotic touch with children: Ethical and developmental considerations. *Journal of Psychotherapy in Independent Practice, 1(3)*, 17–30. DOI 10.1300/J288v01n03_02

Badenoch, B. (2008). *Being a brain-wise therapist: A practical guide to interpersonal neurobiology.* New York: Norton.

Benjamin, B.E., & Sohnen-Moe, C. (2014). *The ethics of touch* (2nd ed.). Tucson, AZ: Sohnen Moe, Associates, Inc.

Bowlby, J. (1988). *A secure base: Parent-child attachment and healthy human development.* New York: Basic Books.

Bratton, S.C., Opiola, K., & Dafoe, E. (2015). Child-parent relationship therapy: A 10-session filial therapy model. In D.A. Crenshaw & A.L. Stewart (Eds.), *Play therapy: A comprehensive guide to theory and practice* (pp. 129–140). New York: Guilford Press.

Brazelton, T.B., & Sparrow, J.D. (2006). *Touchpoints: Birth to three: Your child's emotional and behavioral development,* (2nd ed., rev.). Cambridge, MA: Da Capo.

Brody, V.A. (1997). *The dialogue of touch: Developmental play therapy* (2nd ed.). Northvale, NJ: Jason Aronson.

Brown, S. (2010). *Play: How it shapes the brain, opens the imagination, and invigorates the soul.* New York: Penguin.

Center on the Developing Child. (2016). *Reaching for breakthroughs with science-based innovation.* Harvard University. Retrieved on 31 October, 2016 from: http://developingchild.harvard.edu/

Courtney, J.A. (2013). *The curative touch of a Magic Rainbow Hug*, video recording. TEDx Talk. Retrieved on 29 October, 2016 from: https://www.youtube.com/watch?v=kYZqyjzuaOw

Courtney, J.A. (2014). *FirstPlay practitioner manual.* Boynton Beach, FL: Developmental Play & Attachment Therapies, Inc.

Courtney, J.A. (2015). *FirstPlay parent manual.* Boynton Beach, FL: Developmental Play & Attachment Therapies, Inc.

Courtney, J.A., & Gray, S.W. (2011). Perspectives of a child therapist as revealed through an image illustrated by the therapist. *Art Therapy: Journal of the American Art Therapy Association, 8(23)*, 132–139. DOI:10.1080/07421656.2011.599719

Courtney, J.A., & Gray, S.W. (2014). A phenomenological inquiry into practitioner experiences of developmental play therapy: Implications for training in touch. *International Journal of Play Therapy, 23(2)*, 114–129. DOI:10.1037/a0036366

Courtney, J.A., & Mills, J.C. (2016, March). Utilizing the metaphor of nature as co-therapist in StoryPlay®. *Play Therapy, 11(1)*, 18–21.

Drehobl, K.F., & Fuhr, M.G. (2000). *Pediatric massage for the child with special needs.* New York: Harcourt Health Sciences.

Field, T. (2011). Massage therapy: A review of the recent research. In M.J. Hertenstein & S.J. Weiss (Eds.), *The handbook of touch: Neuroscience: Behavioral and health perspectives* (pp. 455–468). New York: Springer.

Field, T. (2014). *Touch* (2nd ed.). Cambridge, MA: MIT Press.

Gil, E. (1991). *The healing power of play: Working with abused children.* New York: Guilford Press.

Gil, E. (2014). *Play in family therapy* (2nd ed.). New York: Guilford Press.

Goldenberg, H., & Goldenberg, I. (2013). *Family therapy: An overview* (9th ed.). Belmont, CA: Brooks/Cole.

Guerney, L.F. (2015). Foreword. In E. Green, J.N., Baggerly, & A.C. Myrick (Eds.), *Counseling families: Play-based treatment.* Lanham, MD: Rowman & Littlefield.

Kestly, T.A. (2014). *The interpersonal neurobiology of play: Brain-building interventions for emotional well-being.* New York: Norton.

Linden, D.J. (2015). *Touch: The science of hand, heart, and mind.* New York: Penguin Group.

McClure, V. (2000). *Infant massage: A handbook for loving parents* (Rev. ed.). New York: Bantam Books.

Mills, J.C., & Crowley, R.J. (2014). *Therapeutic metaphors for children and the child within* (2nd ed.). New York: Routledge.

Myrow, D.L. (2000). Theraplay: The early years. In E. Munns (Ed.), *Theraplay: Innovations in attachment-enhancing play therapy* (pp. 2–8). Northvale, NJ: Jason Aronson.

O'Brien, M., & Lynch, H. (2011). Exploring the role of touch in the first year of life: Mothers' perspectives of tactile interactions with their infants. *British Journal of Occupational Therapy, 74(3),* 129–136. DOI:10.4276/030802211X12996065859247

Perry, B.D. (2006). Applying principles of neurodevelopment to clinical work with maltreated and traumatized children: The neurosequential model of therapeutics. In N. B. Webb (Ed.), *Working with traumatized youth in child welfare* (pp. 27–52). New York: Guilford Press.

Rawat, P. (2016). *Splitting the arrow: Understanding the business of life.* Nagano, Japan: Bunya Publishing.

Schneider, E.F., & Patterson, P.P. (2010, December). You've got that magic touch: Integrating the sense of touch into early childhood services. *Young Exceptional Children, 13(5),* 17–27. DOI:10.1177/1096250610384706

Schore, A.N. (2012). *The science of the art of psychotherapy.* New York: Norton.

Schore, A.N., & Schore, J.R. (2012). Modern attachment theory: The central role of affect regulation in development and treatment. In A.N. Schore (Ed.), *The science of the art of psychotherapy* (pp. 27–51). New York: Norton.

Spitz, R.A., & Wolf, K.M. (1946). Anaclitic depression: An inquiry into the genesis of psychiatric conditions in early childhood. *Psychoanalytic Study of the Child, 2,* 313–342.

Stern, D.N. (1977/2002). *The first relationship.* Cambridge, MA: Harvard University Press.

Touch Research Institute at the University of Miami. (n.d.). *Welcome to the Touch Research Institute.* Retrieved on 31 October, 2016 from: http://www6.miami.edu/touch-research/

van der Kolk, B. (2014). *The body keeps the score.* New York: Penguin Group.

Webb, N.B. (2011). *Social work practice with children* (3rd ed.). New York: Guilford Press.

Young, C. (2005). *About the ethics of professional touch.* Online Publication. Retrieved on 29 October, 2016 from: http://www.eabp.org/pdf/TheEthicsofTouch.pdf

5 Use of Touch in Theraplay® with ADHD Children in a School Setting

Angela F. Y. Siu

"Touch" is the first language we learn and it remains as our richest means of emotional expression throughout life.
    Dacher Keltner, *Born to Be Good: The Science of a Meaningful Life*

Introduction

Theraplay® is a structured form of play therapy that models responsive, positive, and playful interaction that occurs naturally between parent and child. In this approach, the interaction is at first between the therapist and the child, while the parents observe. Eventually, parents will join in the Theraplay® activities or even take up the role to lead the activities in the session (Booth & Jernberg, 2010). No toys are used. Parents are guided to see that a child's behavior has underlying emotions and intentions. The goals of Theraplay® are to create a secure attachment, and help parents become consistently attuned and responsive to the child's cues and needs. Emphasis is on noticing and promoting the positive aspects of the child and the strengths of the parent. With this focus, the parent gradually develops more attunement and positive perspective of her child, and the child will increase his/her capacity for self-regulation, and consequently improves his/her well-being.

Theraplay® was developed by Ann Jernberg in 1967 when she was the director of the Head Start program in Chicago. Jernberg adopted Bowlby's (1969/1982) theory of attachment as a model to emphasize healthy parent-child interaction for positive development of children. Emphasis was also placed on the importance of a nurturing and soothing relationship between the adult and child, which includes cradling, holding, rocking, and a great deal of physical contact with the child. In addition to its use in the Head Start programs, Theraplay® was later adopted for use in other settings such as preschools, day care centers, foster care, and adoption services, as well as centers for early intervention of special-needs children and those suffering from complex trauma (see Booth & Jernberg, 2010). Research evidence has demonstrated the efficacy of the Theraplay® model for various populations including children who are shy and withdrawn, as well as those from adoptive families (see Siu, 2009; Weir *et al.*, 2013; Wettig *et al.*, 2011).

In this chapter, the characteristics of children with Attention Deficit Hyperactivity Disorder (ADHD) are first described, followed by a discussion on Theraplay® as a play therapy model in addressing the needs of children who have ADHD. Ethical considerations in the use of touch when using Theraplay® are also discussed. The chapter ends with a case study to demonstrate how Theraplay® is applied to a third-grade child who is diagnosed with ADHD.

Attention Deficit Hyperactivity Disorder and School Children

Attention Deficit Hyperactivity Disorder (ADHD) is one of the most common neurobehavioral disorders of childhood (Frank-Briggs, 2013). In the current clinical view, ADHD is described as a disorder of age-inappropriate behavior in two neuropsychological domains, namely inattention and hyperactivity-impulsivity (inhibition). Examples of the former domain include impaired resistance to respond to distractions and poor persistence toward tasks, while examples for the latter are problems in delaying gratification and excessive task-irrelevant movement (Barkley, 2010). ADHD is also described as having deficits in executive function, that is, the capacity for self-regulation (Barkley, 2012). Symptoms of ADHD affect school children in all areas of development, including school achievement, peer relationship, and general adjustment (Imeraj *et al.*, 2013; Uekermann *et al.*, 2010). According to the most recent National Health Interview Survey (Bloom *et al.*, 2012), more than 5 million (10%) of children aged 3 to 17 are diagnosed with ADHD in the United States. ADHD is also a prevalent developmental disorder worldwide (Faraone *et al.*, 2003). When left untreated, ADHD symptoms may even persist into adulthood and affect academic, social, occupational, and familial health, such as inducing the likelihood of alcohol and psychoactive substances abuse (Jin *et al.*, 2014).

Commonly Used Approaches to Work with ADHD Children

Evidence-based psychosocial approaches for treating ADHD children at school included behavioral intervention (see, e.g., DuPaul *et al.*, 2011) and cognitive behavior therapy (see, e.g., DuPaul *et al.*, 2012). Play therapy has also been documented with evidence to support its efficacy for children with ADHD (see, e.g., Bratton *et al.*, 2013; Schaefer, 2014). Panksepp and his team suggested that physical play could reduce impulse control problems (Panksepp, 2007; Panksepp & Scott, 2012) and promote brain development (Gordon *et al.*, 2003).

Theraplay®: An Attachment-Based Play Therapy for Children with ADHD

In *The Social Neuroscience of Education*, Cozolino (2013) wrote about the fundamental ways in which social relationships and the brain interact to form the foundations of how we learn, and how attachment experiences facilitate learning. His views echo those of Siegel (2007), who describes a two-way highway of brain functioning and how it impacts a person. One lane of highway involves the flow of what is coming up from the bottom (in the form of sensation or emotion), while the other involves the flow coming down from the top (in the form of thoughts and stored memories molded by prior experience) (Siegel, 2007). There has been evidence in the literature on affective neuroscience suggesting that "bottom-up" (regulatory/emotional and attachment-based) treatments are more in line with the body-mind connection than those that are "top-down" (cognitive and language based), and Theraplay® is one of those bottom-up therapies. As Gaskill and Perry (2013) put it, it is unlikely that words, reasoning, or ideas will change the primary regulatory networks in the lower areas of the brain in dysregulated children. In the case of such children, most require an atmosphere of enjoyment, safety, and attunement between them and adults. Furthermore, a therapist may need to restrict the environment and control stimuli in the surroundings in order to match the child's developmental needs and avoid overstimulation of the child that may lead to frustration, irritability, and temper tantrums (Siu, 2009). Through bottom-up interventions, the goal is to help the children to become regulated, and to feel safe in order for change of behavior to take place. According to Barkley (2010), a core feature of ADHD is emotional impulsiveness, which is a part of poor inhibition. Emotional impulsiveness is characterized by poor inhibition of inappropriate behavior relating to strong emotions, difficulties in self-regulating (moderating) emotional reactions to evocative events, and impairment in self-motivation and arousal when necessary to support goal-directed action. Given that self-regulation of emotion can be learned, first via external stimuli (adults) and later internally (e.g., self-talk), and that bottom-up therapies can promote such learning, attachment-based therapy (such as Theraplay®) is highly applicable to children with ADHD.

Theraplay® and the Use of Touch

Importance of Touch in Therapy

Touch occurs normally in parent-child attachment formation. Panksepp (2001) stated that loving touch produces oxytocin and releases endogenous opioids. Stack and Jean (2011) further point out that touch constitutes the single most effective component of the complex interpersonal, nonverbal communication system (touch, gaze, vocalization, movement, positioning) that underlies attachment and regulation in early life. Kestly (2014) suggests that an adult's response to a child's signals of anxiety creates secure attachment. Adults can help children reduce anxiety by conveying to them that they are understood by holding and calming them. Maddigan *et al.* (2003) reported that fifteen minutes of daily massage for adolescents with ADHD over a period of two weeks led to an increase in concentration level when working and a decrease in disruptive behavior in the classroom.

Touch and Theraplay®

Touch is an essential part of Theraplay® treatment (Makela, 2003). The overall purpose of touch in Theraplay® is to address the developmental needs of children, that is, to touch carefully and respectfully. The following are descriptions of the types of touch that are used in the Theraplay® intervention model (The Theraplay® Institute, 2014).

1 ***Structuring Touch:*** Theraplay® sessions often start off with an entrance activity that is playful and interactive, and it usually involves structuring contact. Such structuring contact is important in order to create a sense of physical and emotional safety and predictability. Examples of such activities include holding hands and walking together into the room, creating special handshakes, and doing some type of routine that involves close proximity between therapist and child. In the session, the therapist and child most often sit relatively close together and face each other. Activities are alternated between active and quiet ones, thus providing opportunities for modulation of movement and energy. An example of an active game is *Keeping Balloons in the Air* (holding of hands between the child and therapist and making an effort to keep balloons from dropping onto the floor), while an example of a quiet one is *Cotton Ball Guess/Feather Guess* (guessing where one is being touched with a cotton ball or a feather). Touch that gives ADHD children a sense of structure is particularly important because they need to learn self-regulation.

2 ***Engaging Touch:*** In Theraplay®, touch is a means to create a secure relationship, communicate acceptance and playfulness, and also provide children with an experience of gentleness and calmness. The therapist will become attuned to a child's reactions and make touch an acceptable thing. In fact, most of Theraplay® activities are physically engaging and involve a level of physical contact in some form or another. Examples of physically engaging Theraplay® activities include *Clap Patterns* and *Tangle and Untangle*. For children with ADHD, engaging touch is also important to make the games fun so that children enjoy them and pay attention to continue with the games (and the fun).

3 ***Nurturing Touch:*** In Theraplay®, nurturing touch is meant to provide a calming experience for children and to help them to eventually develop the capacity to soothe and calm themselves. Examples of activities include cuddling, rocking, singing to the child, applying lotion, and caring for wounds. Nurturing touch is especially important in response to dysregulation, which is a characteristic of children with ADHD. In addition, children with attention problems or impulsivity are more likely to experience harsh parenting (see, e.g., Khamis, 2006). Offering nurturing touch may help to reduce problems associated with maltreatment.

4 ***Calming Touch:*** This kind of containing touch is especially important when a child has escalated to the point where there is a risk of the child harming himself/herself or the therapist. Examples of this kind of touch include putting an arm around the child, holding him/her on the adult's lap, sitting very close together, and holding both hands firmly in both of the therapist's hands. When working with ADHD children, this kind of calming and containing

touch is unavoidable, as ADHD children tend to have dysregulated behaviors that need soothing in order to help themselves calm down.

Ethical Considerations in the Use of Touch in Theraplay®

Although there have been concerns regarding the use of touch in therapy, including the fear of inappropriate touch, research evidence from both animal and human cases support the importance of touch in therapy (see, e.g., Feldman et al., 2010; Harlow, 1958; see also The Theraplay® Institute, 2014). The following points are worth noting when applying Theraplay® to work with ADHD children (and to child clients in general):

Ethical Issue One: Is the Use of Touch as a Therapeutic Method Culturally Appropriate?

Touch is applicable to all humans, regardless of which culture a person is from. However, the degree of appropriate social touch and therapeutic touch varies among cultures. Community-appropriate touch (e.g., a light kiss on both cheeks) between therapists and children is common in certain Latin, African American, French, and Jewish communities but Northern European, Japanese, or North American children may be less likely to expect physical touch (Smith et al., 1998; Zur, 2007). The cultural background of the therapist is also likely to affect the extent to which touch is used during therapy. For instance, one study illustrated that Brazilian therapists were more likely to deem routine touch that is a part of greeting or comforting behavior (e.g., shaking hands or kissing on the cheek) as appropriate compared to therapists in the United States (Miller et al., 2006). Religion is also another issue related to the appropriate use of touch. For example, touch between strangers or between unrelated members of the opposite sex may not be socially acceptable for Muslims.

In dealing with cultural differences, therapists can consider doing the following:

1 Become familiarized with the understanding of touch in that particular child's culture. How do people view touch and what are some of the taboos in relation to physical contact and touch between one person and another?
2 Talk to the parents/caregivers and find out about their understanding of touch. Acknowledge the differences among cultures. It is important to explain to the adults the role and rationale of touch in Theraplay®.
3 Constantly check with the adults and gain their permission to use touch when working with the child.

Ethical Issue Two: Will Physical Touch in Therapy Frighten the Child (or the Parent)?

Children who have a history of physical or sexual abuse may be afraid of being touched and the act of touching may trigger their negative emotions.

Therapists can consider using the following ways to cope with this:

1 Gather more information about the child (and the parents' developmental history) and see if there is a possibility of history relating to physical and/or sexual abuse.
2 Adjust touch behaviors based on the child's reaction to it.

Ethical Issue Three: Am I (the Therapist) Feeling Comfortable with the Use of Physical Touch in Therapy?

Even if there is evidence that appropriate touch can meet the needs of young children (see, e.g., Carlson, 2006), the therapist may personally feel uneasy having physical contact with his/her clients. This could be related to the gender issue and the age of the client. It may be easy for a female therapist to hold the hands of a five-year-old boy, but it may not be so easy for her to do the same with a ten-year-old boy. Such uneasiness could also be related to the therapist's own developmental history.

Here are several ways to handle this kind of situation:

1 Start to work with children with whom the therapist feels most comfortable when making physical contact, such as younger children and children of the same gender as the therapist.
2 Start with some indirect touch to ease both parties into it at the initial stage. Materials such as cotton balls, feathers, or a scarf may act as "in-between" objects to facilitate the positive feeling of touch. The act of touch can come in a more natural way when providing physical assistance to clients in the case of challenging activities or movement games that require physical support. Direct physical touch can then be gradually included. Sometimes, with the help of the caregiver, the flow from using an object to direct physical touch becomes more natural.
3 Gather more information about the case. Predict whether touch would be necessary for certain children (such as those with a history of violent behaviors or who are mentally challenged) in order to restrain aggressive behaviors and to ensure safety for the child and the therapist.
4 Seek psychological help if physical contact with a child triggers the therapist's own personal issues.

Case of Andy

Brief Child Background

Andy was a third-grade student who was diagnosed with ADHD when he was in the first grade. His academic performance at school was below average and he had difficulty completing his assignments. Socially, he had impulsive tendencies and would easily get involved in arguments with his peers. His parents were very concerned about Andy's situation as he also had temper tantrums at home.

Brief Description of Setting

Theraplay® sessions were conducted with Andy for half an hour after school on a weekly basis. Since Theraplay® focuses on direct interpersonal contact, a small place at the counseling room is good enough for the sessions. The room was specifically arranged to have many cushions around in order to provide a safe and comfortable place. The cushions can also serve as "something in-between" for the personal space and physical boundary.

Assessment

During the interview, Andy was cooperative and followed instructions closely. He reported having good relationships with his parents while looking for better connection with his peers and teachers. The relationship between Andy and his mother was assessed using the Marschak Interaction Method (MIM) (Booth et al., 2011; Marschak, 1960), a method that is used to assess parent-child interactions using the dimensions in Theraplay®: i.e., structure, engagement, nurturing, and challenge (Booth & Jernberg, 2010). Overall, the dyad had some fun together. The mother allowed Andy to take the lead by determining the pace of the tasks. Andy was willing to accept this role. He initiated fun and wanted his mother to follow his lead, but his mother reminded him to get back on track. Limited physical contact was noted throughout the session. Although Andy asked his mother to comb his hair, she responded in a dismissing manner by saying, "You are old enough to take care of yourself," and she added, "You should learn to do things by yourself." The mother seldom acknowledged Andy's effort to complete the tasks or his needs for fun and attention. Andy had difficulty experiencing a calm, focused state of optimal arousal necessary for learning. In addition to his difficulty in connecting to his mother, he also had unmet attachment needs that were necessary to soothe him. Andy's difficulties in his academic and social areas were understandable as both his parents and teachers expected more from him than what he was capable of handling.

Touch-Related Issues in Consideration to Working with Andy

As a female therapist, I was fully aware that pre-adolescent boys sometimes feel uneasy to have close physical distance (or physical contact) with a female adult who is seen as an unfamiliar person. So, I needed to be alert in relating to him at the start. By reviewing the clips of the MIM, I could sense that Andy longed for the attention (including hugging) from his mother. I checked with Andy's mother regarding his response to being touched or having close contact with him, and she stated that Andy would enjoy the touch if he has good rapport with an adult. Given that this child had impulsive tendencies and was reported to have had temper tantrums, I was heightened to the possibility of child-initiated inappropriate touch. This could include him hitting the therapist due to his temper and the potential that I may need to intervene using some type of physical restraints for safety. Because of these concerns, I had to take the lead within sessions and Andy adjusted accordingly without a problem.

Rationale for Using Theraplay® to Work with Andy

Theraplay® is an approach that could help children like Andy to increase their adaptive control of behavior. It could help them to regulate their excitement and activity level (Booth & Jernberg, 2010) and alternate between appropriate stimulation and a state of calmness. When Andy experienced the activities with me (and later on with his mother or father), he learned self-regulation by taking charge of his own sensory and motor experiences. Theraplay® sessions with Andy were structured in the following way: Welcome, Check-up, Activities, Feeding, and Closing. I led the activities, which were fun and engaging. These kinds of activities provided optimal stimulation and excitement, as well as nurturing elements to calm Andy. The challenging activities helped Andy to practice self-regulation and build confidence in dealing with frustration.

Treatment Plan

1. Work with Andy directly while the mother observes. The work was to monitor the level of stimulation and attune to his reactions and regulatory issues.
2. Include mother to join in part of the session (especially during feeding).
3. Guide the mother to lead some or all of the activities.

Stages of Therapy for Andy

Andy attended fifteen Theraplay® sessions. The discussion below focuses on the issues related to touch that came up within sessions.

Initial Phase

With the understanding of Andy's challenges, it was difficult for him to settle down as he laughed and giggled often. This may indicate that he felt uneasy with me sitting close to him. I purposefully sat "at a distance" and played games with him, such as *Guessing Words on Hand* and *Balloon between Two Bodies*, in order to make the structural touch more natural. I also alternated between active and calm activities so that he would not need to sit in one spot throughout the whole session. Surprisingly, Andy liked to participate in *Weather Report*—an activity in which the adult "draws" different types of weather on the back of the child. For example, drawing a large circle would represent a sunny day, while light finger taps would mean a rainy day. Andy accepted this kind of nurturing touch.

However, there were other times when he rejected physical contact. One example was when he placed stickers on his hands and arms. I responded by asking him to put them on me too. In the end, he rejected that idea. I acknowledged his uneasiness and then promised that I would try another game with him in the next session.

Middle Phase

Andy began to present more challenges in the sessions such as not following instructions when asked. Due to his unsafe hyperactivity behaviors, I sometimes needed to stay alert to hold his hands for safety and for calming him down. However, in some activities, he could experience a calm and focused state before he accelerated again. In the activity of *Powder Shapes*, he allowed me to hold his hand, put powder on it, and press his hand on a black card so that the lines of his hands could show clearly. There were also occasions when he was dysregulated. The following interaction exemplified an intervention of touch for calming:

> *At one point during the therapy when we were working on a balancing activity in which Andy was asked to balance two beanbags on his head and walk across the room, he acted normally for a few minutes, but later on threw the beanbag directly at the wall. Worried about him getting hurt, I immediately took his hands and said to him, "I realize that you are very excited about balancing two beanbags on your head ... the beanbag is not for throwing." He did not quite hear my words and started to shake off my hand and walk away. I then held both of his hands again, brought him to the cushion, and made him sit down. I sat next to him and did not say a word for a few minutes. Then, I reflected on his feelings and I held his hands and rhythmically patted on his own knees while singing a song to him. The singing was not a planned activity but was initiated in response to his dysregulation. Holding Andy's hands could be seen as containment in order to protect him from getting hurt or hurting himself. The calming touch in this incident could be seen as an ethically responsible touch.*

Final Phase

Toward the end of the treatment, Andy's mother was guided to take the lead, but he appeared more dysregulated than before. I had to discuss with his mother about her way of doing the activities, as well as her sensitivity in noticing Andy's needs. As the dyad moved on in the sessions, more nurturing activities were completed with initiation by the mother (working together with me). Andy appeared calm and enjoyed the physical contact with his mother. At one point when his mother was holding Andy's hand and talking to him about something when he was young, Andy was engaged and calm, even without reminders from his mother or me.

After all the sessions were over, the mother indicated that her relationship with Andy was less tense. She began noticing Andy's needs more and responded to him in an empathic manner. She was trying her best to be "an external stimulus" to help Andy stay on task before he could be distracted or act impulsively. At school, the teachers saw his progress and could apply the principles of Theraplay® to work with him in the classroom to reduce his impulsivity.

Post-Case Discussion

One of the ethical dilemmas involved was whether to hold Andy or even physically restrain him if he was getting out of control. Given that Andy had ADHD, there was a need for me to stay alert and to evaluate the danger that potentially could arise. Holding his hands firmly and stopping him from recklessly running around was at times necessary. To avoid potential ethical issues concerning touch, I might have used my voice with stronger emphasis to tell him to stop running around. On the other hand, I was aware that touch could be used as a means to calm him down. When I held Andy's hands and reflected his feelings, it only lasted until he was able to re-engage in a calming activity.

Summary

A multi-model approach is needed to help children who are diagnosed with ADHD. In addition to the school-based interventions such as social skills training groups, parent education and involvement is crucial. Theraplay® is an attachment-based play therapy model, with an emphasis on the use of touch. It can help children connect to others, develop self-regulation, and learn adaptive coping skills.

Discussion Questions

1 Based upon the key concepts of Theraplay®, what touch-based activities can you think of that are appropriate to use with ADHD children to help them calm down? Demonstrate the activity with a colleague.
2 What are some possible reasons why Andy appeared more dysregulated when his mother initially took the lead of the activities? If you were the therapist in this situation, what would you do or say? Role play with a colleague your dialogue between mother and therapist.
3 In the case of Andy, the four types of touch (structuring, engaging, nurturing, and calming) were applied. Which types of touch do you think are more essential for working with ADHD children? Why?

References

Barkley, R.A. (2010). Deficient emotional self-regulation is a core component of ADHD. *Journal of ADHD and Related Disorders*, *1*, 5–37. DOI:10.3810/pgm.2011.09.2459

Barkley, R.A. (2012). *Executive functions: What they are, how they work, and why the evolved*. New York: Guilford Press.

Bloom, B., Jones, L., & Freeman, G. (2013). Summary health statistics for U.S. children: National Health Interview Survey, 2012. National Center for Health Statistics. *Vital Health Statistics*, *10(258)*. Retrieved on 29 October, 2016 from: http://www.cdc.gov/nchs/data/series/sr_10/sr10_258.pdf

Booth, P., Christensen, G., & Lindaman, S. (2011). *Marschak interaction method (MIM): Manual and cards* (3rd ed.). Chicago: Theraplay® Institute.

Booth, P.B. & Jernberg, A.M. (2010). *Theraplay®: Helping parents and children build better relationships through attachment-based play* (3rd ed.). San Francisco: Jossey-Bass.

Bowlby, J. (1969/1982). *Attachment and loss. Vol. 1: Attachment*. New York: Basic Books.

Bratton, S., Ceballos, P., Sheely-Moore, A., Meany-Walen, K., Pronchenko, Y., & Jones, L. (2013). Head Start early mental health intervention: Effects of child-centered play on disruptive behaviors. *International Journal of Play Therapy*, *22*, 28–42. DOI:http://dx.doi.org/10.1037/a0030318

Carlson, F. (2006). *Essential touch: Meeting the needs of young children*. Washington, DC: NAEYC.

Cozolino, L. (2013). *The social neuroscience of education: Optimizing attachment and learning in the classroom*. New York: Norton.

DuPaul, G.J., Eckert, T.L., & Vilardo, B. (2012). The effects of school-based interventions for attention deficit hyperactivity disorder: A meta-analysis 1996–2010. *School Psychology Review*, *41*, 387–412.

DuPaul, G.J., Weyandt, L.L., & Janusis, G.M. (2011). ADHD in the classroom: Effective intervention strategies. *Theory into Practice*, *50*, 35–42. DOI:http://dx.doi.org/10.1080/00405841.2011.534935

Faraone, S.V., Sergeant, J., Gillberg, C., & Biederman, J. (2003). The worldwide prevalence of ADHD: Is it an American condition? *World Psychiatry*, *2*, 104–113. Retrieved on 29 October, 2016 from: https://www.ncbi.nlm.nih.gov/pubmed/16946911

Feldman, R., Singer, M., & Zagoory, O. (2010). Touch attenuates infants' physiological reactivity to stress. *Developmental Science*, *13*, 271–278. DOI:10.1111/j.1467-7687.2009.00890.x

Frank-Briggs, A.I. (2013). Attention deficit hyperactivity disorder (ADHD). *Journal of Pediatric Neurology*, *9*, 291–298. DOI:10.3233/JPN-2011-0494

Gaskill, R.L., & Perry, P.D. (2013). The neurobiological power of play: Using the neurosequential model of therapeutics to guide play in the healing process. In C.A. Malchiodi & D.A. Crenshaw (Eds.), *Creative arts and play therapy for attachment problems* (pp. 178–194). New York: Guilford Press.

Gordon, N.S., Burke, S., Akil, H., Watson, J., & Panksepp, J. (2003). Socially induced brain fertilization: Play promotes brain derived neurotrophic factor expression. *Neuroscience Letters*, *341*, 17–20. DOI:10.1016/S0304-3940(03)00158-7

Harlow, H.F. (1958). The nature of love. *American Psychologist*, *13*, 673–685. Retrieved on 29 October, 2016 from: http://psychclassics.yorku.ca/Harlow/love.htm

Imeraj, L., Antrop, I., Sonuga-Barke, E., Deboutte, D., Deschepper, E., Bal, S., & Roeyers H. (2013). The impact of instructional context on classroom on task-behavior. *Journal of School Psychology, 51,* 481–498. DOI:10.1016/j.jsp.2013.05.004

Jin, W., Du, Y., Zhong, X., & David, C. (2014). Prevalence and contributing factors to attention deficit hyperactivity disorder: A study of five- to fifteen-year-old children in Zhabei District, Shanghai. *Asia-Pacific Psychiatry, 6,* 397–404. DOI:10.1111/appy.12114d

Keltner, D. (2009). *Born to be good: the science of a meaningful life.* New York: Norton.

Kestly, T.A. (2014). *The interpersonal neurobiology of play: Brain-building interventions for emotional well-being.* New York: Norton.

Khamis, V. (2006). Family environment and parenting as predictors of attention-deficit hyperactivity disorder among children. *Journal of Social Service Research, 32,* 99–116. DOI:10.1300/J079v32n04_06

Maddigan, B., Hodgson, P., Heath, S., Dick, B., St. John, K., McWilliam-Burton, T., Snelgrove, C., & White, H. (2003). The effects of massage therapy and exercise therapy on children and adolescents with ADHD. *The Canadian Child and Adolescent Psychiatry Review, 12,* 41–44. Retrieved on 29 October, 2016 from: https://www.ncbi.nlm.nih.gov/pmc/articles/PMC2538473/pdf/0120040.pdf

Makela, J. (2003). What makes Theraplay® effective: Insights from developmental sciences. *The Theraplay® Institute Newsletter, Fall/Winter,* 9–11.

Marschak, M. (1960). A method for evaluating child-parent interaction under controlled conditions. *Journal of Genetic Psychology, 97,* 3–22.

Miller, P.M., Commons, M.L., & Gutheil, T.G. (2006). Clinicians' perceptions of boundaries in Brazil and the United States. *Journal of the American Academy of Psychiatry and the Law Online, 34,* 33–42. Retrieved 29 October, 2016 from: http://www.jaapl.org/content/34/1/33.full

Panksepp, J. (2001). The long-term consequences of infant emotions: prescriptions for the twenty-first century. *Infant Mental Health Journal, 22,* 1–2. DOI:10.1002/1097-0355(200101/04)22:1<132::AID-IMHJ5>3.0.CO;2-9

Panksepp, J. (2007). Can PLAY diminish ADHD and facilitate the construction of the social brain? *Journal of the Canadian Academy of Child and Adolescent Psychiatry, 10,* 57–66. DOI:Retrieved on 29 October, 2016 from: https://www.ncbi.nlm.nih.gov/pmc/articles/PMC2242642/

Panksepp, J., & Scott, E.L. (2012). Reflections on rough and tumble play, social development and ADHD. In A.L. Meyers & T.P. Gullotta (Eds.), *Physical activity across lifespan: Prevention and treatment for health and well-being* (pp. 23–40). New York: Springer.

Schaefer, C.E. (2014). *The therapeutic power of play.* Northvale, NJ: Aronson.

Siegel, D.J. (2007). *The mindful brain: Reflection and attunement in the cultivation of well-being.* New York: Norton.

Siu, A.F.Y. (2009). Theraplay® in the Chinese world: An intervention program for Hong Kong children with internalizing problems. *International Journal of Play Therapy, 18,* 1–12. DOI:10.1037/a0013979

Smith, E., Clance, P.R., & Imes, S. (Eds.) (1998). *Touch in psychotherapy: Theory, research and practice.* New York: Guilford Press.

Stack, D., & Jean, A. (2011). Communicating through touch: Touching during parent-infant interactions. In M.J. Hertenstein & S. Weiss (Eds.), *The handbook of touch: Neuroscience, behavioral, and health perspectives* (pp. 273–298). New York: Springer.

The Theraplay® Institute. (2014). *Theraplay®: Level one training manual.* Chicago: The Theraplay® Institute.

Uekermann, J., Kraemer, M., Abdel-Hamid, M., Schimmelmann, B.G., Hebebrand, J., Daum, I., & Kis, B. (2010). Social cognition in attention-deficit hyperactivity disorder (ADHD). *Neuroscience & Biobehavioral Reviews, 34,* 734–743. DOI:10.1016/j.neubiorev.2009.10.009

Weir, K., Song, L., Canosa, P., Rodrigues, N., McWilliams, M., & Parker, L. (2013). Whole family Theraplay®: Integrating family systems theory and Theraplay® to treat adoptive families. *Adoption Quarterly, 16,* 175–200. DOI:10.1080/10926755.2013.844216

Wettig, H.G., Coleman, A.R., & Geider, F.J. (2011). Evaluating the effectiveness of Theraplay® in treating shy, socially withdrawn children. *International Journal of Play Therapy, 20,* 26–37. DOI:10.1037/a0022666

Zur, O. (2007). Touch in therapy and the standard of care in psychotherapy and counseling: Bringing clarity to illusive relationships. *US Association of Body Psychotherapy Journal, 6,* 61–93. Retrieved on 29 October, 2016 from: http://www.zurinstitute.com/touch_standardofcare.pdf

6 Touching Autism through DIRFloortime®

Eva Nowakowski-Sims and Audrey Gregan

Each person in the world is a unique human being. One of the important tasks of growing is the discovery of "who I am" in relation to all those whom I meet.

Fred Rogers, *Life's Journeys According to Mister Rogers*

Introduction

Play is an integral part of development, in that it is often referred to as the "business of childhood." Through play, children stimulate their senses, exercise muscles, build social skills, and work through any emotional difficulties they are experiencing. Children with autism spectrum disorder (ASD) struggle in areas of play that involve imaginary play or peer-group play, yet desire to have friendships and interact with peers; they simply lack the social ability and skills to interact successfully. Because of this, it is challenging to find meaningful play interventions to work with children with ASD that respond to their specific interests and ability levels. The DIRFloortime® approach (where DIR stands for "development, individual difference, relationship-based") is a comprehensive framework for understanding and treating children challenged by autism spectrum and related disorders. It focuses on helping children master the building blocks of relating, communicating, and thinking.

Children and adolescents with ASD exhibit symptoms that vary in intensity from very mild to severe. The most common symptoms include impairments in social skills, communication, and the ability to regulate and modulate emotions; difficulties establishing and creating meaningful relationships; restricted, repetitive, and stereotyped patterns of behavior; sensory processing issues including touch sensitivities; and difficulties handling transitions and change (Coplan, 2010). Therapists' attempts to engage a child diagnosed with autism are often met with rejection. Pretend and imaginary play present a greater challenge for children with autism and therapists should therefore avoid play-based interventions that rely heavily on abstract concepts, pretend play, and metaphor (Grant, 2014). However, research has suggested that children with autism are capable of symbolic and pretend play (Hobson, Lee, & Hobson, 2009). Directive play interventions can help children learn social skills to interact more successfully with peers and participate in group play (Grant, 2014). Developmental methods like

DIRFloortime® tend to have a strong child focus and stress the importance of affect and relationship as key vehicles for change (Greenspan & Wieder, 2006).

DIRFloortime® Approach

Developmental, Individual Difference, Relationship-Based (DIR) Floortime® model is an interdisciplinary framework that enables play therapists, parents, and educators to construct a comprehensive assessment and intervention program based on the child's and family's unique developmental profile that addresses obstacles that children with autism or other developmental disorders face (Greenspan & Wieder, 1999). The model was first developed by Dr. Stanley Greenspan and Serena Wieder, as a developmental relationship-based treatment, to build healthy foundations for social, emotional, and intellectual capacities rather than focusing on skills and isolated behaviors:

- *"D" is for Developmental:* The six developmental milestones (see below) are the building blocks that every child must master as a foundation for healthy emotional and intellectual growth.
- *"I" is for Individual Difference:* Each child has a unique way of taking in the world—sights, sounds, touch, etc.—and responding to it. Difficulties in processing and/or responding to sensory information may be part of a child's individual differences and can interfere with his or her ability to relate, communicate, and think;
- *"R" is Relationship-Based:* Building relationships with primary caregivers is a critical element in helping a child return to a healthy developmental path. Floortime encourages parents to tailor their interactions with their child (ICDL, 2000).

Six basic developmental milestones lay a foundation for all learning and development, which is the standard basis of continuous evaluation in DIRFloortime®. Children without special needs often master these skills relatively easily. Children with challenges struggle to master these skills because their biological abilities often make the mastery more difficult. These foundational milestones are (1) Shared Attention and Regulation, (2) Engagement and Relating, (3) Purposeful Emotional Interaction, (4) Social Problem Solving, (5) Creating Ideas, and 6. Connecting Ideas Together, Thinking Logically.

Floortime™ is a way of connecting with children through play that utilizes motivation to achieve goals. A fundamental goal of Floortime™ is to follow the children's lead or harness their natural interests. It relies on the use of relationship as a vehicle for change and emphasizes the importance of affective interactions (Coletti, 2011). A secondary goal of Floortime™ is joining children in their world and pulling them into a shared emotional experience in order to help master the fundamentals of emotional, social, language, and intellectual development (Greenspan & Wieder, 1999). Some examples of this include engaging children in high interest activities such as bubbles and whistles, or sitting closely beside a child who is resistant to touch, mirroring their every move. The goal is to create an environment of sensory stimulation through activities that children enjoy.

Sessions typically last 20 to 30 minutes and take place on the floor, where a parent or therapist joins children in play activities. The goal is to follow the children's lead on one hand but create opportunities and challenges that help them master functional, emotional, and developmental goals (FEDLs) (Hess, 2012) on the other. FEDLs are central in DIRFloortime® assessment and treatment. Each FEDL demands high levels of emotional and intellectual engagement on the part of the therapist, who is responsible for helping children master the stages one by one and resume a healthy developmental trajectory (Coletti, 2011). Often, the therapist utilizes DIRFloortime® using a strengths-based approach; this involves a therapist validating children's attempts to master a challenging task. Once children feel validated, they are more likely to allow the therapist to challenge them more (Hess, 2009).

To date, limited research has examined the effectiveness of DIRFloortime® when working with children with autism. Mercer (2015) reviewed research studies supporting the effectiveness of DIRFloortime® and concluded that DIR can be considered a possibility for evidence-based practice (EBP), but not as an evidence-based treatment (EBT). Solomon *et al.* (2014) conducted a randomized controlled trial of the DIR approach on the Play and Language for Autistic Youngsters (PLAY) project, in a sample of 128 children, and found significant improvement relative to the control group on interaction skills, functional development, and autistic symptoms. Rentz (2015) found that children who received DIRFloortime® had significantly greater improvement in social-emotional functioning over time than children who received alternative community treatment. Rentz also concluded that DIRFloortime® intervention increased caregivers' ability to support their child's social-emotional functioning. Casenhiser, Shanker, and Stieben (2013) investigated the outcomes of a DIR-based intervention, in a sample of 51 children, and found that the quality of social interactions in the treatment group improved significantly. Pajareya and Nopmaneejumruslers (2011) found significant decreases in autistic symptoms with high parental satisfaction of the intervention in a small randomized control study with 28 participants. Lal and Chhahbria (2013), in a study of 26 children, found significant improvements in behavioral indicators associated with autism and social skills. In a sample of 26 parents, Pilarz (2009) conducted a week-long DIRFloortime® parent training and found significant increases in the quality of parent–child interactions as well as significant increases in the child's developmental level. Although DIRFloortime® has been recognized as an emerging evidence-based practice, further research in DIRFloortime® is needed.

Parent's Role

One of the most important components of DIRFloortime® is family involvement. Parents and caregivers are encouraged to employ DIRFloortime® techniques at home to help their child master the developmental levels (Greenspan & Wieder, 1999). Floortime's emphasis on parental/caregiver participation coupled with the stress associated with parenting a child with ASD can be overwhelming. Research on DIRFloortime® treatment that included parent training has demonstrated significant increases in the quality of parent-child interactions and improvements in family life and family resilience (Pilarz, 2009).

Touch in Working with Children on the Autism Spectrum

The usefulness of touch in therapy has long been debated, some arguing that the risk outweighs the benefit (Alyn, 1988). However, touch is one of the most fundamental human experiences and is directly linked to secure attachment (Jernberg & Booth, 2010). Weiss *et al.* (2000) found that high frequency of positive touch is correlated with a sense of closeness with others, which is essential for learning, emotion regulation, and social interactions. Touch has also been identified as an essential component of treatment for children with autism as they often have an aversion to being touched (Brody, 1997; Courtney, 2012; Grandin, 1992). Jennings (1999) uses the body and its relationship with other bodies, through touch and other senses, to form the basis for identity development. This development is supported by movement and collaboration with another, especially an adult body, to work both with and against in movement and connection. This encourages experiences of both "we" and "I," the development of trust in oneself and in another, and the understanding of one's "body self." Experiences of both safety and "ritual" through rocking, soothing touch, and being held assists in developing healthy attachments (Jennings, 1999, 2005). Developmental play therapy (DPT, which the author, Gregan, utilizes to inform her work in ASD) is another relationship-based treatment modality that addresses children's physical and emotional well-being (Courtney, 2012; Courtney & Gray, 2014). Touch is an essential component of DPT where the therapeutic interaction is focused on the playful activities between therapist and child and/or parent and child.

In working with children with ASD, touch has been beneficial when a trusting relationship has been established. Children with autism have difficulty expressing themselves, but can do so through bodily stimulus and senses. Many children coming for therapy spontaneously enter into a therapeutic regression, knowing to which stage they need to return. However, for children with autism they may need support to progress through their developmental stages. In this case the therapist has to meet children where they are developmentally and create an environment that provides them with experiences of success in order for them to move forward. The therapist has to take the role of nurturing parent who can regulate stress and meet the therapeutic needs of children. Touch becomes essential when the therapist takes on the role of nurturing parent in a therapeutic setting. Touch-centric models of treatment, such as DPT, work to bridge the bond between parent and child, as the therapist models for the parents how to touch and connect with their children (Brody, 1997; Courtney, 2012).

Ethical Considerations of Touch

Touch in clinical practice has been long debated with polarized views on its purpose. Westland (2011) highlighted the research support for including touch in psychotherapy, and identified the purpose of touch when working with childhood developmental deficits and trauma. Research found touch to be successful: When working with clients incapable of verbal communication and are in need of symbolic mothering (Bosanquet, 1970; Toronto, 2006); in play when mirroring a child (McNeely, 1987); when a non-developed child is seeking a physical connection to experience the presence of the therapist (Goodman & Teicher, 1988); to help a child connect body sensations with touch, and to bridge physiological awareness with feelings (Eiden, 1998); and to facilitate the client's capacity for organization and sustaining emotional and interpersonal structure (Cornell, 1998).

Because touch and physical contact has been questioned and sometimes stigmatized in the mental health caring profession, best practice recommendations and guidelines have been established to address criticism of this polarizing issue that is mostly driven by fear and misunderstanding.

The Association for Play Therapy's (APT) *Paper on Touch: Clinical, Professional, and Ethical Issues* (2015), recommended best practices for therapists to follow in their use of touch in clinical practice. APT identifies the need for the play therapist to first carefully evaluate and understand their own motivations for using or not using touch, and whether or not this decision meets the needs of the child. Of importance is the need for informed consent. Westland (2011) encourages therapists to discuss the role of touch at the initial contracting stage and explain why it is included in the therapeutic session.

Jennings (2005) highlighted the significance of explaining the use and importance of embodied processes in detail to both parents and children before the intervention begins and incorporating it into the therapeutic contract as strategies for addressing the issue of touch. Aquino and Lee (2000) suggest collecting assent of the child where developmental considerations permit. Additionally, Westland (2011) argues that the client should be comfortable with touch, where "the touch should be considered as an aspect of the relationship and its discussion from a meta-perspective can strengthen the therapeutic alliance" (p. 25). Finally, Aquino and Lee (2000) talk about the importance of teaching children clear boundaries with regard to touch.

The Role of Culture

Touch is a universal form of communication that varies based on cultural background. Research supports the link between culture and acceptance of another's touch (DiBiase & Gunnoe, 2004). Anthropologist Ashley Montagu (1995) believes that touch is adaptive in evolution as a form of social communication that can cross species, cultures, genders, and age groups. However, acceptance of touch is based on contact and non-contact cultures (Hall, 1976). When working with children, the therapist needs to consider both his/her own cultural acceptance of touch as well as the cultural influences of the children. When using the DIRFloortime® approach, the therapist is sensitive to the client's needs. Thus, when clients may need nurturing, touch becomes essential. Understanding how one's culture receives and gives touch is an inherent part of building the therapeutic relationship and becomes known through the process of getting to know one another.

Case of Sean

The following case study, conducted by the author (Gregan), illustrated how touch was used as part of the DIRFloortime® approach. The following case study, Sean, highlights child-initiated and therapist-initiated touch, and all identifying information has been changed to protect confidentiality. There was a presenting need for early nurturing work where Sean needed skills to connect with the people close to him in order to build meaningful relationships.

Presenting Problem

Sean, age seven, was referred for DIRFloortime® and play therapy services upon entrance to the special school for children with autism. He was extremely withdrawn, tense, and tearful, had no speech, walked on his tip toes, and was fearful of unfamiliar environments. Sean was being fed by bottle with formula milk and did not eat solids. He found touch by strangers frightening and it was difficult for him to engage with people. He was the eldest child with two younger siblings, which left Sean's parents feeling overwhelmed with his care, and which led to much stress. The family sought out therapeutic assistance to address problems associated with Sean's eating and socialization. The therapist began therapy sessions by sitting quietly on the floor with Sean and watching him attentively. This practice of non-directive play therapy utilized DIRFloortime® methods by focusing attention on activities led by the child.

Initial Phase (Sessions 1–9)

Sean initially presented as a very distant and fearful child, but showed a need for connection. His infantile and very sensitive nature put him at an early stage of development. The therapy room was simply a quiet room with cushions and soft padding on the walls, big windows that let in light, and different sizes of soft colorful balls. Initially, Sean was nervous, fearful and distant, but willing to come along into the playroom. For four weeks (three days a week for thirty minutes) Sean explored the soft balls and cushions. Sometimes the therapist would blow bubbles to get Sean's attention to make him aware of her presence. Sean would engage with the colorful balls, but kept his distance from the therapist. The therapist would call his name but Sean found it difficult to make eye contact. Slowly, over time, Sean would begin to raise his head in response to the therapist calling his name, as he tried to make a connection. Gradually he accepted the therapist's presence and the sound of her voice. As more time progressed, Sean would connect with the therapist giving her a slight glance eye-to-eye. It was during these moments that the therapist initiated further connection by calling Sean's name and rolling the ball toward him. At first he did not roll the ball back, but after a couple of sessions, Sean began to pick up the ball and roll it back, but away from the therapist.

> **Special Note:** *It seemed that Sean was using the ball as a transitional object to enhance his emotional security. The above scenario demonstrated how the therapist utilizes the DIRFloortime® approach by first accepting Sean as he was. In order to support and help develop Sean's emotional process at his stage in development, the therapist is providing missed experiences that embraced the use of all the senses that have a synergistic effect on the developing brain.*
>
> (Dawson, 2008)

Middle Phase (Sessions 10–15)

As the therapy progressed, Sean increasingly spent time in close proximity to the therapist, initiating both eye and physical contact. Sean's social interaction increased as he began to gesture without the use of words. Additionally, Sean would initiate physical contact by roughly jumping into the therapist's lap. The therapist, knowing that Sean did not understand how to make appropriate contact, would then model for Sean socially acceptable forms of making physical connection. For example, the therapist stated, "*Oh, you want to jump.*" And then, while maintaining secure contact through hand holding and being sensitive to not reject his initiation for making contact, the therapist would stand up and say, "*Let's jump together like this,*" while jumping up and down on the cushions. At this point, all touch between Sean and the therapist was initiated by Sean and the therapist would follow his lead.

> **Special Note:** *Here the child initiates the use of touch with the therapist, and therapist redirects appropriate contact. Because Sean is emotionally at a very early stage of development, he needs nurturing to develop an attachment and relationship. The developed trust between the child and the therapist allows the use of nurturing touch to help Sean feel safe. This then directs Sean to satisfy his intrinsic need to explore emotionally and physically through sensory play.*

Advanced Phases of Treatment (Sessions 16–25)

By the fifteenth session, Sean presented as less fearful and more relaxed; he was aware of the boundaries in the room as evidenced by his attempts to throw the ball out the door and then smile at the therapist. Such testing of boundaries indicated that the therapist (and the playroom) represented security to Sean and that an attachment with the therapist was beginning to take root.

> ***Special Note:*** *Research has documented the significance of having a secure attachment between therapist and child when working with ASD. In Gerhardt (2010) a nursery school study demonstrated that what a young child needs is an adult who is emotionally available and tuned in to help regulate his state. Edith Sullwood described the therapist's role as having the responsibility of providing a surrogate lap when working with children*
> (as cited in O'Connor & Schaefer, 1994)

Sean had progressed to a more integrated play therapy room with a variety of tactile toys. As he explored the new objects in the room, the therapist mirrored his behavior. Although Sean was still nonverbal, he communicated by using the Picture Exchange Communication System (a program used for nonverbal children) to get his needs met. He was much happier and was more interested in exploring new places and making contact with people around him. His play improved, it became more symbolic and interactive while still including the therapist in much of it. There was more contact and touch as both played the game of chase or assistance with hand drying after water play.

Final Phase (Sessions 26–40)

The therapist and Sean had worked hard to establish a trusting relationship. Sean no longer needed the therapy room and could move away from non-directive play strategies toward more interaction with peers. To prepare him for the move to a classroom, the therapist held Sean's hand as they walked around the building to familiarize him with the environment (see Figure 6.1). He was able to meet staff and look into different classrooms to reduce his fear of unknown places. Initially, Sean found it overwhelming, but accepted the presence of his peers as he sat removed from them and watched what the others did. This move initiated new relationships, that is, with teachers and special need assistants. By involving others, the therapist helped to reduce Sean's dependency on her.

The next intervention goal was to introduce solid food to Sean. The therapist first introduced, "Messy Play," where Sean and the therapist played with pureed food, tasting it using their hands. This process was very slow and sometimes very upsetting to Sean; he wanted to try and taste the food but was afraid. Sean would use his sense of smell to try the foods; he would smell the food and put the food toward the therapist to smell. As one would do when introducing solids to a baby, the therapist would model chewing with dry foods such as crackers. The therapist invited Sean to feed her and displayed delight in tasting the food. Sean would then try a small portion of food from the therapist's finger. She then encouraged him to feel the food on his own lips. Eventually, Sean became independent and

Figure 6.1 Holding the therapist's hand enabled Sean to feel safe exploring his new environment.

Source: © Depositphotos.com/Olechowski

started to feed himself. Sean's parents came to observe some of the sessions and found them to be helpful and, with support, the interventions were transferred to the home environment. The feeding program went on for more than ten weeks; although the process was slow, the intervention was successful. Sean was feeling secure, happy, and relaxed, which also led to less stress on the family.

> ***Special Note:*** *Here, the client-directed use of touch in feeding the therapist was successful because the therapeutic environment was a safe space where Sean was allowed to be himself. Sean got autonomy in the presence of an adult who was non-judgmental and was able to enter his world as a follower and be fully present with him in every moment.*

As Sean's treatment continued, his confidence grew and he began to take part in group activities with his class. He made great progress with his speech and was able to develop friendships with peers by using music and singing in a group. He is now a happy and independent young man who will do very well in the adult program with the proper support to meet his and his family's needs.

Countertransferences and Cultural Considerations

It must be noted that the therapist in this case was female and a member of a high-contact culture, where Sean came from a culture considered more low contact. Having awareness of this cultural difference was paramount and the role that touch would have in the therapeutic sessions was discussed with Sean's family in the contracting stage of therapy. Also, the therapist was aware of possible countertransference situations with Sean as she wanted to respond to his need for nurturing immediately with a hug, but knew she needed to wait and follow his lead and respond to his initiation of touch. Empathy played a critical role in facilitating trust, which was essential to establishing safety surrounding touch interactions during the therapy with Sean. Because working with Sean was overwhelming at times, the therapist sought out supervision to help her manage her emotions and stay positive.

Post-Case Discussion and the Role of Touch in Treatment

Touch, as a form of communication, acts as a support and protection that is integral to achieving secure attachment between parent and child. However, parents with children on the autism spectrum may not always be available to fulfill that responsibility in their child's life. Sean's mother was feeling overwhelmed with life's responsibilities and was not able to attend to Sean's emotional needs, therefore unintentionally reinforcing Sean's behavioral difficulties. When a parent is not available to provide a child with nurturing touch, therapists may serve the role of symbolic mothering. With Sean, therapeutic touch was able to satisfy his unmet needs for nurturing, thus creating a more secure attachment with the therapist, his mother, and then extending out to other people close to him.

Aquino and Lee (2000) reinforced the notion that the helping professional needs to understand the reasons for the use of therapeutic touch and/or lack of touch in different situations. Some children with ASD prefer not to be touched while others seek and crave touch. For Sean, his presenting problem to therapy was his inability to be comfortable with touch or to appropriately provide touch to others. By the end of therapy Sean had awakened from his closed off and isolated world and accepted touch from others. He was then able to enjoy interaction and even began to initiate appropriate touch with others. For example, Sean would touch the therapist's lips looking for her reaction and reassurance that eating the food was going to be okay. This client-initiated touch helped Sean to feel safe enough to take the necessary risks to try something new.

The case with Sean reinforced that human touch is a vital element in a child's development of attachment. Because of the child's need to be touched, the therapist used a DIRFloortime® approach, an intervention that supports the use of nurturing touch in clinical practice. Duhn (2010) pointed out the need for successful interventions that highlight the positive experience of caring human touch. DIRFloortime® is one such intervention, where therapists strive to create safety, create security, and create protection (both physical and emotional) for clients.

Conclusion

Play is a wonderful tool for helping children with autism to engage with others and move beyond autism's self-absorption into real, shared interaction. Play can allow children to explore their feelings, their environment, and develop relationships with parents, siblings, and peers. It is widely known that intensive, early intervention is critical for the maximization of therapeutic benefits for children with ASDs (see, e.g., Dawson, 2008). DIRFloortime® treatment approach is a systematic way of working with a child to help him climb the developmental ladder and is the heart of the developmental approach to therapy. It takes a child back to the very first milestone he may have missed and begins the developmental process anew. By working intensively with parents and therapists, the child can climb the ladder of milestones, one rung at a time, to begin to acquire the skills he is missing (Wieder & Greenspan, 2003).

The case study with Sean was not about changing his personality, but rather about understanding how he saw the world differently and the therapist's need to accept him unconditionally. There is a lot of work to be done in developing trusting relationships and respect for children diagnosed with autism. Early intervention with play therapy can help a child with autism reach his or her developmental milestones. Touch is a critical part of play therapy, a powerful communication tool used to establish trust. It is in this connection with others that children feel nurtured and are able to develop healthy relationships in life.

Discussion Questions

1. Reflecting on the case example presented, discuss with a colleague how the DIRFloortime® approach served the client's need for nurturing through the use of touch.
2. Conduct an Internet search and discover more about DIRFloortime®. Locate at least three other interventions that work therapeutically with children diagnosed with autism. Respond to the following:
   - How does DIRFloortime® compare to those other treatment interventions?
   - Compare the differences in these treatment approaches related to what is involved in receiving training and/or certification with profoundly developmentally delayed children with ASD.

References

Alyn, J.H. (1988). The politics of touch in therapy: A response to Willison and Masson. *Journal of Counseling and Development*, 66, 432–433.

Aquino, A.T., & Lee, S.S. (2000). The use of nonerotic touch with children: Ethical and developmental considerations. *Journal of Psychotherapy in Independent Practice*, 1(3), 17–30. DOI:10.1300/J288v01n03_02

Association for Play Therapy. (2015). *Paper on touch: Clinical, professional, & ethical issues.* Retrieved on 1 November, 2016 from http://c.ymcdn.com/sites/www.a4pt.org/resource/resmgr/Publications/Paper_On_Touch_2015.pdf

Bosanquet, C. (1970). Getting in touch. *Journal of Analytical Psychology*, 15(1), 42–57.

Brody, V. (1997). *The dialogue of touch: Developmental play therapy* (2nd ed.). Northvale, NJ: Jason Aronson.

Casenhiser, D.M., Shanker, S.G., & Stieben, J. (2013). Learning through interaction in children with autism: Preliminary data from a social-communication-based intervention. *Autism*, *17*, 220–241.
Coletti, K.C. (2011). *The experiences of parents who implement a floortime intervention program for a young child with an ASD*. (Doctoral dissertation). Available from ProQuest Dissertations and Theses database (UMI No. 3459690).
Coplan, J. (2010). *Making sense of autistic spectrum disorders: Create the brightest future for your child with the best treatment options*. New York: Random House.
Cornell, W.F. (1998). Touch and boundaries in transactional analysis: Ethical and transferential considerations. In Conference Proceedings of the USA Association for Body Psychotherapy, Creating Our Community, Boulder, Colorado. Retrieved on 1 January, 2016 from: http://www.cbpc.org.uk/TouchInPsychotherapy.htm
Courtney, J.A. (2012). Touching autism through developmental play therapy. In L. Gallo-Lopez & L.C. Rubin (Eds.), *Play-based interventions for children and adolescents with autism spectrum disorders* (pp. 137–157). New York: Routledge.
Courtney, J.A., & Gray, S. (2014). A phenomenological inquiry into practitioner experiences of developmental play therapy: Implications for training in touch. *International Journal of Play Therapy*, *23(2)*, 114–129.
Dawson, G. (2008). Early behavioral intervention, brain plasticity, and the prevention of autism spectrum disorder. *Development and Psychopathology*, *20(3)*, 775–803.
DiBiase, R., & Gunnoe, J. (2004). Gender and culture differences in touching behavior. *Journal of Social Psychology*, *144*, 49–62.
Duhn, L. (2010). The importance of touch in the development of attachment. *Advances in Neonatal Care*, *10(6)*, 294–300. DOI:10.1097/ANC.0b013e3181fd2263
Eiden, B. (1998). The body in psychotherapy, the use of touch in psychotherapy. *Self and Society*, *26(2)*, 3–41.
Gerhardt, S. (2010). *Why love matters: How affection shapes a baby's brain*. New York: Routledge.
Goodman, M., & Teichner, A. (1988). To touch or not to touch. *Psychotherapy*, *25(4)*, 492–500. DOI:doi/10.1037/h0085374
Grandin, T. (1992). Calming effects of deep touch pressure in patients with autistic disorder, college students, and animals. *Journal of Child and Adolescent Psychopharmacology*, *2(1)*. Retrieved on 1 January, 2016 from http://www.grandin.com/inc/squeeze.html
Grant, R.J. (2014). *Play based interventions: For autism, ADHD, neurodevelopmental disorders, and developmental disabilities*. Springfield, Missouri: R.J.G. Publishing.
Greenspan, S., & Wieder, S. (1999). A functional developmental approach to autism spectrum disorders. *Journal of the Association for Persons with Severe Handicaps*, *24*, 147–161. DOI:10.2511/rpsd.24.3.147
Greenspan, S.I., & Wieder, S. (2006). *Engaging autism*. New York: Da Capo.
Hall, E. (1976). *Beyond culture*. New York: Knopf
Hess, E.B. (2009). Introduction to Floor/Time: A developmental/relational approach to the treatment of autism. *Play Therapy*, *4(1)*, 16–19.
Hess, E.B. (2012). DIR/Floortime®: A developmental/relational play therapy approach for treating children impacted by autism. In L. Gallo-Lopez & L.C. Rubin (Eds.), *Play-based interventions for children and adolescents with autism spectrum disorders* (pp. 231–248). New York: Routledge.

Hobson, P., Lee, A., & Hobson, A. (2009). Qualities of symbolic play among children with autism: A social-developmental perspective. *Journal of Autism and Developmental Disorders, 37*, 1107–1115.

Interdisciplinary Council for Developmental and Learning Disorders (2000). *ICDL Clinical Practice Guidelines*. Bethesda, MD: ICDL Press. Retrieved on 1 January, 2016 from: www.icdl.com

Jennings, S. (1999). *Introduction to developmental play therapy*. London: Jessica Kingsley.

Jennings, S. (2005). *Creative play with children at risk*. Bicester, UK: Speechmark.

Jernberg, A., & Booth, P. (2010). *Theraplay: Helping parents and children build better relationships through attachment based play* (3rd ed.). San Francisco: Wiley.

Lal, R., & Chhahbria, R. (2013). Early intervention of autism: A case for Floor Time approach. *Recent Advances in Autism Spectrum Disorders, 1*, 691–717. DOI:10.5772/54378

McNeely, D.A. (1987). *Touching, body therapy and depth psychology*. Toronto: Inner City Books.

Mercer, J. (2015). Examining DIRFloortime® as a treatment for children with autism Spectrum disorders: A review of research and theory. *Research on Social Work Practice, 20*, 1–11. DOI:10.1177/1049731515583062

Montagu, A. (1995). Animadversions on the development of a theory of touch. In T.M. Field (Ed.), *Touch in early development*. Mahwah, NJ: Lawrence Erlbaum.

O'Connor, K.J., & Schaefer, C.E. (1994). *Handbook of play therapy. Vol. II: Advances and innovations*. New York: Wiley.

Pajareya, K., & Nopmaneejumruslers, K. (2011). A one-year prospective follow-up study of a DIRFloortime® parent training intervention for pre-school children with autism spectrum disorders. *Journal of the Medical Association of Thailand, 95*, 1184–1193. DOI:10.1177/1362613310386502

Pilarz, K. (2009). *Evaluation of the efficacy of a seven-week public school curriculum based DIRFloortime® parent training program for parents of children on the autism spectrum*. (Doctoral dissertation). Available from ProQuest Dissertations and Theses database (UMI No. 3337233)

Rentz, E.A. (2015). *Autism spectrum disorders: Developmental, individual difference, relationship-based (DIRFloortime®) Outcomes*. (Doctoral dissertation). Available from ProQuest Dissertations and Theses database (UMI No. 3722233).

Rogers, F. (2005). *Life's journeys according to Mister Rogers*. New York: Hyperion.

Solomon, R., van Egeren, L.A., Mahoney, G., Huber, M.S.Q., & Zimmerman, P. (2014). PLAY project home consultation intervention for young children with autism spectrum disorders: A randomized controlled trial. *Journal of Developmental and Behavioral Pediatrics, 35*, 475–485.

Toronto, E.L.K. (2006). A clinician's response to physical touch in the psychoanalytic setting. *International Journal of Psychotherapy, 7(1)*, 69–81.

Weiss, S.J., Wilson, P., Herenstein, M.J., & Campos, R. (2000). The tactile context of a mother's caregiving: Implications for attachment of low birth weight infants. *Infant Behavioral Child Development, 23*, 91–111.

Westland, G. (2011). Physical touch in psychotherapy: Why are we not touching more? *Body, Movement and Dance in Psychotherapy, 6(1)*, 17–29. DOI:doi/abs/10.1080/17432979.2010.508597

Wieder, S., & Greenspan, S.I. (2003). Climbing the symbolic ladder in the DIR model through floor time/interactive play. *Autism, 7*, 425–435.

Part III
Healing Children Traumatized by Touch

7 Healing Touch

Working with Children Impacted by Abuse and Neglect

Joanne Whelley, Andrea Raasch, and Shakti Sutriasa

> I will believe your touch before I believe your words.
> Virginia Satir, *The New Peoplemaking*

The efficacy of touch in psychotherapy has long been debated (Westland, 2011). Nowhere is touch more controversial than in its use with children who have experienced abuse and neglect. Touch is the first of the senses to develop in the human infant (Montagu, 1986) and is considered a human's first language (Zur & Nordmarken, 2016). Touch is central to cognitive, emotional, developmental, and behavioral aspects of our lives (Linden, 2015), and how the world is perceived and experienced by the infant is largely defined by touch. The skin is the largest and most sensitive organ in the body and touch has powerful effects as the nervous system quickly transmits the information to the brain. It could be said that humans are hard wired to need touch (Field, 2014).

Touch appears to stimulate our bodies to react in very specific ways. The emotions that are communicated by touch can shape our behavior (Field, 2014). According to Linden (as cited by Konnikova, 2015), "The body talks to the brain, the brain to the body." The right kind of touch can lower blood pressure, heart rate, and cortisol levels; stimulate the hippocampus; and drive the release of hormones that have been linked to positive and uplifting emotions (Field, 2010). It has been recognized for over four decades that touch that is absent, inappropriately sexualized, cold, or abusive can communicate emotions such as stress that trigger biological responses, which may shape behavior that draws us inward or to strike out.

Child Abuse and Trauma

Child abuse and neglect are among the United States' most serious concerns (U.S. Department of Health and Human Services, 2016, p. 21). The U.S. Department of Health and Human Services indicated that in 2014 there were approximately 702,000 children who experienced abuse in the United States.

Among those children, 58,105 or 8.3 percent were sexual abuse cases. (U.S. Department of Health and Human Services, 2016, p. 25). In instances of physical and sexual abuse, touch may be the predominating vehicle for the traumatic event. In the case of neglect, it is the absence of touch that may be the root of the trauma.

Abuse in children causes the biological phenomenon of stress. Brain scans have shown that, during a flashback of a traumatic event, the right side of the brain is activated while the left side is deactivated. The right brain stores the sensory experience of trauma. When the left brain is not functioning, the person is left without logic to help process the experience. Specifically, the prefrontal cortex, the seat of rational thinking, shuts down, making it impossible to use logic to confront traumatic memories (van der Kolk, 2014).

Many studies document the fact that traumatic memories are encoded in our brains as sensations and images, not as language, as Broca's area of the brain is disabled during trauma (Newhouse, 2015). Herman (1992) reports that, "in states of high sympathetic arousal, the linguistic encoding of memory is inactivated, and the central nervous system reverts to the sensory and iconic forms of memory that predominate in early life" (p. 39). This results in the child having great difficulty reconstructing a narrative of their traumatic memories (van der Kolk, 2014). There are literally no words for these traumatic memories. This makes these memories hard to access and not amenable to "talk therapy."

When triggered, the trauma is experienced by the child as if it were happening in the present (van der Kolk, 2014). The body physically responds to these threats as the amygdala sends hormones that ready us for fight or flight, increasing heart rate and blood pressure. When the child is traumatized, the freeze response of the primitive brain prevents the action responses of the animal brain, fight or flight, from going into action. The energy resulting from the flood of unused stress hormones from the amygdala to ready the person for flight or fight is stored in the body. The very mechanisms nature intended to propel humans to safety and action instead immobilizes those who are traumatized. The stress hormones remaining in the body may result in rage and outbursts once the tonic immobility lessens. The goal of therapy, therefore, is to restore the fight or flight responses that were overwhelmed. Van der Kolk (2014) states "the fundamental issue in resolving traumatic stress is to restore the proper balance between the rational and emotional brains" (p. 205).

Learning theory suggests that animals rely on environmental cues to learn new behaviors (Bryden *et al.*, 2011). Studies have consistently shown that when participants are engaged in cognitively demanding tasks, the anterior cingulate cortex (ACC) and lateral areas within the prefrontal cortex (PFC) are critically active (Ridderinkhof *et al.*, 2004). Since trauma disables the left anterior cingulate, children are less able to filter out distractions, less able to focus on environmental cues, and, therefore, less able to learn (Newhouse, 2015). Because traumatized children may not be able to express their traumatic memories in words, those buried traumatic memories may lead to increased stress hormones that are slow to dissipate, and learning is compromised.

Vignette A: Case of Mary

Mary is a 9-year-old female sexual abuse client working with a female therapist. The therapist is attempting to teach the client a butterfly hug, which is a bilateral stimulation technique often used as an emotional regulation tool. Although the therapist is demonstrating the technique for the client, the client appears confused about how and where to place her arms. The therapist believes the intervention will be a useful coping skill for Mary and is not able to describe or demonstrate the technique in a different manner. She sits beside Mary hoping that Mary can copy what she is doing, but Mary is still confused. The therapist asks for permission to show Mary how to place her arms and hands by putting them in the correct position saying,

> "Mary, I think this coping skill will be really helpful and I want to make sure you can do it properly. Is it okay if I take your arms and place them in the proper position?"

Mary agrees. Mary is then able to do the technique properly with the therapist's assistance.

Touch and Working with Traumatized Clients

Touch has been seen as an essential component of healing since ancient times (Bowlby, 1952). Well before the surge in neurobiological knowledge about trauma and touch, the helpfulness of touch in psychotherapy was recognized (Hunter & Struve, 1998). Even with the victims of sexual abuse, Horton et al. (1995) noted that almost 75 percent of patients with a history of abuse indicated that touch increased a sense of trust, empowerment, and self-esteem. Additionally, some participants also felt that touch restored a feeling of self-worth and re-enforced that they were deserving of being appropriately and respectfully touched (Horton et al. 1995).

Lawry (1998) pointed out that touch can serve as a healer to Finklehor's (1986) four traumagenic factors. With stigmatization, she argues that touch helps the client not to feel separate, different, or unworthy of touch. Touch also serves as an antidote to betrayal and sexualization because, in a therapeutic setting, it can be received with the goal of healing, nurturing, and caring. Providing a client with the ability to voice an opinion addresses powerlessness, by simply allowing a client to say "yes" or "no" to touch. Touching, especially when a client has been maltreated, can provide empathy and remind the client that she or he is worthy of being touched (Horton et al., 1995).

Research and practice concur that developing a safe place for a child to process his or her abuse experiences is critical (Rose & Philpot, 2005). Touch lets clients know that they are safe. Attuned touch, such as being touched, hugged, and rocked, helps with excessive arousal and makes us feel comforted, bonded, safe, and in control (Aquino & Lee, 2000). These are not only antidotes to the neurobiological effect of trauma, but are also elements of a warm, trusting therapeutic relationship. The right kind of touch, especially when a client has been maltreated, can provide empathy and remind the client that she or he is worthy and deserving of human touch.

Within the population of children who have experienced abuse or neglect, touch can also express acceptance and boost or repair self-esteem and body acceptance, as well as develop trust (Phelan, 2009). With a growing body of knowledge around maltreatment and its effects on neurobiology, healing might best be served through body-oriented therapies (van der Kolk, 2014). Body therapies engage the safety system of the brain before trying to address trauma cognitively. They concentrate on overwhelming sensations and emotions before eliciting the story (van der Kolk, 2014). To have clients begin to tell their story without first ensuring their emotional safety may be unethical.

Vignette B: Case of Natasha

Natasha is a 16-year-old female who has been in sexual abuse therapy for five months. The therapist is using Trauma-Focused Cognitive Behavioral Therapy (TF-CBT), and Natasha is in the phase of treatment involving preparation of her trauma narrative. During the session, as Natasha started writing the details of her personal story about sexual abuse, she became noticeably upset. Her tears turned into uncontrollable crying, she was physically shaking, and she had difficulty calming herself down even with the therapist's prompting. The therapist knew that Natasha was experiencing emotional dysregulation likely triggered by exposure to the trauma. Not only would Natasha need to return her body to a calmer state so that she could refocus on the therapeutic work, but it would be important for Natasha to feel supported in the sharing of such a painful memory.

The therapist felt compelled to reach out to offer support and reassurance to Natasha and also to help her "come back" to her physical body, regrounding her to the present moment rather than getting carried away by her strong feelings. Before the therapist initiated touch, she considered the therapeutic alliance which she believed was strong. Natasha had been actively engaged in her sessions and her mother reported to the therapist that Natasha looked forward to coming to therapy and always seemed better afterward. The therapist herself felt comfortable with touch and so she reached out to place her hand on Natasha's shoulder to offer consolation and reassurance. The therapist remained aware, watching for any signs that the touch might be experienced by Natasha as uncomfortable, such as pulling away, tension in her body, increased crying, and other signs of continued dysregulation. None of those signs were apparent so the therapist kept her hand on Natasha's shoulder and made a gentle patting motion, being fully present with Natasha in the moment and continuing to prompt Natasha to use her breathing skills. Natasha seemed responsive to the touch and was able to follow the therapist's lead and eventually calmed down. A few minutes later she was able to continue working on her trauma narrative without disruption.

Neglect and the Absence of Touch

Absence of touch, which may be seen in children who have been neglected, also influences development, attachment, bonding, and all future relationships (Aquino & Lee, 2000). In their studies of Romanian orphans, Carlson and Earls (1997) found that those infants who experienced the sensory deprivation typical in Romanian orphanages displayed "muteness, blank facial expressions, social withdrawal, and bizarre stereotypic movements" (as cited in Konnikova, 2015, para. 2). These infants had differing levels and timing of cortisol release than their counterparts who received sensory enrichment. Cortisol fluctuations in the enriched infants approximated those of home-reared infants, indicating that the detrimental effects of the absence of touch could be mitigated. However, the positive change was not sustained when touch was again reduced (Carlson & Earls, 1997), suggesting that the need for touch is ongoing.

The majority of children seen by social services in the United States are there for reasons of neglect. Studies indicate that children who are neglected in early childhood present traits similar to those children raised in institutions (Sheridan et al., 2012). Nurturing a child early in life may help him or her develop a larger hippocampus, the brain region important for learning, memory, and stress responses. Brain images show that children of nurturing mothers had hippocampal volumes 10 percent larger than children whose mothers were not as nurturing (Castro, 2012). Beyond the neurobiological implications, an environmental context (home, school, therapy, etc.) absent of touch may send a message to a child that she or he is not valued or is worthless.

Ethical Considerations

Despite the vast scientific data on the importance of touch for human development, communication, and its effectiveness in healing, the field of psychotherapy has generally shunned its use (Bonitz, 2008; Hunter & Struve, 1998). The negative perceptions of touch arise from the history of psychotherapy, cultural implications, and, in public arenas, societal pressure on professionals not to touch children (Halley, 2007). Opinions and perspective on touch are also colored by culture (Halley, 2007). American culture is among one of the cultures identified as low touch (Zur & Nordmarken, 2016). From the Western viewpoint, there are cultural taboos around touch with the opposite sex, the same sex, with one's self, and with strangers (Hunter & Struve, 1998). An individual is often reluctant to speak about touch particularly if his or her views differ from the cultural norm (Halley, 2007).

Although no professional organization sees touch as unethical in all circumstances (Zur & Nordmarken, 2016), and evidence continues to mount on the efficacy of touch in the therapeutic process for children who have experienced abuse and neglect, touch remains a point of controversy. Often, clinicians are taught or told about or perceive touch as inherently sexual, potentially harmful, inappropriate, or unprofessional. However, Aquino and Lee (2000) suggest that the absence of touch in the therapeutic endeavor could cause a child to blame him or herself for the previous abuse, and they point out that not allowing a child to embrace a therapist could possibly devalue the child.

Touch should always be done only for the client's benefit and be a part of the treatment plan (Zur & Nordmarken, 2016; Bonitz, 2008). It is not helpful to use a deontological approach in determining the "rightness" of touch in the therapeutic setting. As with all clinical decisions, certain considerations must be addressed. Zur and Nordmarken (2016) have developed guidelines for the clinical use of touch. These guidelines encourage client safety, address issues of power and control, and implore the clinician to not act out of fear of legal reprisal, but rather practice competently and develop evidence-based treatment plans.

Boundaries and Clear Guidelines

Children who have experienced abuse have had multiple boundaries violated, not only boundaries among and between self and others, but also boundaries between self as distinct from the outside world. Scared people cannot tell where their bodies begin and end. The constant questioning of "who am I" and "where am I" is manifested through hypervigilance. Through warm and reassuring touch people experience the boundaries of their bodies and this helps to promote a sense of control and safety (van der Kolk, 2014). The following vignette is an example of setting clear boundaries and guidelines.

Vignette C: Case of Sarah

> *Sarah is a 6-year-old female sexual abuse client who has been working with a male therapist for just a few sessions. Sarah makes constant attempts during sessions to be physically close to the therapist and touching him in some manner that makes the therapist uncomfortable. If they are sitting on a couch, Sarah will position herself so close to the therapist that their legs and hips are touching. She also attempts to crawl on the therapist's lap when he sits on a chair. The therapist is aware that a man sexually abused*

Sarah. This inappropriate touch and physical proximity may have distorted her perceptions of appropriate boundaries. In addition to providing some verbal instructions about space and touch between them in sessions, the therapist also uses intentional seating arrangements, objects as physical barriers, and caregiver support to reinforce boundary concepts.

When sitting on the couch with Sarah, the therapist uses strategic placement of pillows between them to prevent Sarah from getting close enough that their body parts are touching. If the therapist is sitting in a chair and Sarah comes up and tries to sit on his lap, the therapist issues a verbal reminder, "Remember, one of our rules is that you don't sit on my lap." He then moves to sit on the floor, and asks Sarah to sit across from him. He also intentionally places a therapeutic activity or game between them as a preventative measure from her reaching out to touch or grab him. During home visits, the therapist never has a session alone in a room with Sarah, behind closed doors, or in her bedroom. He makes sure her mother is within a distance that allows her to see them at all times. As the therapist maintains consistency of these physical boundaries, in combination with verbal psycho-education, Sarah's attempts to engage in these behaviors decrease.

Power Dynamics

Therapists working with child victims of sexual abuse need to be mindful of power dynamics (McNeil-Haber, 2004). Touch is an expression of social power and, given that children have experienced touch as a violation, they often have issues with power, trust, safety, and control (Halley, 2007; Rose & Philpot, 2005). Touch can accidentally reinforce a negative or harmful power dynamic in which the client feels less powerful than the therapist. One way to address the power issue directly is to offer several choices to the child. Choice empowers all children. Abused children, in particular, have had no choice and may feel powerless. When, where, and in what manner to be touched are important areas of choice. Once rapport and emotional engagement are established, the therapist must be clear about the types of touch that will occur and confirm that the child agrees to be touched (Hunter & Struve, 1998; Zur & Nordmarken, 2016).

Vignette D: Case of Brendan

Six-year-old Brendan was living in a shelter with his mom after both had experienced physical abuse from his dad. The director of the shelter reported that Brendan was displaying frequent aggressive behaviors and felt that he and his mother might benefit from nurturing massage therapy. With the treating counselor leading the session, the intervention plan was *for the massage therapist to demonstrate the massage techniques and then mom, in turn, would massage Brendan. However, Brendan refused to allow his mother to massage him. As the massage techniques were demonstrated, his mom would continue to ask Brendan for permission to massage him, and he said "no," which the mother respected. He instead asked a teddy bear's permission and would massage the bear. As it came time to massage the face, the counselor had an idea. After Brendan practiced massage on the teddy bear's face, the counselor suggested Brendan ask mom if she would like a massage on her face. He liked this idea and scooted in front of his mom, warmed his hands and asked permission. Brendan watched diligently as the counselor demonstrated each massage stroke on her own face. He lovingly placed his hands on mom's cheeks and provided gentle strokes. Brendan asked her if the massage was too hard. Mom said no, it felt good, as the tears streamed down her cheeks.*

(Adapted from Allen, 2013)

Competence

There is so much misunderstanding about the potential therapeutic power of touch in the general and professional communities, it is imperative that therapists seek out training in the proper use of touch. In some states the perception of therapeutic touch as negative is so strong that legislation has been passed. In Florida, for example, the Florida Board of Massage Therapy has concluded that touch for compensation requires one to be licensed as a massage therapist (Rand, 2007). By contrast, the Veterans Health Administration hospital system, a leader in the treatment of post-traumatic stress disorder, has instituted a training program in holistic methods including Reiki, meditation, guided imagery, Tai Chi, and reflexology (Rappaport, 2012). Although the NASW Code of Ethics (2008) does not forbid the use of touch, it does require that "social workers should exercise careful judgment and take responsible steps (including appropriate education, research, training, consultation, and supervision) to ensure the competence of their work and to protect clients from harm" (Section 1.04B).

As always, the therapeutic endeavor begins with self-awareness by the therapist. The therapist's own issues with touch and nurturing and physical ways of showing support and building relationships need to be examined. This involves exploring one's personal beliefs, values, and comfort level around touch (McNeil-Haber, 2004). When working with child victims of sexual abuse, it is critical that the therapist pay attention to his or her emotional reactions to the child as they uncover the story (Wickham & West, 2002). Touch awareness with this population relies upon the therapist being ever vigilant and self-reflective (Wickham & West, 2002). It also means the therapist being mindful of emotional, physical, and sexual boundaries that are constantly changing and always evolving (McNeil-Haber, 2004). The therapist must be clear about his or her own opinions on touch.

Training is critical as therapists do not receive specific guidance within traditional therapeutic training on touch issues other than for restraint policies. Strozier, Krizek, and Sale (2003) note that 82 percent of social workers surveyed said there was a lack of training around touch in graduate schools and in supervision. In a study comparing therapists who touch with those who do not, it was found that those who utilized touch had supervisors who valued the efficacy of touch (Milakovich, 1992 as cited in McGuirk, 2012).

Supervision is clearly important (Bonitz, 2008) and is required under the NASW Code of Ethics (2008) for competent practice (Section 1.04 a, b, c). Supervision allows a practitioner to process sessions and offer a "third ear" (McQueen, 2008). It offers therapists a safe place to openly discuss issues that arise in sessions and is a place to process therapeutic issues and mitigate the effect of vicarious trauma (Harrison, 2007). Therapeutic interventions such as Trauma-Focused CBT and Trauma-Focused Integrated Play Therapy (Gil, 2012; Gil & Shaw, 2014) are trauma-specific and require specialized training and supervision. Even more importantly, body therapies, such as Reiki, meditation, guided imagery, Tai Chi, and reflexology also require training and supervision.

Case of John

When working with a child sexual abuse victim, a therapist may be touched by the client in an unexpected way that is experienced by the therapist as provocative, sexual, and intrusive. This can be extremely alarming, upsetting, and uncomfortable. The therapist may worry about her ability to address, stop, and resolve the inappropriate touch, and about the potential ramifications of professional liability. There are several steps that can be taken to assist a therapist with handling inappropriate client-initiated touch in sessions, including comprehensive and ongoing assessment, boundary-specific treatment strategies, and utilization of supervision to address therapist self-awareness and professionalism. The following case study illustrates how a therapist addressed her client's inappropriate touch in sessions.

Case Background

John is a 6-year-old client who was a victim of sexual abuse for more than two years by his mother's boyfriend. The sexual abuse incidents involved oral and anal sex as well as exposure to pornography. John was removed from his home and placed in foster care where he received home-based therapy. John scored in the clinically significant ranges for anxiety, post-traumatic stress arousal, and sexual concerns when the Trauma Symptom Checklist for Young Children (TSCYC) was administered at intake. It was reported that he had sexual behavior problems primarily related to the inappropriate touching of private body parts of adults and peers at home and school.

John also exhibited inappropriate touching behaviors toward the female therapist assigned to the case. Initially, he would run up to the therapist and wrap his arms around her body in a bear hug with his head resting against her lower abdomen and call her his "girlfriend" and squeeze her tightly for several seconds. The therapist reported feeling uncomfortable with the interaction, but did not want to make John feel rejected or potentially disrupt the therapeutic alliance. In other sessions, John reached out and grabbed the therapist's breasts and buttocks. The therapist reported experiencing anxiety over how to handle what she perceived to be aggressive, provocative, sexual touch. She wasn't sure what to say to John without shaming him or causing him to disengage.

Supervisory Support

The supervisor utilized multiple interventions to help the therapist identify and address John's touching behaviors as well as to bring more self-awareness to the work. The therapist was first encouraged to explore her views about touch, specifically with clients, children, and trauma victims. The supervisor also assisted the therapist in clarifying her views and perceptions of acceptable boundaries in sessions. The supervisor assisted the therapist in understanding the context for John's touching behaviors that were based upon assessment findings including that he may struggle with disruptive thoughts, feelings, fears, and behaviors related to his sexual trauma. The therapist would need to provide John with consistent education and practice role-plays in order to internalize what he learned about boundaries. It would also be important to help John identify the types of abusive touches he experienced in order to increase his awareness that the touches he was initiating may be reactions to his sexual abuse, but were unacceptable. The supervisor helped the therapist identify language to use when talking with John about personal boundaries and space, and also helped the therapist brainstorm therapeutic interventions and activities.

Therapist Implementation of Supervisory Suggestions and Client's Response

The therapist first clarified her role to John as his counselor and not his girlfriend. She then explained to John why his hugs felt uncomfortable to her and then demonstrated an appropriate hug. In particular, John was taught how to hug the therapist gently, without tightly squeezing her or placing his head on her abdomen. She had John practice the hug and then talked with him about alternative touches that would be acceptable in their therapy sessions, such as high fives or fist bumps. This helped the therapist and John become clear on an acceptable greeting ritual.

The therapist then talked with John about personal space and boundaries, including what types of touches were appropriate with what types of people and in what contexts. The therapist utilized a play activity called Space Scotch (see this chapter's Appendix A) to engage John in practicing and internalizing what he learned. The session activities helped as John was subsequently able to hug the therapist the way they practiced and was also able to recall the information learned about boundaries and touch. The therapist assessed John's environment and any potential triggers, and she provided corrective experiences for him. The therapist came up with a baseline for John's sexual behavior problems and potential triggers that might arouse sexual concerns. The results indicated that John's arousal was related to general anxiety. The therapist then taught John calming strategies including breathing, mindfulness, and muscle relaxation to cope with his anxious feelings.

Summary

The use of touch in treatment of children who have been abused and neglected is a multifaceted issue. Biology informs us of the importance of touch in our bodies' communication, not only with the outside world, but also our bodies' communication with our brain. Inappropriate, sexualized, or absent touch may have long-standing effects on physical, emotional, and social development. Touch has been used to help regulate emotions, calm anxiety, and communicate safety. Touch has also been instrumental in reversing or mitigating developmental delays in infants who experienced lack of nurturing touch. When and how to use touch has been controversial, and advocacy for its use has been cyclical throughout the centuries. Much of the disdain for using touch in therapeutic ways stems from both cultural taboos and risk management considerations. Use of touch is not an "always" or "never" prospect. Touch needs to occur within parameters that respect both child and therapist boundaries, is practiced with clinical competence, and recognizes the influence of perceived power. Turning touch that has harmed into touch that can heal may be the ethical imperative.

Discussion Questions and Exercises

1   Reflect on your feelings about touch based on your personal history. How might these affect your work with a child impacted by abuse?
2   With a colleague choose one of the case vignettes and take turns role playing the therapist and child and practice therapeutic touch interventions that can help the child to calm and self-regulate. Process your experience.
3   Reflecting back on the case study of John, if you were the therapist in this case, what other interventions could you use that address boundary and touch violations that may occur in sessions?

Appendix A

Space Scotch: A Game of Space and Boundaries

Description

This exercise is designed to help children identify appropriate types of emotional and physical space and boundaries between people, depending upon the relationship and circumstances.

Figure 7.1 Example of Space Scotch: A Game of Space and Boundaries. (Used with permission from Andrea Raasch.)

Suggested items needed

- Large white sheet with permanent markers (or chalk for a sidewalk)
- Large poster board
- 6 different colors of construction paper
- Markers, stickers, and glue
- Small prizes as rewards

Preparation

- Draw a hopscotch game on a large white sheet using permanent markers, color-coding each step with one of six colors, i.e., 1 = pink, 2 = blue, 3 = green, 4 = yellow, 5 = purple, and 6 = red. Depending upon how large your game is, you may need to repeat the colors. For example, 1 and 10 might both be pink.
- On the poster board, line up and glue six different colors of construction paper vertically and write one of the following space/boundary categories next to each color:

pink = me, blue = my family, green = relatives and close friends, yellow = people I know, purple = neighbors and helpers, and red = strangers. The six different colors must match the colors used on the sheet, so you may have 1 = pink = me, etc.
- Using the same 6 colors of construction paper, cut them into card size and write space/boundary scenarios on the back of one side. You will have 6 piles of scenarios, i.e., the pink pile includes scenarios about space/boundaries related to the individual.

Instructions/Directions

1 Using a stress ball or other game piece, have the child throw it onto the first number on the hopscotch game board.
2 The child hops to the number, you read a scenario card from the corresponding color scenario deck, the child answers the question and hops back to the start.
3 The child continues to hop to all numbers on the game board, repeating the game if necessary with the goal of answering as many questions as possible in 20 minutes.
4 For each correct answer, the child will get to collect a prize.
5 At the end of the game, review any answers the child did not get correct before the child is able to collect the prizes.

References

Allen, T. (2013). *Healing touch: Using massage to break the cycle of abuse.* Retrieved on 1 April, 2016 from: http://www.massagetoday.com/mpacms/mt/article.php?id=14562
Aquino, A., & Lee, S. (2000). The use of nonerotic touch with children. *Journal of Psychotherapy in Independent Practice, 1(3)*, 17–30. DOI:10.1300/J288v01n03_02
Bonitz, V. (2008). Use of physical touch in the "talking cure": A journey to the outskirts of psychotherapy. *Psychotherapy, Theory, Research, Practice, Training, 45(3)*, 391–404. DOI:http://dx.doi.org/10.1037/a0013311
Bowlby, J. (1952). *Maternal care and mental health: A report on behalf of the World Health Organization.* Geneva, Switzerland: World Health Organization.
Bryden, D., Johnson, E., Tobia, S., Kashtelyan, V., & Roesch, M. (2011). Attention for learning signals in anterior cingulate. *Journal of Neuroscience, 31(50)*, 18266–18274. Retrieved on 1 November, 2016 from: http://jneurosci.org/content/31/50/18266.full
Carlson, M., & Earls, F. (1997). Psychological and neuroendocrinological sequelae of early social deprivation in institutionalized children in Romania. *Integrative Neurobiology of Affiliation, 807*, 419–428.
Castro, J. (2012). *How a mother's love changes a child's brain.* Retrieved on 10 April, 2016 from: http://www.livescience.com/21778-early-neglect-alters-kids-brains.html
Field, T. (2010). Touch for social emotional and physical well-being: A review. *Developmental Review, 30(4)*, 367–383. Retrieved on 7 March, 2015 from: http://www.sciencedirect.com/science/article/pii/S0273229711000025
Field, T. (2014). *Touch* (2nd ed.). Cambridge, MA: MIT Press.

Finklehor, D. (1986). *A sourcebook on child sexual abuse*. Beverly Hills, CA: Sage.

Gil, E. (2012). Trauma-focused integrated play therapy. In P.G. Brown (Ed.), *Handbook of child sexual abuse: Identification, assessment, and treatment* (pp. 151–178). New York: Wiley & Sons.

Gil, E., & Shaw, J.A. (2014). *Working with children with sexual behavior problems*. New York: Guilford Press.

Halley, J.O. (2007). *Boundaries of touch: Parenting and adult-child intimacy*. Urbana, IL: University of Illinois Press.

Harrison, G. (2007). In Brooke, S. (Ed.), *The use of the creative therapies with sexual abuse survivors* (pp. 301–310). Springfield, IL: Charles C. Thomas.

Herman, J. (1992). *Trauma and recovery: The aftermath of violence—from domestic abuse to political terror*. New York: Basic Books.

Horton, J., Clance, P., Sterk-Elifson, C., & Emshoff, J. (1995). Touch in psychotherapy: A survey of patient's experiences. *Psychotherapy, 32(3)*, 443–457. Retrieved on 1 November, 2016 from: https://www.researchgate.net/publication/232507028_Touch_in_psychotherapy_A_survey_of_patient's_experiences

Hunter, M., & Struve, J. (1998). *The ethical use of touch in psychotherapy*. Thousand Oaks, CA: Sage.

Konnikova, M. (2015). The power of touch. *The New Yorker*. Retrieved on 7 March, 2015 from: http://www.newyorker.com/../maria-konnikova/power-touch

Lawry, S.S. (1998). In E.W.L. Smith, P.R. Clance, & S. Imes (Eds.), *Touch in psychotherapy: Theory, research, and practice* (pp. 201–210). New York: Guilford Press.

Linden, D. (2015). *Touch: The science of hand, heart and mind*. New York: Viking.

McGuirk, J. (2012). The place of touch in counseling and psychotherapy and the potential for healing within the therapeutic relationship. *Inside Out, 68(3)*. Retrieved 10 April, 2016 from: http://iahip.org/inside-out/issue-68-autumn-2012/the-place-of-touch-in-counselling-and-psychotherapy-and-the-potential-for-healing-within-the-therapeutic-relationship

McNeil-Haber, F. (2004). Ethical considerations in the use of nonerotic touch in psychotherapy with children. *Ethics & Behavior, 14(2)*, 123–140. DOI:10.1207/s15327019eb1402_3

McQueen, D. (2008). *Psychoanalytic psychotherapy after child abuse: Psychoanalytic psychotherapy in the treatment of adults and children who have experienced sexual abuse, violence, and neglect in childhood*. London: Karnac Books.

Montagu, A. (1986). *Touching: The human significance of the skin* (3rd ed.). New York: Harper & Row.

NASW (2008). *Code of Ethics*. Washington, DC: NASW. Retrieved on 10 April, 2016 from: http://www.socialworkers.org/pubs/code/code.asp

Newhouse, E. (2015). Vets experiencing trauma can't respond to reason. *Psychology Today*. Retrieved on 9 April, 2016 from: https://www.psychologytoday.com/blog/invisible-wounds/201512/vets-experiencing-trauma-cant-respond-reason

Phelan, J.E. (2009). Exploring the use of touch in the psychotherapeutic setting: A phenomenological review. *Psychotherapy: Theory, Research, Practice, Training, 46*, 97–111. DOI:10.1037/a0014751

Rand, W. (2007). Florida, Reiki and the Board of Massage. *The International Center for Reiki Training*. Retrieved on 10 April, 2016 from: http://www.spiritualone.com/online/sept04/flreikiandmassage.htm

Rappaport, R. (2012). Holistic nurses joining forces to care for veterans. *Beginnings: Journal of the American Holistic Nurses, 32(5)*, 14–16.

Ridderinkhof, K.R., van den Wildenberg, W.P., Segalowitz, S.J., & Carter, C.S. (2004). *Brain Cognition, 56*, 129–140. Retrieved on 1 November, 2016 from: https://www.ncbi.nlm.nih.gov/pubmed/15518930

Rose, R., & Philpot, T. (2005). *The child's own story: Life story work with traumatized children*. London: Jessica Kingsley.

Satir, V. (1988). *The new peoplemaking*. Mountain View, CA: Science and Behavior Book, Inc.

Sheridan, M.A., Fox, N.A., Zeanah, C.H., McLaughlin, K.A., & Nelson, C.A. (2012). Variation in neural development as a result of exposure to institutionalization early in childhood. *Proceedings of the National Academy of Sciences of the United States of America, 109(32)*, 12927-32. Retrieved on 1 November, 2016 from: https://www.ncbi.nlm.nih.gov/pubmed/22826224

Strozier, A., Krizek, C., & Sale, K. (2003). Touch: Its use in psychotherapy. *Journal of Social Work Practice, 17(1)*, 49–62.

U.S. Department of Health and Human Services, Administration for Children and Families, Administration on Children, Youth and Families, Children's Bureau. (2016). *Child maltreatment 2014*. Retrieved on 1 November, 2016 from: http://www.acf.hhs.gov/programs/cb/research-data-technology/statistics-research/child-maltreatment

van der Kolk, B. (2014). *The body keeps the score*. New York: Penguin Group.

Westland, G. (2011). Physical touch in psychotherapy: Why are we not touching more? Body, movement and dance in psychotherapy. *An International Journal the Theory, Research and Practice, 6(1)*, 17–29. DOI:10.1080/17432979.2010.508597

Wickham, R.E., & West, J. (2002). *Therapeutic work with sexually abused children*. London: Sage Publications.

Zur, O., & Nordmarken, N. (2016). *To touch or not to touch: Exploring the myth of prohibition on touch in psychotherapy and counseling*. Retrieved on 10 April, 2016 from: http://www.zurinstitute.com/touchintherapy.html

8 Hands Are Not for Hitting

Redefining Touch for Children Exposed to Domestic Violence

Rachel Scharlepp and Melissa Radey

> When the need for touch remains unsatisfied, abnormal behavior will result.
> Ashley Montagu, *Touching*

Overview

Touch is a fundamental sense, essential for human growth and development. Trauma exposure, particularly in cases of domestic violence, can disrupt normal functioning of touch for individuals and families. This chapter provides a brief history of touch and examines the empirical foundation for using touch in child psychotherapy. A case study is presented, describing how a therapist facilitated nurturing touch using Kinesthetic Storytelling® with a mother–daughter dyad to repair their attachment relationship affected by domestic violence. The chapter concludes with ethical and clinical implications for using touch in child therapy.

Theoretical and Research Base

Background

Sensory receptors serve as single access points to the world in all species. Humans have up to twenty-one uniquely identified senses, many of which correspond to experiencing touch. Senses involved with touch are the first to develop in embryos and inspire the development of all other senses. Not only the first to develop, touch is the only reciprocal sense; one cannot touch without being touched. Touch is critical to development (Ardiel & Rankin, 2010). Second to survival, touch can improve life quality, overall functioning, and reverse the effects of adversity. Initially studied by Harlow (1973) with infant rhesus monkeys, research on the effects of touch has increased tremendously.

Researchers have found that the sensory stimulation of touch, as opposed to cognitively processing the concept of being touched, is the key component to optimal development. Kolb and Gibb (2007) found an exciting example of this when they linked touch with healing physical brain injury in rats. They found functional recovery and synaptic reorganization occurred as the result of simply *stroking* rats with brain lesions (Kolb & Gibb, 2007). Furthermore, stroking a pregnant rat had the effect of *preventing* lesions in her offspring (Kolb & Gibb, 2007). Bredy *et al.* (2004) researched the effects of parental touch on adult outcomes of rat pups. They identified parental differences in the beneficial effects of touch, with rat pup fathers playing an influential role on development only when their parenting style included touch (i.e., licking and grooming). Although strong evidence supports healing properties of touch with rats and their pups, is touch salient in healing human emotional pain and scars?

Empirical Support for the Use of Touch in Psychotherapy

Although the biological basis supporting the benefits of touch was suspected as early as the 1930s in Bellevue Hospital's delivery unit (Day, 2013) and empirically established in the 1950s with rhesus monkeys (Harlow, 1973), the therapeutic use of touch, especially in working with children, is still emerging. Available work indicates that appropriate touch plays a salient role in the therapeutic relationship (APT, 2015; Smith *et al.*, 1998; Zur & Nordmarken, 2016). Hernandez-Reif *et al.* (2007) found that therapeutic touch decreased stress reactions and increased serotonin and dopamine levels in preterm infants, all vital to achieving the emotional safety required for healing to occur. Hunter and Struve (1998), in their exploration of ethical considerations of touch in adult psychotherapy, found that combining touch and talk within the therapeutic relationship can increase a sense of empathy, sympathy, safety, calm, and comfort, whereas talk therapy without touch is restrictive. Others agree that touch, when used appropriately, can increase connectivity, strength, and trust among the therapy duet (McNeil-Haber, 2004; Smith *et al.*, 1998; Zur & Nordmarken, 2016).

Child psychotherapy requires special consideration because: first, children, in many ways, are more vulnerable than their adult counterparts and are biologically dependent on adults for safety and basic needs; and second, children naturally relate to using touch and veering away from touch may create a contrived sense of the therapeutic relationship.

Although touch, if used therapeutically, can be an imperative part of healing, are there exceptions? What about situations in which touch has been the culprit, creating danger, threat, pain, and control? Who should provide the touch: therapist or parent?

Impact of Domestic Violence on Children and the Importance of Touch

Experts have estimated that approximately 10 million children are exposed to domestic violence (DV) each year in the United States, with the majority of survivors under the age of 6 years old (American Academy of Child and Adolescent Psychiatry, 2013). The U.S. Department of Justice (2015) defines DV as "a pattern of abusive behavior in any relationship that is used by one partner to gain or maintain power and control over another intimate partner" (What is domestic violence section, para. 1). DV does not stay within the confines of the abusive relationship. In fact, child witnesses of DV may be more at risk of traumatization than the intended victim, especially if the victim is their primary caregiver (van der Kolk, 1996).

People often believe that younger children are less at risk of poor outcomes as a result of DV due to their age and inability to explicitly store memories. Conversely, younger children are more vulnerable because children under the age of three years are at a critical stage for attachment; they depend on adults for survival, and they have difficulty understanding and processing the complexities of DV (Carpenter & Stacks, 2009; De Bellis *et al.*, 2005; van der Kolk, 1996). Van der Kolk (1996) explains that "the earliest and possibly the most damaging psychological trauma is the loss of a secure base" (p. 204). A child watching her caregiver controlled, intimidated, threatened, or physically assaulted by another adult consequently raises questions about her caregiver's ability to protect.

Children are hardwired to attach to their caregiver in order to maintain safety. When children witness their caregiver being abused, their secure base, the basis for future development, is threatened. When the abuser is a trusted adult or a parental figure, the negative effects increase exponentially (Scharlepp *et al.*, 2012; van der Kolk, 1996). In households with DV, touch as a bonder and nurturer is warped into an intimidator and abuser. Additionally, Tsavoussis *et al.* (2014) found evidence of multiple structural changes in all key areas of the brain in child witnesses of DV. For these children touch needs to be redefined, as they have learned that touch is not to connect, but a tool of control (Gil, 2015). Brains and bodies need to relearn that touch can be for comfort, communication, and connection.

For relearning to occur, touch needs to be reintroduced, not through cognitive reframing, but through the touch of an attuned caregiver. Indeed, maternal licking decreases hypothalamic-pituitary-adrenal (HPA) stress reactions in rats (Liu *et al.*, 1997). The HPA axis, part of the neuroendocrine system, is a complex set of feedback circuitry responsible for regulation of the system under stress. When activated, digestion decreases, immune responses are triggered, mood/emotional reactions are activated, and energy storage increases as expenditure decreases. Liu and colleagues (1997) found that the simple act of touch calms this cascade reaction. Conversely, the lack of touch or the presence of abusive touch has been found to cause this system to be hypersensitive, resulting in unproductive or counterproductive reactions.

Importantly, the introduction of appropriate touch to a system already wired for vigilance due to misuse of touch can both calm an activated system and inspire neural pathway changes with a healthier stress response over a lifetime (Ardiel & Rankin, 2010; Bredy *et al.*, 2003; Liu *et al.*, 1997; Lovic & Fleming, 2004). (See Figure 8.1 that revealed the impact of DV on two siblings during an initial assessment.)

Empirical Support for the Use of Touch Following Traumatic Events

Research on the therapeutic benefits of touch is growing. Field (1998), in her review of a series of findings from the Touch Research Institute (see

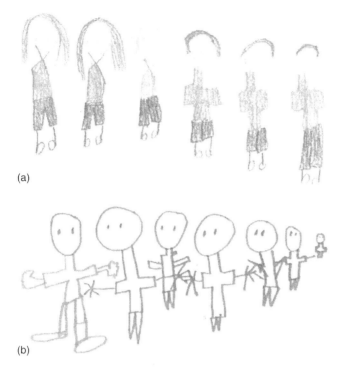

Figure 8.1 The salience of touch in domestic violence is evident in these two family drawings created by a brother and sister. The violence was kept a family secret until disclosed through the drawings. (a) The girl (aged eight) added details, but left off arms and hands; while (b) the boy (aged five) drew hands, but showed "Dad" with "big fists." (Drawings used with permission.)

http://www6.miami.edu/touch-research/), concluded that therapeutic massage significantly enhanced attention and alertness among children with autism and attention-deficit/hyperactivity disorder; alleviated stress, depression, and anxiety among children with post-traumatic stress disorder from experiencing Hurricane Andrew; improved body image and decreased depression among adolescent girls with bulimia; and increased sociability, soothability, and emotionality among massaged infants.

To examine the effects of touch for adults, Kaiser *et al.* (2010) designed a randomized controlled study testing the effects of sensory integration therapy in treating post-traumatic stress disorder. The treatment group received vestibular stimulation and the study findings suggest that sensory integration is a promising treatment modality for treating traumatization (Kaiser *et al.*, 2010). Field et al. (1997) found that 30-minute, twice weekly massage therapy sessions reregistered the body's openness to touch and decreased anxiety, depression, and chemical stress responses after one month of treatment among female survivors of sexual and physical abuse. Women in the comparison group who had never been sexually or physically abused also experienced a decrease in anxiety and depression, but not in the chemical stress response, suggesting an added benefit of touch to the healing process.

Although some psychotherapists warn against the use of touch due to the inherent legal risks, most agree that touch can be therapeutically beneficial for abuse survivors (Hunter & Struve, 1998). To better assist child practitioners in considering the use of touch, the Association for Play Therapy (APT) published *Paper on Touch: Clinical, Professional, & Ethical Issues* (2015), providing a summary of the clinical, professional, and ethical issues regarding touch in work with children. One special consideration is using touch in treating children who have experienced trauma. As with other populations, the therapist needs to be attuned to the child's needs and response to touch. Therapist sensitivity is especially critical with children who have experienced trauma because of the risk of retraumatization (APT, 2015; Brody, 1992).

The following case example (implemented by Rachel Scharlepp) explores the detrimental effects of DV, specifically the potential consequence of distorting nurturing touch into threatening touch. This case includes clinical and ethical complexities and depicts what Brody (1992) described as the *dialogue* that touch inspires. A discussion of the key ethical dilemmas follows.

Case of Mama P. and Sally

Background and Presenting Problem

Mama P., a 28-year-old African American, has two children, 3-year-old Sally and 3-month-old Josiah. Extended family and church members adequately support the family, although Mama P. expresses the fact that she feels lonely much of the time. The family lives modestly in a clean and quiet government-subsidized housing complex. Mama P. has a college degree and works full-time as an administrative assistant. I saw Sally in an outpatient community mental health center predominantly serving Medicaid recipients. Because I was the only child therapist at the center, Sally was automatically assigned to me. During the intake process, Mama P. disclosed that I was the sixth therapist to work with Sally in the past six months, explaining that the other therapists were unable to help Sally because Sally was "so terrible." I was newly licensed and working to complete the requirements to become a Registered Play Therapist. I had recently started advanced training in infant mental health and had recently attended a workshop on Kinesthetic Storytelling® (Courtney, 2014) and its use as an intervention to redefine touch in the parent–child relationship.

Mama P. had been worried about Sally for quite some time, fearing she was a "sociopath" like her father. Sally's father was sentenced to 15 years' imprisonment for attempted murder of his girlfriend. Prior to this he was violently abusive toward Mama P. and, by proxy, their two children. Mama P. explained that the father started out as controlling, which she initially interpreted as over-protectiveness and found endearing. The father's controlling behavior spiraled into violent rages triggered by jealousy over the mother's attention for their children. The father repeatedly interrupted Mama P.'s precious time of nursing Josiah by raping her with their newborn sandwiched between them and Sally watching from across the room. The father would then leave for days and return with gifts and charm, making Mama P. question and minimize the abuse. Sally witnessed many of these attacks and one day mustered the courage to attempt to protect her mom. As the father raped Mama P. for what would become the last time, Sally jumped on his back, pulled his hair, and screamed for him to stop. The father turned his attention to her, biting her side and kicking her in the forehead with his steel-toed boot. Once the father left, Mama P. found that Sally was severely bleeding from the bite and took her to the ER where the story of abuse was disclosed and reported.

Informed Consent and Assessment

The agency's informed consent did not include specific policies and procedures surrounding touch. The therapist, however, addressed the ethics of touch by informing Mama P. of the times when touch was used as an intervention tool, educating her on its use, and having her present during the touch-based interventions. In order to better understand Sally, Mama P., and their relationship, I administered the Semi-Structured Observation of Parent-Child Interactions (Crowell & Feldman, 1991). The results indicated that both mom and child were traumatized, and the traumatization had damaged their relationship. Without direct intervention, the prognosis for the dyad and Sally's developmental trajectory was bleak.

Ethical Rationale for Utilizing a Touch-Based Intervention

Foundational to child-centered play therapy (Landreth, 2012), special attention to the therapeutic relationship is essential prior to introducing anything other than child-directed touch in therapy (Gil, 1991; McNeil-Haber, 2004). Even though their relationship had been damaged by DV, Sally developmentally required access during sessions to her secure base, Mama P. The dyad needed me to model how to give and receive nurturing touch (Gil, 2015). Sally's touch felt dangerous and "gross" to Mama P., often causing Sally to frantically cling to her mother for affection. I closely monitored Mama P.'s and Sally's responses to the touch-based interventions. When Mama P. would start to withdraw out of discomfort or because of her trauma, I was able to offer support by enhancing her and Sally's understanding of each other's needs to foster emotional security (Gil, 2015).

Treatment Plan

Goals | Objectives

1 Build therapeutic relationships
  - 1.1 Conduct individual child-centered play therapy with Sally focused on processing past trauma and current relationships.
  - 1.2 Conduct parent guidance sessions with Mama P. focused on finding effective ways to parent a child with a history of traumatization.
  - 1.3 Assess the parent–child relationship.

2 Redefine touch for the dyad
  - 2.1 Transition dyad into child–parent psychotherapy focused on processing past trauma.
  - 2.2 Use Kinesthetic Storytelling® to introduce touch to both mom and child.
  - 2.3 Monitor Mama P.'s and Sally's reactions to maintain emotional safety.
  - 2.4 Encourage Mama P.'s ability to respond to Sally's needs as opposed to reacting from a place of traumatization.

3 Process past trauma
  - 3.1 Return to child-centered play therapy with a parent guidance component.
  - 3.2 Refer Mama P. to individual therapy to work through her traumatization.
  - 3.3 Monitor parent–child interactions to determine if or when to initiate additional child–parent psychotherapy.

Introducing Corrective and Reparative Touch

When I felt that the therapeutic relationship with the dyad was at a point in which therapist-directed touch was safe, therapy entered the next phase, focused on providing *corrective* and *reparative* experiences for the dyad (Gil, 1991). Mama P. shared the information that she carried a heavy burden of guilt surrounding her inability to give affectionate touch to Sally. Mama P. described having an instinctual response of disgust when Sally touched her. I had witnessed Mama P.

jump back repulsed at Sally's slightest affectionate gesture (e.g., sitting close to Mama P.'s side).

Mama P.'s response to her child clashed with what she knew Sally needed, thus reinforcing a deep guilt each time Sally triggered Mama P.'s trauma. Helping Mama P. understand her response in terms of her own traumatization dissipated some of Mama P.'s guilt and advanced our work to redefine touch. With each physical rejection, Sally's efforts to acquiesce her developmental need for touch magnified to the point of demanding touch. Helping Sally to understand Mama P.'s reaction and meeting Sally's developmental need for nurturing touch became the prominent goal of treatment (Allen, 2012).

Treatment progressed quickly after Mama P. and Sally understood their own and each other's needs and transitioned from individual work to child–parent psychotherapy (Lieberman & Van Horn, 2005). I utilized a kinesthetic story, *The Magic Rainbow Hug©* (Courtney, 2013), to provide Mama P. with a script. The book is uniquely designed to help children find emotional refuge through relaxation techniques and utilizing structured touch activities. Asking permission from Mama P., I told the story on her back to illustrate the story's kinesthetic touch activities before introducing it to Sally. Mama P. was initially squirmy and embarrassed, but I could feel her relax as she allowed herself to engage in the story. In the discussion that followed, Mama P. said that she had not been safely touched since she was a child around Sally's age. She reflected that touch felt "awkward and weird" at first, then "ok," and, eventually "natural and good." We also discussed the importance of giving and receiving respectful touch (Allen, 2012).

Facilitating Kinesthetic Storytelling® with Mama P. and Sally

At the next session, Mama P. showed Sally *The Magic Rainbow Hug©* and explained that the book was going to help them heal and grow. For a few minutes, Mama P. and Sally shared memories of the father's abuse. For the first time, Mama P. spoke openly about the events that Sally had witnessed. When the dyad indicated that they were ready for the story, we lined up on the floor. Mama P. mimicked my request and considerately asked Sally if she was comfortable with a "Back Story." I sat behind Mama P. and read the story while also drawing the activities on her back. Simultaneously, as Sally sat in front of Mama P., Mama P. drew the activities on Sally's back. Mama P. felt safer and more relaxed touching Sally with me as a close guide modeling touch. As the story progressed, I could feel Mama P. relaxing and strengthening her core as she built her confidence. (See Figure 8.2 for a story activity example.)

We finished the story and Sally immediately asked to go through it again. Mama P. hesitantly agreed. Noticing her pause, I checked in with her to assess how she was doing. Mama P. indicated that she wanted to tell the story again. During the second reading, I had the dyad add personal details to the story. I left the book with Mama P. and Sally and encouraged them to read it as many times as they wanted. I coached Mama P. on how to communicate to Sally when she was

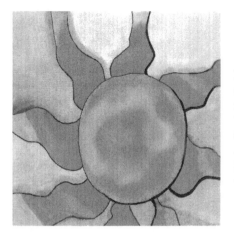

SUN Parent Directions—Make your hand into a fist and slowly make three circular rotations clockwise on the upper middle part of the back. Next, use your fist to draw "rays" of light moving out in all directions. (Excerpt from *The Magic Rainbow Hug©*. Illustration used with permission from Developmental Play & Attachment Therapies, Inc.)

Figure 8.2

overwhelmed or felt triggered. Mama P. and I also coached Sally on ways to show and request affection that were less likely to trigger Mama P.'s trauma response.

In the sessions that followed, touch was prescribed using Kinesthetic Storytelling®. The dyad personalized the story more and more as sessions progressed. As the end of this stage of treatment neared, the family and I went for a walk outdoors. I watched as Sally and Mama P. chatted as they walked ahead and I warmly observed Mama P. naturally grab Sally's hand and pull her to her side. This was the first time I had witnessed Mama P. initiate any type of nurturing contact with Sally. Sally leaned in to her mother with a look of contentment. This exchange evidenced that Mama P. and Sally had successfully redefined touch.

Later Stages of Therapy

Mama P. and Sally's simple exchange during the walk indicated that treatment had progressed into the final stage: processing other aspects of trauma for both Mama P. and Sally. Mama P. was still accepting phone calls from the incarcerated father. She felt a strong loyalty to the idea that he was the father of her children and she had not fully acknowledged the impact of abuse. Mama P. also disclosed throughout the course of treatment that she had grown up in a home rife with DV. I was convinced that Mama P. could benefit from individual therapy from an external therapist to further address the depths of her traumatization, and she agreed.

I continued therapy with Sally for an additional six months to process her mixed feelings about her father, to develop her self-concept and progress toward increased independence, and to develop healthy relationships with authority figures. Sally reached her treatment goals and soon no longer needed my help.

Sally and Mama P. had developed both as individuals and they had successfully healed their attachment relationship. Termination was planned and the final session together with Mama P. and Sally was a celebration of our three years together.

Ethical Considerations of Touch

Few guidelines exist when it comes to touch in psychotherapy with children, thus raising ethical questions. Children naturally use touch to express, connect, and achieve safety. Denying child-initiated touch is potentially harmful and to do so raises ethical concerns (McNeil-Haber, 2004). However, there are ethical risks for therapists using therapist-initiated touch as a therapeutic intervention. Using touch in psychotherapy with children exposed to DV requires the therapist to be extra sensitive to their history of touch (APT, 2015). As with Mama P. and Sally, the decision-making process regarding the use of touch should include close assessment of the therapeutic relationships, the parent-child relationship, and the treatment plan goals.

The approach of facilitating attuned touch between Mama P. and Sally minimized ethical concerns of liability as the therapist was able to monitor for physical and emotional safety (Gil, 2015). The predominant ethical dilemma in this case study emerged early in treatment. Mama P. brought Sally to treatment with the preconception that Sally needed to be "fixed." Initially, Mama P. was not eager to participate in therapy because she did not understand her role. However, Sally's age and the presenting problem (Sally's and Mama P.'s dual traumatization) indicated the need for child–parent psychotherapy centered on redefining touch.

I consulted with colleagues in the infant mental health field and they unanimously agreed with the treatment plan that I had developed. It was difficult to convince Mama P. to join her daughter in treatment and she did not agree until after we had strengthened our therapeutic alliance, a process that took two months. Treating Sally individually would have been easier; however, I firmly believe that the family's growth would have been subsequently stunted. Sally needed to receive nurturing touch from her mother, not exclusively from a therapist. Although I might have provided Sally with moments of emotional safety and examples of safe touch, she needed heavy doses of safe touch between sessions and, due to her developmental stage, she needed safe touch from her mother.

A secondary ethical dilemma revolved around Mama P.'s need to redefine touch. Through redefining touch, I risked re-traumatizing Mama P. in my efforts to help Sally. I again consulted a trusted colleague and we agreed that I should discuss redefining touch with Mama P. Mama P. eagerly agreed to proceed with the proposed treatment. Although solving this dilemma was simpler than the first, I feared that Mama P. was not the best judge of her capacity at the time, due to her unresolved trauma. To ensure Mama P.'s safety throughout the process, I monitored her responses closely, checked in with her frequently, and allowed her to set the pace.

The last ethical dilemma key to my work with this family arose at the point when Mama P. disclosed childhood exposure to DV. She was able to do so because of the trust within the therapeutic relationship. I knew that I could not explore childhood DV issues further with Mama P. because of my role with Sally. Mama P. needed her own therapist to process childhood experiences of abusive touch. Mama P. was surprised and disheartened when I explained my decision. She understood the conflict in roles; however, she struggled to identify the subtle distinction between work with a dyad and individual work. I was reassured of the appropriateness of my referral a few weeks later when Mama P. excitedly told me about her first individual session with her therapist, whom she had located and contacted independently.

Countertransference and Cultural Considerations

This was the most horrific case I had ever come across. It was difficult to hear Mama P. tell the story of violence and abuse, but it was heart wrenching to watch her instinctually reject Sally's attempts for affection. I was aware of my own impulse to provide Sally with the nurturance she needed. Mama P.'s continued phone contact with the incarcerated father was also perplexing and upsetting. I had to work diligently to remind myself that Mama P. was acting from a place of traumatization and not mal-intent. My ability to identify and rein in countertransferences came from frequent supervision, which gave me the opportunity to sort through my feelings. My additional research on the cycle of abuse and DV and attachment theory strengthened my ability to empathize from a professional stance with the mother.

Another point of countertransference that arose during sessions was rooted in Mama P.'s use of corporal punishment, which included frequent use of a belt, and required for me to be sensitive to cultural differences. Although I offered Mama P. discipline alternatives, I understood that African American parenting practices are noted as having higher levels of physical discipline than European Americans (Yildirim & Roopnarine, 2015). Research has found that maternal warmth is not strong enough to combat the negative impact of physical discipline on a child (Yildirim & Roopnarine, 2015). Dr. Stacy Patton (2015), in her quest to educate African American parents on the harmful effects of physical discipline, suggested that these practices were inserted into African American culture by slave masters and are not native cultural practices (Patton, 2015). The influence of culture, compounded by a history of DV exposure, was likely to have greater negative effects on Sally and it called for an exponential increase in Mama P.'s maternal warmth, which she was gradually able to provide as her own trauma healed. As maternal warmth increased, so did Sally's positive behaviors, reducing the need for any type of punishment.

Clinical Implications

Touch can be an imperative part of treating trauma caused by DV exposure. Training child therapists in the therapeutic benefits and ethics of touch is necessary to ensure appropriate application (APT, 2015). Similar to how new parents are often trained to read their babies' cues to determine soothing touches or distressing touches, therapists can acquire the same level of attunement needed to appropriately and therapeutically use touch (Zur & Nordmarken, 2016). In addition to attunement, therapists can benefit from learning cultural, gender, and age differentials and their roles of giving and receiving touch.

Fuller (2006) urges trainees to consider the ethical principles of beneficence and no maleficence, justice and integrity, fidelity and responsibility, and respect for clients' rights and dignity when learning new ways to use touch as a therapeutic tool. This can include therapist-facilitated touch within parent–child relationships. Also important, especially for child therapists new to using touch in treatment, is the understanding that appropriate and effective touch with one child can be inappropriate and damaging to another. Because of the intensity and reciprocal nature of touch, therapists using touch need to participate in clinical supervision, consultation, and training to ensure the appropriate use of touch (Courtney & Gray, 2014) and to prevent vicarious traumatization (Carpenter & Stacks, 2009).

Discussion Questions

1. Sally was actively seeking to touch and be touched by Mama P. How might the therapist approach treatment differently if Sally were *actively avoiding* touch?
2. If you were a therapist of the opposite gender of your client, how might you approach touch differently?
3. The therapist worked diligently to curb countertransferances. What countertransferances arose for you while reading the case study? How would you work to keep these out of the therapeutic relationship and treatment?

References

Allen, T. (2012). Healing touch: Using massage to break the cycle of abuse. *Massage Today, 12(4)*. Retrieved on 5 October, 2016 from: http://www.massagetoday.com/mpacms/mt/article.php?id=14562

American Academy of Child & Adolescent Psychiatry. (2013). *Domestic violence and children.* Retrieved on 5 October, 2016 from: http://www.aacap.org/AACAP/Families_and_Youth/Facts_for_Families/FFF-Guide/Helping-Children-Exposed-to-Domestic-Violence-109.aspx

Ardiel, E.L., & Rankin, C.H. (2010). The importance of touch in development. *Pediatric Child Health, 15(6)*, 153–156. DOI:10.1097/ANC.0b013e3181fd2263

Association for Play Therapy (APT). (2015). *Paper on touch: Clinical, professional, & ethical issues.* Retrieved on 31 March, 2016 from: http://c.ymcdn.com/sites/www.a4pt.org/resource/resmgr/Publications/Paper_On_Touch_2015.pdf

Bredy, T.W., Humpartzoomian, R.A., Cain, D.P., & Meaney, M.J. (2003). Partial reversal of the effect of maternal care on cognitive function through environmental enrichment. *Neuroscience, 118(2)*, 571–576. DOI:10.1016/S0306-4522(02)00918-1 571

Bredy, T.W., Lee, A.W., Meaney, M.J., & Brown, R.E. (2004). Effect of neonatal handling and paternal care on offspring cognitive development in the monogamous California mouse. *Hormones and Behavior, 46(1)*, 30–38. DOI:10.1016/j.yhbeh.2003.09.017

Brody, V.A. (1992). The dialogue of touch: Developmental play therapy. *International Journal of Play Therapy, 1(1)*, 21–30. DOI:10.1037/h0090232

Carpenter, G.L., & Stacks, A.M. (2009). Developmental effects of exposure to intimate partner violence in early childhood: A review of the literature. *Children and Youth Services Review, 31(8)*, 831–839. DOI:10.1016/j.childyouth.2009.03.005

Courtney, J.A. (2013). *The magic rainbow hug*. Palm Beach Gardens, FL: Developmental Play & Attachment Therapies.

Courtney, J.A. (2014). *FirstPlay Therapy Practitioner Training Manual*. Palm Beach Gardens, FL: Developmental Play & Attachment Therapies.

Courtney, J.A., & Gray, S.W. (2014). A phenomenological inquiry into practitioner experiences of developmental play therapy: Implications for training in touch. *International Journal of Play Therapy, 23(2)*, 114–129. DOI:10.1037/a0036366

Crowell, J.A. & Feldman, S.S. (1991). Mothers' working models of attachment relationships and mother and child behavior during separation and reunion. *Developmental Psychology, 27*, 597–605. DOI:http://dx.doi.org/10.1037/0012-1649.27.4.597

Day, N. (2013). *Baby meets world: Suck, smile, touch, toddle: A journey through infancy*. New York: St. Martin's Press.

De Bellis, M., Hooper, S., & Sapia, J. (2005). Early trauma exposure and the brain. In J. Vasterling, & C. Brewin (Eds), *Neuropsychology of PTSD: Biological, cognitive, and clinical perspectives*. New York: Guilford Press.

Field, T.M. (1998). Massage therapy effects. *American Psychologist, 53(12)*, 1270–1281. DOI:http://dx.doi.org/10.1037/0003-066X.53.12.1270

Field, T., Hernandez-Reif, M., Hart, S., Quintino, O., Drose, L.A., Field, T., Kuhn, C., & Schanberg, S. (1997). Effects of sexual abuse are lessened by massage therapy. *Journal of Bodywork and Movement Therapies, 1(2)*, 65–69. DOI:10.1016/s1360-8592(97)80002-2

Fuller, D.K. (2006). Training students on the ethics of touch in psychotherapy. *Association of Directors of Psychology Training Clinics Newsletter, 8(2)*. Retrieved on 5 October, 2016 from: http://www.aptc.org/news/112006/article_one.html

Gil, E. (1991). *The healing power of play: Working with abused children*. New York: Guilford Press.

Gil, E. (2015). Reunifying families after critical separations: An integrative play therapy approach to building and strengthening family ties. In D.A. Crenshaw, & A.L. Stewart (Eds.), *Play therapy: A comprehensive guide to theory and practice* (pp. 353–369). New York: Guilford Press.

Harlow, H. (1973). A variable-temperature surrogate mother for studying attachment in infant monkeys. *Behavior Research Methods, 5(3)*, 269–272. DOI:10.3758/bf03200181

Hernandez-Reif, M., Diego, M., & Field, T. (2007). Preterm infants show reduced stress behaviors and activity after 5 days of massage therapy. *Infant Behavior and Development, 30(4)*, 557–561. DOI:10.1016/j.infbeh.2007.04.002

Hunter, M., & Struve, J. (1998). *The ethical use of touch in psychotherapy (and political culture)*. Thousand Oaks, CA: Sage. DOI:10.4135/9781483328102

Kaiser, E.M., Gillette, C.S., & Spinazzola, J. (2010). A controlled pilot-outcome study of sensory integration in the treatment of complex adaptation to traumatic stress. *Journal of Aggression, Maltreatment & Trauma, 19*, 699–720. DOI:10.1080/10926771.2010.515162

Kolb, B., & Gibb, R. (2007). Brain plasticity and recovery from early cortical injury. *Developmental Psychobiology, 49*, 107–118. DOI:10.1002/dev.20199

Landreth, G. (2012). *Play therapy: The art of the relationship* (3rd ed.). New York: Routledge.

Lieberman, A.F., & Van Horn, P. (2005). *Don't hit my mommy! A manual for child–parent psychotherapy with young witnesses of family violence*. Washington, DC: Zero to Three.

Liu, D., Diorio, J., Tannenbaum, B., & Meaney, M.J. (1997). Maternal care, hippocampal glucocorticoid receptors, and hypothalamic-pituitary-adrenal responses to stress. *Science, 277*, 1659–1662. DOI:10.1126/science.277.5332.1659

Lovic, V., & Fleming, A.S. (2004). Artificially-reared female rats show reduced prepulse inhibition and deficits in the attentional set shifting task: Reversal of effects with maternal-like licking stimulation. *Behavioral Brain Research, 148*, 209–219. DOI:10.1016/S0166-4328(03)00206-7

McNeil-Haber, F.M. (2004). Ethical considerations in the use of nonerotic touch with children. *Ethics and Behavior, 14*, 123–140. DOI:10.1207/s15327019eb1402_3

Montagu, A. (1986). *Touching: The human significance of the skin* (3rd ed.). New York: Harper & Row.

Patton, S. (2015). *A message from Spare the Kids, Inc. creator*. Retrieved on 23 March, 2016 from: http://sparethekids.com/a-message-from-spare-the-kids-creator/

Scharlepp, R., Cleveland, A.D., & Barlow, S.M. (2012). *The power of play: Supporting survivors and their children through the healing journey*. Tallahassee, FL: Florida Coalition Against Domestic Violence.

Smith, E., Clance, P.R., & Imes, S. (Eds.) (1998). *Touch in psychotherapy: Theory, research, and practice*. New York: Guilford Press.

Tsavoussis, S., Stawicki, S., Stoicea, N., & Papadimos, T.J. (2014). Child-witnessed domestic violence and its adverse effects on brain development: A call for societal self-examination and awareness. *Frontiers in Public Health, 2(October)*, 1–5. DOI:10.3389/fpubh.2014.00178

United States Department of Justice. (2015). *Domestic violence*. Retrieved on 3 October, 2016 from: http://www.justice.gov/ovw/domestic-violence

van der Kolk, B.A. (1996). The complexity of adaptation to trauma. In B.A. van der Kolk, A.C. McFarlane, & L. Weisaeth (Eds.), *Traumatic stress*. New York: Guilford Press. DOI:10.1176/ajp.153.7.83

Yildirim, E.D., & Roopnarine, J.L. (2015). The mediating role of maternal warmth in the associations between harsh parental practices and externalizing and internalizing behaviors in Hispanic American, African American, and European American families. *Cultural Diversity and Ethnic Minority Psychology, 21(3)*, 430–439. DOI:10.1037/a0038210

Zur, O., & Nordmarken, N. (2016). *To touch or not to touch: Exploring the myth of prohibition on touch in psychotherapy and counseling*. Retrieved on 3 October, 2016 from: http://www.zurinstitute.com/touchintherapy.html

9 Ethical Use of Touch and Nurturing-Restraint in Play Therapy with Aggressive Young Children, as Illustrated through a Reflective Supervision Session

Roxanne Grobbel, Kristina Cooke, and Norma Bonet

> Too often we underestimate the power of a touch, a smile, a kind word, a listening ear, an honest compliment, or the smallest act of caring, all of which have the potential to turn a life around.
>
> Leo Buscaglia, *Love: What Life Is All About*

Introduction

The number of preschool children who demonstrate significantly disruptive, aggressive behaviors is increasing, especially among disadvantaged children (Barfield et al., 2012). This is of concern because these behaviors place them at risk for future social and emotional problems and at greater risk for future mental health problems (Foulkrod & Davenport, 2010). Children with disruptive behaviors have also been found to be lacking school readiness (National Center of Children in Poverty, 2012) and have a greater expulsion rate from preschool, at a rate three times higher than the rate for K-12 students (Gilliam, 2005). Since aggressive behaviors are the most common reason for child referrals for therapy (with 33% to 50% of cases referred for outpatient treatment) (Kazdin, 2011), therapists will likely work with aggressive children often in their careers, which may require the use of restraint. Unfortunately, many therapists have had little or no education regarding the use of restraints, especially in the use of nurturing-restraint (Westland, 2011). Therefore, they may not be prepared for children's physical aggression or have the basic skills needed to physically intervene.

Aggressive Behavior in Young Children

During the typical course of development, young children (toddlers and preschoolers) often have periods of aggressive and oppositional behaviors, which typically decrease as language develops and they have an alternative means to express themselves. Most children reach the peak of aggression in kindergarten, with the majority no longer exhibiting physical aggression by the end of elementary school (Ray et al., 2009). However, children's anger, aggression, and deficits in emotional regulation can be symptoms associated with trauma (van der Kolk, 2014). Traumatized children often overreact to minor stressors and struggle to calm themselves when stressed (van der Kolk, 2014). Since their emotional reactions are overwhelming, they can often express their anger in the form of external aggression in the play therapy room (Foulkrod & Davenport, 2010; Robinson & Grobbel, 2008). Therapists may need to physically intervene and, if done appropriately, this can help provide a feeling of safety, process trauma, and resolve emotional issues.

The Importance of Touch in Child Development and Healing

Touch has been noted to be one of the most critical components of human development, overriding all other human senses (Montagu, 1986). It is a meaningful manner of communication, a means of attachment, and a powerful healing force. In fact, research has found that a lack of touch can cause failure to thrive, attachment disorders, aggressive behavior, and an inability to self-regulate (Ardiel & Rankin, 2010; van der Kolk, 2014). When human beings are deprived of touch at an early age, the need for holding and touch will often remain (Perry & Szalavitz, 2006) and/or abnormal behavior can develop (Montagu, 1986). Within a clinical setting, the importance of touch for a child's development and healing has long been documented (Brazelton & Sparrow, 2006; Field, 2014). Brody (1992) stated that "a child who experiences touch from a capable toucher will grow toward healthy maturity and will heal from earlier trauma and neglect" (p. xiv).

Appropriate touch can soothe emotional and physical dysregulation, foster growth from childhood developmental deficiency and trauma, deepen the attachment relationship, and provide nurturance (Field, 2014). Additionally, Perry and Szalavitz (2006) found that children who experienced neglect and trauma responded to physical interventions (such as rocking and being held) that would be developmentally appropriate for the age at which they experienced the trauma, but not necessarily for their chronological age. Westland (2011) reminds us that touch is not just a technique; it is relational, and therefore, for touch to be healing, it must be genuine and congruent.

Ethical Considerations Regarding the Use of Touch

Despite its positive potential, touch within the clinical setting is an issue laden with ethical considerations (Courtney & Gray, 2014). Due to the inherent power difference between therapist and child, clients are often at a disadvantage because of their vulnerability and this can be amplified when touching occurs (McNeil-Haber, 2004). Some therapists may also refrain from touching clients altogether out of fear that it will lead to misunderstandings and potential legal consequences (Zur & Nordmarken, 2016). Touch is a natural part of a young child's play and many child-initiated touches often happen. Mental health professional associations do not prohibit the use of appropriate touch in therapy (Zur & Nordmarken, 2016). Therefore, adopting a "no touch" policy across the board may not be the most clinically or ethically appropriate stance for child therapists (McNeil-Haber, 2004). While all therapists can agree that any touch that is punitive, sexual, or may be interpreted as sexual, is unethical and forbidden, there are still ethical concerns regarding touch with children, particularly when it comes to working with aggressive children whose behaviors pose safety concerns to self and others.

Aggressive Behaviors in Children and the Ethical Use of Restraint

Therapists providing services to aggressive young children need to consider ethical issues regarding the use of restraints in particular because, as the Association for Play Therapy (2015) stated, there may be times when "the play therapist's ability to effectively and safely restrain the child is essential to maintaining the child's safety in the playroom" (p. 3). The word "restraint" itself often conjures up negative associations of frightened children being traumatized as they panic, scream, and try to kick themselves free, leaving them exhausted, distraught, and mistrusting.

Restraint of children can carry a risk of physical harm (even death) and/or traumatization (or retraumatization), potentially making them feel powerless (Valenkamp et al., 2014). As such, the use of restraints can violate the ethical principle of "do no harm" (McNeil-Haber, 2004). However, the discussions surrounding the restraint of children can be difficult because, in the literature, definitions of restraint vary (Valenkamp et al., 2014). It has been used to describe anything that "immobilizes or reduces the ability of a student to move his or her torso, arms, legs, or head freely" (U.S. Department of Education, 2012) to a very dangerous method of forcing a child to the floor with one or more adults using their bodies or mechanical devices to immobilize the child (Couvillon et al., 2010).

The literature reveals a movement toward preventative multistrategy interventions in order to de-escalate crisis situations and ensure restraint is only used as a last resort (Valenkamp et al., 2014). However, there is minimal literature addressing young children (under six years of age) in residential settings. There is no literature on the benefit of restraint, besides ensuring safety, and previous literature regarding holding therapy has been internationally challenged in recent years (Mercer, 2002). The authors did not discover any literature addressing the use of restraint with young children in nonresidential, therapy settings (e.g., playrooms), but they were able to find articles regarding ethical issues which arise when touch or restraint is used with children, as mentioned earlier.

Ethical Considerations in the Use of Physical Restraint

McNeil-Haber (2004) developed a comprehensive list of ethical factors for therapists to consider when using any form of touch, and the authors of this chapter have adapted this list to specifically address these ethical considerations in the use of physical restraint with children:

- Is restraint of the child necessary to keep the child or play therapist safe?
- Are there precautions that can be taken to avoid the use of physical restraint?
- Can the restraint be structured in a therapeutic nurturing manner?
- Is the therapist cognizant of the mental state required for co-regulation?
- Has the therapist identified countertransference (e.g., bias or the therapist's unchecked anger)?
- Is the therapist clear about institutional policies regarding restraint of children in therapy?
- How does culture and gender influence how the use of restraint will be perceived?
- How does the child's diagnosis and history of abuse influence the use of restraint?
- Is the therapist cognizant of the power dynamics within the therapist–child relationship?
- Does the informed consent address when and how physical restraint may be used?
- Is there a person available for prevention or assistance when restraint may be indicated?
- Does the therapist seek supervision, consultation, or training regarding the use of restraint in therapy?
- Is the therapist thoroughly documenting any use of restraint in therapy and informing the parents?

A Nurturing-Restraint Approach

Consistent with these factors and the research on touch, the authors of this chapter are offering a nurturing-restraint approach that can be used when working with aggressive children. This approach is also intended to be used as a last resort, when all other attempts to de-escalate and redirect fail (e.g., verbal limit-setting or the use of a pillow/bear as a barrier or object for physical release of aggression) and the therapist deems that the child's aggressive behaviors pose a significant safety concern for the child or the therapist. The nurturing-restraint approach varies from other types of restraints described earlier in the chapter in that it is essential that the therapist remains empathetically connected with the child.

With warmth and understanding, a therapist can use nurturing-restraint to produce a state of safety and an opportunity for co-regulation that can assist the child in developing self-regulation. Our brains are wired to detect and differentiate safety, danger, and threats to our life. When we perceive danger the fight–flight response is automatically initiated and these perceptions can be distorted by insecure attachment as well as numerous other developmental, mood, and anxiety disorders (Siegel, 2015); yet this fight–flight response is inhibited when safety is detected.

By meeting the aggressive child's anger and surging emotions with warmth and empathy, the therapist can provide a secure holding space in which the child can develop the inner resources to regulate (Badenoch, 2008). Children learn to self-regulate by responding to an adult's emotional communication and the alignment of states of mind (they internalize the adult's response) (Siegel, 2015). This co-regulation develops through right-brain to right-brain attunement between the therapist and client, and allows for brain development, linking limbic area to the prefrontal areas (Badenoch, 2008). This right-brain way of connection is communicated through one's tone of voice, caring gestures, kindness in one's eyes, relaxed breathing, and accepting posture (Badenoch, 2008). When the aggressive child's powerful emotions arise, the therapist can understand their source and respond with an attuned response that facilitates regulation. This response requires that the therapist has knowledge of their own mental health and a keen awareness of their own feelings and self-regulation in order to serve in this capacity (Badenoch, 2008).

Thus, it is essential that the therapist maintains a warm and empathetic attitude with a safe, attuned, sensitive touch during the nurturing-restraint, and remains acutely aware of their own feelings and self-regulation throughout the intervention. The actual nurturing-restraint hold is based on a form of loose cradling, with the therapist standing behind the child (or sitting behind if the child is young), while utilizing focused, patterned, repetitive somatosensory activities (such as tapping or rocking), related to self-regulation, attention, arousal, and impulsivity, to help the brain organize (Gaskill & Perry, 2014; Perry & Szalavitz, 2006), while at the same time acknowledging and reflecting the child's wants, needs, and feelings to make the child feel heard and understood (Landreth, 2012).

The nurturing approach incorporates the following essential elements: (1) the therapist's self-regulation and physical and emotional expression of warmth and empathy; (2) the therapist's soothing voice and calm body language; (3) acknowledgment of feelings, use of grounding statements, and reflection of positive changes ("I'm noticing you are feeling calmer"); (4) gentle, loose holding— only to the extent required—with the possibility of transforming the hold into a cradling or positive holding; and (5) repetitive somatosensory activities related to self-regulation, arousal, and impulsivity. These repetitive somatosensory activities include: soothing sounds such as humming and singing, and rhythmic movement such as rocking, swaying, gentle tapping, and patting (see Figure 9.1).

The therapist successfully used this method in the case study below. However, as the case shows, working with aggressive children and using nurturing-restraint can bring up a range of emotional and clinical issues for the therapist. Reflective supervision is shown as an effective forum for sorting through these considerations as it provided a safe space to examine emotions and reactions to the clinical experiences (refer to the end of the chapter for a sample parental informed consent form for the use of nurturing-restraint).

Ethical Use of Nurturing-Restraint 125

Figure 9.1 The therapist helps the child to regulate by using a nurturing-restraint.
Source: ©iStock.com/Vesna Andjic

Reflective Supervision

Reflective supervision can best be described as the practice of a supervisor and therapist examining the thoughts, feelings, actions, and reactions that the therapist experiences while working with clients, with the purpose of improving clinical practice skills (Eggbeer *et al.*, 2010; Seymour & Crenshaw, 2015). It was developed in the 1980s within the infant mental health field for practitioners dealing with the emotionally laden nature of relationship-based work with vulnerable young children and families (Eggbeer *et al.*, 2007; Schafer, 2007). These practitioners needed a supervision style that allowed them to step back and reflect on what they were experiencing and their emotional responses to the challenging work (Weatherston *et al.*, 2010). Since that time, reflective supervision has grown to be used in a variety of fields, including play therapy, and can be especially useful with emotionally charged situations like working with aggressive children.

Case of Amy and Michael

The following case illustrates how reflective supervision was used to process a challenging session that arose when working with a young, traumatized child who demonstrated aggressive behavior toward the supervisee. For confidentiality, the case details have been altered and the supervisor and supervisee consented to the use of their supervision session for this chapter. The case illustrates the gray areas when using nurturing-restraint with aggressive children and it will be shown how reflective supervision helped a supervisee resolve ethical issues and develop clinical skills needed to handle future similar situations. The supervisee's reflective process and how she attained insight into her thoughts, feelings, and actions have been highlighted.

Supervisor and Supervisee Description

The supervisor was a Registered Play Therapist-Supervisor through the Association for Play Therapy with training in reflective supervision. The supervisee, Amy, a recent Masters of Social Work graduate, was six weeks pregnant, which she had not revealed to anyone.

Case Background

The client, Michael, was a five-year-old African American male who lived in a single-parent home with his mother and three siblings in a high-crime neighborhood. His mother worked full time but their family income was below the poverty level. Michael had no contact with his biological father who was in prison, and there was no other family in the area.

Assessment

Michael was referred by his teacher for on-site play therapy services, due to disruptive and aggressive behaviors in the classroom. Michael's mother disclosed that he had witnessed episodes of his father's domestic abuse toward her. Further assessment revealed a diagnosis of post-traumatic stress disorder indicated by the following symptoms: nightmares; dissociation; avoidance and aggressive reaction to triggers related to the domestic violence; poor social skills; inability to self-regulate; and difficulty concentrating and following directions.

Treatment

Michael had been receiving small-group, child-centered play therapy two to three times a week for three months. Services were provided on-site in a playroom at Michael's preschool. His play was repetitive, aggressive, and initially included re-enactment of the domestic violence.

The Issue Brought to Supervision

Amy sat across from her supervisor with her head down and tears swelling in her eyes. She haltingly explained that the session with Michael had been relatively uneventful until she had given the warning that there were five minutes left. At that point, Michael reportedly "went wild" and became aggressive toward her. Sounding defeated, Amy described it as a disaster and a failure as she had to restrain him. The following excerpts highlight only a select portion of the supervision to give the reader a glimpse into the dialogue that transpired and the trusting, caring relationship between the supervisor and supervisee.

Reflective Supervision Session Excerpts

AMY: "It was horrible. It was a disaster; he was out of control. I couldn't do anything."

SUPERVISOR: "Okay, take a minute."

AMY: "I really messed up. I had no control ... I didn't do anything right." (*She starts to cry.*)

SUPERVISOR: "It sounds like this was really difficult for you." (*Supervisor places her hand on the supervisee's knee to anchor her within the moment.*) "Take a breath, let's talk about it."

AMY: "Everything was fine, until I said there was 5 minutes left in the session. It was all so fast. He went wild and began throwing the toys. I reflected to him that he didn't want to leave the playroom, and set the limits like we normally do, but that seemed to make it worse. Then Michael began hitting and kicking at me, and he even hit my stomach."

SUPERVISOR: "It sounds out of control."

AMY: "It was really scary. I should have been able to stop it. I failed, it was my fault."

(The supervision session continued with Amy "beating herself up" for not being able to de-escalate the aggressive behaviors. She then began to describe her intervention in more detail.)

AMY: "But, I did manage to stop him. I got my arms around him and held him. I was scared of being punched. I worry about using restraint and I felt so bad. But I had to."

SUPERVISOR: "You were worried about restraining him."

AMY: "Yes, but I realize that I did start rocking him and humming to him. As he relaxed, I reflected, 'you're starting to relax ... feeling better'. It did help because he was able to calm down and he even hugged me before leaving the playroom."

SUPERVISOR: "That had to be hard. Being afraid and needing to restrain him, yet it sounds like you used a nurturing-restraint. And as you said, you were able to help him regulate by holding and rocking him ... I have seen you calmly take charge with some pretty aggressive children. It sounds like this time was more emotional. I am wondering what was different this time?"

AMY: (*After a long pause and eyes tearing up again ...*) "This time was more emotional. I didn't really feel like myself. I couldn't even handle this. This time was different ... He hit me in the stomach ... and I am pregnant. I haven't told anyone. I was so scared." (*Tears begin to flow.*)

SUPERVISOR: "Ah, so you were worried about your pregnancy ... your baby. Maybe that has something to do with your strong emotional response."

AMY: "I think so. It changed how I felt ... that he hit my stomach. I guess it affected how I felt about everything. I just felt so upset and helpless. As I think about it, I know I was able to make reflections and rock him while it was happening. I used a nurturing-restraint with him; I wasn't restraining him harshly. I really didn't get emotional until afterwards."

Reflective Supervision for Amy and Michael's Case: Clinical and Ethical Considerations

Amy worried that any restraint of Michael could possibly traumatize him due to his domestic violence history. However, after supervision, she had gained new insight. Amy's actions had not been punitive or excessive; rather, she had intervened to ensure safety in the playroom. She had remained calm throughout the session. During reflective supervision, she was able to recognize that she had used nurturing-restraint by wrapping her arms around him in a gentle hug and rocked him while softly humming a sing-song rhythm, which had calmed him.

Her training and knowledge of nurturing-restraint had taken effect without her having to think about it. With this method, he was able to regulate himself. Amy demonstrated how nurturing touch, when used appropriately, can be used to co-regulate a child, and thereby de-escalate rather than escalate a situation. Consequently, the nurturing-restraint approach had been utilized in accordance with ethical guidelines. Many other items on the adaptation of McNeil-Haber's (2004) list of ethical factors were also addressed: Amy was aware of the power dynamics of the therapist–client relationship, of how the client's background, diagnosis, and abuse history might impact his perception of the nurturing-restraint, and of her agency's policies on touch. Amy had also immediately contacted Michael's mom and explained the circumstances related to the nurturing-restraint, and also documented the incident thoroughly. Finally, she sought supervision to process the experience and worked on identifying countertransference concerns.

Together with her supervisor, Amy also worked on implementing other clinically appropriate interventions with Michael to help him process and work through the issues causing his aggressive behaviors. These included reflective listening statements that more accurately reflected his feelings of fear, helplessness, and being attacked, which Amy and her supervisor thought Michael had been projecting during the session. Amy and her supervisor also worked on improving her ability to identify the child's feelings in general, her use of therapeutic limit-setting and giving choices (Landreth, 2012), as well as using a variety of creative gross motor/play interventions for Michael to be able to express his feelings in more appropriate ways.

While Michael continued to display aggression in following sessions, his aggression was increasingly expressed through symbolic play rather than destruction of property or physically attacking the therapist. Amy reported to her supervisor that Michael also began to seek out appropriate nurturing touch from the therapist (requesting to be rocked, wanting to play baby). By the time he graduated preschool three months later, the teacher reported that he had shown significant improvement in his ability to regulate and focus in the classroom.

The Importance of Reflective Supervision for Recognizing Countertransference and Projection

Reflective supervision allowed Amy to step back and realize that there may have been countertransference and projection occurring. Countertransference occurs frequently when working with young children, partially due to their behavioral and emotional unpredictability and aggressive nature, and it includes the thoughts, feelings, and behaviors that the therapist experiences in relation to the client (Gil & Rubin, 2005). Amy realized that due to her pregnancy she was more emotional and responded in a "motherly" protective manner; worried about herself, her unborn child, and Michael. She understood that many emotions affected her feelings and view of her use of restraint, including worrying about possibly harming Michael, anxiety regarding not being good enough, and fearing for her own safety and that of her unborn child. Processing these thoughts and feelings in a safe environment helped her move forward with confidence.

Conclusion

Touch is a powerful sense and can have great healing potential when used appropriately in a clinical setting. This chapter has presented a novel nurturing-restraint approach. However, caution must be taken when using any physical restraint to prevent harm including traumatizing or retraumatizing a child. Implementing nurturing-restraint with aggressive children requires a therapist to exercise a considerable amount of self-awareness, self-regulation, and self-control to regulate their own feelings and behaviors when using this approach. This in turn will help children to calm and self-regulate. Nurturing-restraint should not be used without prior training and consideration of ethical factors involved in the clinical use of touch.

Therapists must also be aware of any countertransferences that may occur when working with aggressive young children, and ongoing reflective supervision is a valuable method to support self-reflection process and professional growth and development. This chapter's adaptation of McNeil-Haber's (2004) comprehensive list of ethical factors can serve as a guide for therapists to consider. Likewise, a sample parental informed consent regarding nurturing-restraint protocols (see box) was developed and included for therapists and agencies to use in developing, reviewing, and discussing with parents the considerations involved regarding the use of nurturing-restraint as a last resort option, and only to maintain safety.

Consent for Use of Nurturing-Restraint for Young Children under 6 Years of Age

At *(name of agency)*, we advocate the use of nurturing touch for the optimum safety and well-being of young children. We also advocate for children's inherent right to accept and refuse touch as they see fit for their own personal comfort.

There are times, however, when a child's safety is at risk. When this happens, we may use touch without the child's permission. Examples would include to keep a child safe from harm (e.g., physically preventing a child from running from the building or climbing onto shelves) and to stop a child from harming himself or herself or another person.

When touch is used for restraint, a therapist will use a nurturing-restraint to hold a child to keep him or her safe. With this method, the therapist maintains calm control and a caring demeanor. The therapist holds the child gently and loosely—only to the extent required—with the possibility to transform the hold into a cradling or positive holding. During this holding, the therapist uses a calm acknowledgment of feelings, grounding statements, a reflection of positive changes ("I'm noticing you're feeling calmer"), and/or repetitive somatosensory activities related to self-regulation (soothing sounds such as humming and singing, and rhythmic movement such as rocking, swaying, gentle tapping, and patting). The use of a nurturing-restraint by the therapist (if necessary) can help a child to develop self-regulation, build trust, and gain a sense of safety. The therapists' use of a calm, soothing voice to reflect the child's feelings reminds children that they are only being held long enough to ensure their safety.

Children will never be bound, held down in a face-down position, or restrained in anger, as these actions are physically and emotionally harmful. Children will not be threatened with restrictive holding in an effort to control their behavior.

Nurturing-restraint will only be used after exhausting all other preventative measures (the use of a pillow/bear as a barrier or object for physical release). Physical restraint, through the use of nurturing-restraint, is not a long-term solution. Instead, it is a short-term intervention that will be used only in extreme circumstances. If the need to restrain a child through nurturing-restraint occurs, the parent or guardian will be informed. The notification will include: (a) name of therapist administering the nurturing-restraint; (b) description of the activity in which the client was engaged immediately preceding the use of the nurturing-restraint; (c) the behavior that prompted the nurturing-restraint; and (d) the efforts made to de-escalate the situation and alternatives to the nurturing-restraint that were attempted prior to the nurturing-restraint intervention.

Name of child		
Signature of parent/guardian	Name of parent/guardian	Date
Signature of parent/guardian	Name of parent/guardian	Date
Signature of Therapist	Name of Therapist	Date

Discussion Questions

1 After reading that touch is essential for a child's emotional and physical development, discuss with a colleague your thoughts and feelings about touch occurrences that may arise within a playroom setting.
2 Imagine that you were just assigned to work individually with an aggressive child. Discuss with a colleague what type of ethical factors you need to consider prior to the first session. List any concerns you may have in working with aggressive children. Discuss what a reflective supervisor might say to help to work through such concerns.
3 Read the consent form in the box above, and discuss with a colleague how you might go about implementing these considerations in your practice.

References

Ardiel, E., & Rankin, C.H. (2010). The importance of touch in development. *Pediatric Child Health, 15(3),* 153–156. Retrieved on 8 November, 2016 from:https://www.ncbi.nlm.nih.gov/pmc/articles/PMC2865952/

Association for Play Therapy. (2015). *Paper on touch: Clinical, professional, & ethical issues.* Retrieved on 1 December, 2015 from: http://c.ymcdn.com/sites/www.a4pt.org/resource/resmgr/Publications/Paper_On_Touch_2015.pdf

Badenoch, B. (2008). *Being a brain-wise therapist: A practical guide to interpersonal neurobiology.* New York: Norton.

Barfield, S., Dobson, C., Gaskill, R., & Perry, B.D. (2012). Neurosequential model of therapeutics in a therapeutic preschool: Implications for work with children with complex neuropsychiatric problems. *International Journal of Play Therapy, 21(1),* 30–44. DOI:10.1037/a0025955

Brazelton, T., & Sparrow, J. (2006). *Touchpoints: Birth to three* (2nd ed.). Cambridge, MA: DeCapo Press.

Buscaglia, L. (1972). *Love: What life is all about.* New York: Ballantine Books.

Brody, V.A. (1992). The dialogue of touch: Developmental play therapy. *International Journal of Play Therapy, 1,* 21–30. DOI:http://dx.doi.org/10.1037/pla0000021

Courtney, J.A. & Gray, S.W. (2014). Phenomenological inquiry into practitioner experiences of developmental play therapy: Implications for training in touch. *International Journal of Play Therapy, 23(2),* 114–129. DOI:10.1037/a0036366

Couvillon, M., Peterson, R.L., Ryan, J.B., Scheuermann, B., & Stegall, J. (2010). A review of crisis intervention training programs for schools. *TEACHING Exceptional Children, 42(5),* 6–17. Retrieved on 21 December, 2015 from: https://www1.maine.gov/education/rulechanges/chapter33/022411dbutlercitreviewofrestraintsinschoolsinschools.pdf

Eggbeer, L., Mann, T.L., & Seibel, N.L. (2007). Reflective supervision: Past, present, and future. *Zero to Three, 28(2),* 5–9.

Eggbeer, L., Shahmoon-Shanok, R., & Clark, R. (2010). Reaching toward an evidence base for reflective supervision. Zero to Three, *31(2),* 39–50. Retrieved on 8 November, 2016 from: http://zttcfn.convio.net/site/DocServer/31-2_Eggbeer.pdf?docID=12862target=

Field, T. (2014). *Touch* (2nd ed.). Cambridge, MA: MIT Press.

Foulkrod, K., & Davenport, B.R. (2010). An examination of empirically informed practice within case reports of play therapy with aggressive and oppositional children. *International Journal of Play Therapy, 19(3),* 144–158. DOI:10.1037/a0020095

Gaskill, R.L., & Perry, B.D. (2014). The neurobiological power of play using the neurosequential model of therapeutics to guide play. In C.A. Malchiodi & D.A. Crenshaw (Eds.), *Creative arts and play therapy for attachment problems* (pp. 178–194). New York: Guilford Press.

Gil, E., & Rubin, L. (2005). Countertransference play: Informing and enhancing play therapist self awareness through play. *International Journal of Play Therapy, 14(2),* 87–102. DOI:10.1037/h0088904

Gilliam, W.S. (2005). *Pre-kindergartens left behind: Expulsion rates in state prekindergarten programs* (FCD Policy Brief Series 3). New York: Foundation for Child Development. Retrieved on 14 December, 2015 from: http://ziglercenter.yale.edu/publications/National%20Prek%20Study_expulsion%20brief_34775_284_5379.pdf

Kazdin, A.E. (2011). Evidence-based treatment research: Advances, limitations, and next steps. *American Psychologist, 66(8),* 685–698. DOI:10.1037/a0024975

Landreth, G.L. (2012). *Play therapy: The art of the relationship* (3rd ed.). New York: Brunner-Routledge.

McNeil-Haber, F.M. (2004). Ethical consideration in the use of nonerotic touch in psychotherapy with children. *Ethics and Behavior, 14(2),* 123–140. DOI:10.1207/s15327019eb1402_3

Mercer, J. (2002). Child psychotherapy involving physical restraint: Techniques used in four approaches. *Child and Adolescent Social Work Journal 19(4),* 303–314. DOI: 10.1023/A:1016353812731

Montagu, A. (1986). *Touching: The human significance of the skin* (3rd ed.). New York: Harper & Row.

National Center of Children in Poverty. (2009, November). *Basic facts about low-income children, 2008: Children under age 6*. Retrieved on 30 October, 2016 from: http://nccp.org/publications/pub_896.html

Perry, B.D., & Szalavitz, M. (2006). *The boy who was raised as a dog: And other stories from a child psychiatrist's notebook—What traumatized children can teach us about loss, love, and healing*. New York: Basic Book.

Ray, D., Blanco, P., Sullivan, J., & Holliman, R. (2009). An exploratory study of child-centered play therapy with aggressive children. *International Journal of Play Therapy, 18(3)*, 162–175. DOI:10.1037/a0014742

Robinson, E.J., & Grobbel, R. (2008). Play therapy techniques with very young at-risk children in child care settings. In C.E. Schaefer, S. Kelly-Zion, & J. McCormack (Eds.), *Play therapy for very young children* (pp. 199–247). Lanham, MD: Rowman & Littlefield.

Schafer, W. (2007). Models and domains of supervision and their relationship to professional development. *Zero to Three, 28(2)*, 10–16.

Seymour, J.W., & Crenshaw, D.A. (2015). Reflective practice in play therapy and supervision. In D.A. Crenshaw & A.L. Stewart (Eds.), *Play therapy: A comprehensive guide to theory and practice* (pp. 483–495). New York: Guilford Press

Siegel, D.J. (2015). *The developing mind. How relationships and the brain interact to shape who we are* (2nd ed.). New York: Guilford Press.

U.S. Department of Education. (2012). *Restraint and seclusion: Resource document*. Retrieved on 14 December, 2016 from: https://www2.ed.gov/policy/seclusion/restraints-and-seclusion-resources.pdf

Valenkamp, M., Delaney, K., & Verheij, F. (2014). Reducing seclusion and restraint during child and adolescent inpatient treatment: Still an underdeveloped area of research. *Journal of Child and Adolescent Psychiatric Nursing, 27(4)*, 169–174. DOI:10.1111/jcap.12084

van der Kolk, B. (2014). *The body keeps the score*. New York: Viking Books.

Weatherston, D., Weigand, R.F., & Weigand, B. (2010). Reflective supervision: Supporting reflection as a cornerstone for competency. *Zero to Three, 31(2)*, 22–30.

Westland, G. (2011). Physical touch in psychotherapy: Why are we not touching more? *Body, Movement and Dance in Psychotherapy, 6(1)*, 17–29. DOI:10.1080/17432979.2010.508597

Zur, O., & Nordmarken, N. (2016). *To touch or not to touch: Exploring the myth of prohibition on touch in psychotherapy and counseling*. Retrieved on 5 January, 2016 from: http://www.zurinstitute.com/touchintherapy.html

10 Healing Adolescent Trauma

Incorporating Ethical Touch in a Movement and Dance Therapy Group

Carol Golly, Daniela Riccelli, and Mark S. Smith

> As we tap into deep sources of bodily wisdom through creative art expression, we dance the renewal, recreation, and healing of ourselves and the world.
> Anna Halprin, "Empowering Creativity through Movement, Metaphor and Dance"

Introduction

The available literature describing the use of therapeutic touch focuses on its use with young children; very little is dedicated to its use with adolescents. This chapter first reviews the literature regarding physical touch, adolescents, and trauma; second, describes the implications for adolescents who experience a lack of touch; third, describes interventions for trauma that utilize touch, including movement and dance therapy; fourth, presents a movement and dance therapy session in a group setting; and fifth, discusses the ethics of using touch for practitioners.

The skin is the first sense organ to develop, as a baby in utero receives significant information through the amniotic wall (Field, 2014; Montagu, 1986). Much of the newborn's world is discovered through touch, as they reach, grasp, hold, and are held and cuddled. Physical contact between caregiver and infant is critical for bonding and attachment to occur, which provides a scaffold for the future emotional and physical well-being of the infant. Subsequently, the need for touch remains salient throughout the life span. Touch is used as a term in the clinical domain to refer to nonerotic touch that is not sexual in either content or intent. Touch in the early years is of critical importance to physical and social growth, in resistance to stress, and in managing anxiety levels (Field, 2014).

There is little information in the literature regarding physical touch and adolescents. Adolescence is a critical time of emotional and physical metamorphosis in an individual's life. Puberty is a time of many developmental changes for the adolescent, including acceptance of one's own body, self, and sexual roles; moving toward more complex information processing and neural growth; identity formation; and moral and spiritual changes (Yamuna, 2013). During this life stage, conflict can occur between the adolescent and his or her parents, friends, and teachers. Parents typically replace affectionate touches with more casual, friend-like touches (Jones, 1994).

Tiffany Field, founder of the Touch Research Institute at the University of Miami, has made significant contributions to understanding the relevancy of touch throughout the life span, including adolescence. Field (1999) found French parents demonstrated physical affection to their children more often than American parents. French adolescents touched each other more frequently than did American adolescents and were less verbally and physically aggressive than American adolescents. Field's further research with adolescents showed that depressed or anxious adolescent inpatient psychiatric patients reported fewer depressive or anxious symptoms when they received daily 30-minute massages, and nurses reported increased positive affect and cooperation (Field, 2014). It would appear that children do not outgrow a need for touch once they attain adolescence.

Touch Deprivation and Negative Touch

Research indicates that touch deprivation in childhood may result in increased aggressive behaviors in adolescence (Field, 2002). Pearce *et al.* (1994) found that adolescents associated "caring" parents with frequent positive physical contact. They further found that frequent negative touch experiences for adolescents, in addition to infrequent positive touch experiences, were related to increased reports of suicidal ideation and self-harm. The findings suggest that both quantity and quality of touch experiences may be risk factors for self-harm and suicidal ideation for adolescents. Field (2005) argued that touch deprivation in infancy and early childhood could be a causal factor in adolescent suicide. Peifer (2008) noted that "[o]verall, the period of adolescence is characterized by unfulfilled needs for touch. When touch by parents comes to a drastic halt, teenagers turn to other relationships and behaviors to meet their tactile needs" (p. 13). Physically painful touch and lack of nurturing touch appear to result in a multitude of serious consequences for the developing child.

Aggression and antisocial behavior problems are associated with maltreatment occurring in childhood and adolescence (Trickett *et al.*, 2011). Touch deprivation in the early years and in adolescence has been suggested by researchers as contributing to adult violence (Field, 1999). The most critical relationship in a human being's life is the attachment of an infant to a primary caregiver, and Perry (2016) advised, "Many researchers and clinicians feel that the maternal-child attachment provides the working framework for all subsequent relationships that the child will develop" (p. 2). Children without touch, stimulation, and nurturing can literally lose the capacity to form any meaningful relationships for the rest of their lives (Green *et al.*, 2013).

John Bowlby (1988) proposed Attachment Theory to explain the biological function of a child's ties with his or her primary caregiver. A secure attachment relationship with a parent or primary caregiver in infancy and early childhood is required in order to form healthy relationships with others throughout the life span, while an insecure attachment with a primary caregiver is related to various emotional and behavioral difficulties (Bowlby, 1988). The role of touch and sensory input in attachment is paramount and includes holding, rocking, feeding, gazing, and physical proximity. Touch and warmth increase oxytocin hormone levels for children and adults, which helps in calming and managing stress (Field, 2014). Viola Brody (1997), founder of Developmental Play Therapy (DPT), a therapeutic method of treating at-risk children, advanced the theory that touch ultimately produces the conditions for a child to develop an "inner self," a basic human need for growth.

Complex Relational Trauma in Adolescents

According to one of the leading contemporary authorities on trauma, Bessel van der Kolk (2005), the single largest public health challenge in America is probably childhood abuse, neglect, and trauma. "Complex trauma" is a term introduced to describe diagnostic implications and associated symptomologies with children and adolescents who have experienced "multiple, chronic and prolonged, developmentally adverse traumatic events, most often of an interpersonal nature and early-life onset" (van der Kolk, 2005, p. 401). Such "events" are generally perpetrated upon a child by their caregiving system or other humans and include physical, emotional, and sexual abuse; neglect; war; and community violence. "Developmental trauma" is another term used in describing children and adolescents' repeated exposure to adverse events such as abuse and neglect perpetrated by a caregiver. Regrettably, the number of adolescents exposed to multiple adverse events has been increasing for the past decade (Ogle *et al.*, 2013). Trauma deteriorates trust in self and others. Trust is violated in a way that causes lifelong physical changes in the brain's neurocircuitry and therefore changes the individual's ability to cope with emotions when the traumatic event is recalled in some way (van der Kolk, 2014).

The Adverse Childhood Experiences (ACE) longitudinal study of more than 17,000 adults reported rates of such abuse to be between 11 percent and 32 percent, depending on the type of trauma (Anda *et al.*, 2006). The ACE study findings led the authors to conclude that child maltreatment was the "most costly public health issue in the United States" (van der Kolk, 2016, p. 267). Anda *et al.* (2006) found that chronic trauma can be long-lasting for adolescents, and was associated with depression, suicide attempts, alcohol and drug abuse, sexual acting out, domestic violence, obesity, heart disease, and other chronic medical and psychological problems.

A diagnosis of post-traumatic stress disorder (PTSD) does not adequately capture the damage wrought by chronic interpersonal trauma. In fact, many forms of interpersonal trauma do not meet the criteria for a definition of a traumatic event, according to van der Kolk (2014). Childhood traumas are often impossible to retrace, and children often have no explicit memory of them, although such an event memory is one of the criteria for a PTSD diagnosis (Elbrecht & Antcliff, 2015). Children exposed to such interpersonal trauma suffer PTSD symptoms and self-regulatory and relational impairments into adulthood, including substance abuse, borderline and antisocial personality, attention deficit hyperactivity disorder (ADHD), conduct disorder, or eating, dissociative, affective, somatoform, cardiovascular, metabolic, immunologic, and sexual disorders. Effects of complex trauma on adolescents include impairments in attachment, biology, cognition, affect regulation, behavioral control, and self-concept; chronic medical illness; impairments from dissociation; binge eating; and self-mutilation (Cook et al., 2005; D'Andrea et al., 2012; Green & Myrick, 2014).

In adolescence, areas of the brain that are responsible for executive functioning are rapidly developing (Cook et al., 2005). These areas, located in the prefrontal cortex, are primarily responsible for autonomous functioning and negotiating relationships. Features include self-awareness, ability to assess meanings of emotional input and experience, and an ability to problem-solve a course of action based on past knowledge and learned understandings regarding the perspectives of others (Cook et al., 2005). Both prior and presently occurring trauma can result in significant problems for adolescents: "Traumatic stressors or prior deficits in self-regulatory abilities that manifest during adolescence, in the absence of sustaining relationships, may lead to disruptions in regulation of affect, behavior, consciousness, cognition, and self-concept integration" (Cook et al., 2005, p. 391). Antisocial behavior in adolescence and peer rejection were found by several researchers to be related to physical and emotional abuse in early childhood (Kim & Cicchetti, 2010).

Dance/Movement Therapy

Dance/movement therapy (DMT) is defined as "the psychotherapeutic use of movement to further the emotional, cognitive, physical, and social integration of the individual" (American Dance Therapy Association, 2016, para. 1). Grounded in the understanding associated with mind–body connection theories, and in the power of movement as essential communication, dance/movement therapy is an effective method of psychotherapy for the treatment of trauma, addiction, PTSD, and other effects of abuse and trauma (van der Kolk, 2014). Trauma exposure causes physical changes in the brain, and individuals who have experienced trauma frequently "dissociate" from the remembered traumatic events, thus blocking access to the healing process by preventing the expression of the event through the use of language. Recent neurobiological research on trauma indicates that body movement is a particularly well-suited approach for the treatment of trauma (van der Kolk, 2014). Siegel advised that activities that include "sensate body focusing, guided imagery, and practice in using and picking up non-verbal cues explicitly stimulate the development of the right side of the brain in order to help people who have an impoverished sense of their own past integrate brain function" (as cited in Milliken, 2008, p. 13).

There is little available information regarding adolescents and movement and dance therapy. LeFeber (2014) advised that dance may provide an opportunity for children to explore and discover their bodies in a supportive environment where creative choices exist. The author finds that "[t]his creates an affirming environment, where children feel heard on a kinesthetic level and are able to experience the value of belonging" (LeFeber, 2014, p. 126). Green and Myrick (2014) stated it is more comfortable for some adolescents to find expression in creative, nonverbal modalities such as play, art, and movement than through traditional talk therapy. The authors state: "Adolescents *talking* about traumatic experiences in psychotherapy are insufficient for the mind and brain to integrate images and cognitions into a unified whole" (Green & Myrick, 2014, p. 140). Because dance uses movement as the principal means of expression, the body can affectively express suffering, and healing can occur. Memories that may be too difficult to express verbally can be shared through movement, while dissociated feelings can be recognized as they arise in the body (Halprin, 2000).

In discussing the significance of interventions for adolescents with insecure attachment histories, Green *et al.* (2013) wrote that, through creative expressions, "adolescents come to understand (a) that their feelings have value, (b) they are supported by caring adults who do not judge them, and (c) attention to their inner emotional landscape is a vital key to their ongoing psychological development" (p. 99). The authors suggested that healing for insecurely attached adolescents most likely occurs through experiencing unconditional acceptance by a securely attached adult who can provide a corrective emotional experience. Central to this experience is a therapist–adolescent client relationship characterized by safety, trust, and mutual respect.

Adolescents, Touch, and Professional Ethics

A centuries-old debate has framed discussions of ethics and touch in the therapeutic setting (Matherly, 2013). It would appear very important to understand actual client experiences of touch in therapy before making claims regarding harm or prescribing standards of care. As previously noted, while studies exist that address young children and touch in psychotherapy, very few studies examine touch experiences of adolescents. Peifer's (2008) qualitative study of adolescents' experiences of touch in psychotherapy found that adolescents considered touch as a significant form of communication in therapy, and that adolescent meaning-making of touch in therapy could only be ascribed on a case-by-case, individual basis. The adolescents in Peifer's study emphasized that practitioners should consider many factors prior to using touch in psychotherapy. These included "asking permission" prior to initiating any kind of touch, and holding a discussion with their clients to inform them how touch may be helpful to the client and listening carefully for client feedback. Peifer's (2008) study participants emphasized that "using touch in therapy requires a special sensitivity, and should be critically considered by clinicians" (p. 60). Further, they expressed the importance of building a therapeutic alliance and a trusting relationship prior to initiating touch.

Adolescents may be wary of aspects of control regarding physical contact, and may react negatively to overly familiar or patronizing touch (Jones, 1994). Zur and Nordmarken (2016) warned that adolescents may respond to touch in a manner in which the clinician did not intend. Gill Westland, founder of the Cambridge Body Psychotherapy Centre, states that clinicians should hold ongoing discussions regarding touch and have regular process reviews (Westland, 2011). This author postulates that "the client and the therapist *at this moment and with this client* should be comfortable with touch" (Westland, 2011, p. 25).

Clearly there is a need for utmost care in the ethical use of touch with clients. Several professional organizations exist that address guiding clinicians in the ethics of touch in therapy. These include the National Association of Social Workers (NASW), the United States Association for Body Psychotherapy (USABP), the American Dance Therapy Association (ADTA), the American Psychological Association (APA), and the Association for Play Therapy (APT). *None* of these professional associations prohibit non-sexual or non-hostile touch in therapy, while *all* of them regard sexual contact or violent touch as unethical (Zur and Nordmarken, 2016). The APA does not specifically mention touch or physical contact that is used in therapy. The NASW *Code of Ethics* (2008) states that social workers "should not engage in physical contact with clients when there is a possibility of psychological harm to the client as a result of the contact. Social workers who engage in appropriate physical contact with clients are responsible for setting clear, appropriate, and culturally sensitive boundaries that govern such physical boundaries."

The USABP Code of Ethics states "[b]ody psychotherapeutic methods, including language, gesture, and touch, when used in responsible and competent ways, make an essential contribution to the psychotherapeutic process by including the missing and often alienated aspects of our being" (USABP, 2007, p. 1). Ethical standards for body psychotherapy include maintaining competence and integrity; education and training; privacy and confidentiality; providing informed consent; avoiding harm and multiple relationships; and maintaining respect for colleagues. The ADTA ethical standards are similar and provide guidelines for the use of touch in dance therapy (ADTA, 2016). While acknowledging the fundamental value of using touch in therapy, dance therapists must make intentional, informed decisions to use touch, and provide verbal or written informed consent information and agreements with clients at regular intervals throughout treatment. Such consent includes the right of the client to refuse touch or rescind consent at any time.

Movement and Dance Therapy Group Session Example

This section presents the first meeting of a uniquely designed 12-session movement and dance group therapy workshop conducted by the author (Riccelli), who has an extensive training background in dance, movement, and trauma treatment. As in many somatic therapies, this group session example illustrates how touch can be effective with adolescents coping with trauma and addictions.

Background

The group encompassed seven adolescents (six females and one male) recovering from addiction and trauma-related issues. Collectively, many of the traumatic events experienced by the participants included repeated childhood sexual abuse, abandonment, grief and multiple losses, drug overdoses, and seriously damaged attachment relationships. The practice sessions took place in an art studio that was once a garage. The windows and doors were open, allowing the breeze to flow through the room. The temperature in the room was pleasant due to the large trees surrounding the studio, and group members were able to hear the sounds of wind and leaves while the therapy was in progress. Dance and movement therapy activities were utilized as a healing approach to trauma and addiction, incorporating the power of positive, ethical, and responsive touch.

Ethical Education and Discussion Regarding Touch in Group Sessions

The first meeting began with all the group members sitting on their mats forming a circle on the floor. The facilitator explained the benefits of dance and movement therapy, and that it may involve incorporation of respectful and caring touch in the healing of trauma. Sensitive topics regarding touch were discussed, and group members had the opportunity to ask questions. The facilitator explained that some activities involved touch among group members. Group members agreed to ask permission to touch one another during group activities and to avoid touching the front of the torso, the neck, the face, or any private parts, and agreed to follow these discussed guidelines regarding respectful touch. If individuals felt uncomfortable with touching each other at any time, they could withdraw from the activity or ask the facilitator for support. Also, group members were asked for their verbal permission to be touched by the facilitator to assist with grounding, positioning of the body, communicating, and stretching.

Since touch can be a trigger for adolescent trauma, the members were advised to raise their hands as a signal to the facilitator that they were feeling uncomfortable with touch, and this would inform the facilitator that they opted out of the activity touch experience or needed further support. Clients were also advised that they had the option to participate as observers at any time during an activity, or participate by sitting in chairs positioned around the perimeter of the room. In addition, group members signed informed consents to participate in the sessions (see form at end of chapter). The following two activities were offered in the first session:

Activity One: Mind–Body Connection: Breathing, Relaxation, Grounding, Stretching

The facilitator led group members in a 20-minute relaxation, stretch, and guided-meditation activity in order to assist them to develop a mind–body awareness,

Healing Adolescent Trauma 141

Figure 10.1 The group facilitator is connecting through attuned touch. (Illustration used with permission from Susan Clark.)

a common disconnect with those who have experienced trauma (van der Kolk, 2014). While lying on their mats, members were asked to practice deep breathing as the facilitator walked around the circle, touching members' feet, holding their ankles firmly but gently, and extending their legs to stretch out the hips and lower spine. The facilitator circled the group, stretching their shoulders, arms, and hands gently, but firmly opening them (to receive touch, warmth, connection with another human being, among other unexpected sensations) as they focused on their breath with their eyes closed. Members were asked to mentally connect with their bodies and observe what feelings and thoughts came up for them while they were moving in certain positions or being touched (see Figure 10.1). Metaphors and visualization were utilized during this part of the activity in order to bring group members to the present moment, slow down brain processes and metabolism, and decrease levels of anxiety and/or stress.

Member Comments Highlighting Touch following Activity One

Clients sat in a circle and shared comments, which included their experiences of touch by the facilitator (they also had another opportunity to journal their experiences). One said, "I felt more relaxed and the touch felt good." Another youth

142 C. Golly, D. Riccelli, and M. S. Smith

agreed, saying, "I forgot about all my stress and I was here in the moment, not worrying about anything, totally present and I liked the touch, it felt good and I was able to release stress." Still another reported, "It really helped my craving; I was wanting to use [substances] really badly before the group and I was shaking. This exercise helped me to stop the shaking, let go of the craving, and the touch felt that I was loved." One particularly vulnerable member said, "It was peaceful, the touch felt comfortable although usually I am not comfortable with touch. It helped me relax, and the touch felt safe."

Activity Two: Moving Freely through Space and Communicating through Touch

The final exercise was chosen because group members were observed to be comfortable in the movement therapy session and appeared grounded and relaxed, allowing for creativity and free expression. As soft instrumental African music played in the background, group members were prompted to listen to an inner calling of their bodies, with no judgments regarding shape or flow, and to begin moving freely through the space while listening to the music in the background. As they approached peers, they were asked to connect through respectful positive

Figure 10.2 The group members connect with each other through movement and dance. (Illustration used with permission from Susan Clark.)

touch and dance. Clients appeared engaged and moved freely through the space while using dance and respectful touch with one another (see Figure 10.2).

Member Session Comments Following Activity Two

The session ended with processing, and clients shared comments such as, "I really liked this activity as there were no rules and I was moving freely"; "It was nice to connect with others"; "Hugs felt good"; "We should start every morning like this"; "Can we do this more?"; "I was grateful and open to the opportunity of touching and being touched"; and "I liked the freedom of no judgment, another way of opening up and letting it all go."

Facilitator Cultural Considerations, Countertransference, and Self-Care

The facilitator of this group (Riccelli) was raised in a Hispanic culture with Italian and Spanish roots, all considered high-touch cultures and I experienced plenty of hugs and kisses and what could be considered positive touch. When incorporating touch in the movement dance therapy sessions, I remained mindful of potential cultural difference regarding touch with clients as well as the sensitivity to the understanding of abuse trauma histories related to the adolescents in the group. My natural impulse was to provide caring touch stemming from my cultural background; however, my personal awareness dictated that I respond and be attuned to the varied needs of the adolescent group members as they arose. As well, I always asked the client's permission prior to any touch provided, as well as the other safety measures indicated in the informed consent. Additionally, although the groups were very rewarding, I was often very exhausted at the end of each session. There was a tremendous amount of physical and emotional energy output. To address any concerns of burnout or secondary trauma, I took care of myself in several ways such as meditating, attending yoga classes, swimming in the ocean, walking in nature, and connecting with friends, among other self-care activities.

Conclusions

There is little information in the clinical literature regarding physical touch and adolescents, yet touch is of crucial importance to human physical and psychological development and functioning. Physically painful touch and lack of nurturing touch are associated with lifelong medical and psychological problems. American children are among the least touched in comparison with other societies. Childhood abuse and neglect are among the most commonly cited risk factors for violence and aggressive behavior in adolescents.

Maltreatment that occurs in childhood and adolescence may result in subsequent interpersonal trauma, which results from chronic developmentally adverse events occurring within a caregiving or interpersonal context. Meanwhile, adolescent trauma is believed to be increasing.

Movement and dance group therapies are a well-established intervention for the treatment of trauma, addictions, PTSD, and other effects of abuse and neglect. They may provide a better therapeutic fit for adolescents, many of whom are more comfortable with creative, nonverbal modalities such as play, art, and movement than with traditional talk therapy. Movement as the principal means of expression can affectively express suffering, therefore allowing healing to occur. As illustrated in the case presentation, the adolescents were able to address deep issues related to touch experiences and connection to others. While dancing in a group setting, individuals were able to relate to each other, "see and be seen" through direct participation, and engage in action and relationship. They were able to connect with themselves and others, getting in touch with repressed feelings, emotions, and sensations, thus formulating new neural pathways in the brain. Touch was thoughtfully and carefully used in the group by both the facilitator and the members. Ethical concerns were addressed through using informed consent, both in written formats and through ongoing verbal explanation and check-ins with group members. The facilitator provided grounding, safety, and containment in the group, in addition to establishing safe utilization of touch for healing. Through the creative expression and safety of the group, the adolescent participants were able to experience feelings of being valued, accepted, and supported; and explore their inner emotional world in a non-judgmental setting.

Sample Movement and Dance Group Informed Consent

We are introducing the use of an experiential therapeutic approach to the healing process of addiction and trauma in a group setting. We incorporate respectful, caring, ethical, and healing touch, movement, and dance to communicate and express feelings and thoughts that at times are difficult to express through the use of words.

We are defining touch as contact between group members and their therapists, and among the participant and other group members. Forms of touch can be: touching of the hands, hugging, holding or rubbing backs, and gentle or firm stretching of extremities. To maintain safety among the group, we ask that vulnerable areas such as the front of the torso and neck are avoided and, additionally, any private areas, including buttocks. Please be respectful of the healing process and safety among the group.

Touch can also be considered when it occurs between the participant and inanimate objects.

We ask that you "observe" what comes up for you during contact times and share or write during processing of the experience.

If you feel uncomfortable with the touch, you can raise your hand as a signal to stop at any time, or you can choose to withdraw from the activity in progress at any time, sit, and/or observe. You can choose not to participate in the activity at any time.

Participation in this workshop and its activity is completely voluntary.

We will ask that you complete a series of questions at the end, which also is voluntary.

We hope that this experience can be of benefit to you in your healing process and help us better understand the power of touch in the healing of trauma and addiction.

CONSENT:

- I am being offered the opportunity to participate in a Dance/Movement Therapy workshop, which is introducing ethical, caring, healing, and respectful touch into the healing process. I understand that in giving my consent to participate I will be asked to complete some multiple-choice and open-ended questions at the end about my experiences.
- I understand that the information gathered will remain entirely confidential and that any identifying data will be disguised both in this workshop and in any publication. No information which could identify me will be used. The original questionnaire data will be destroyed one year after the completion of the workshop.
- I understand that participation is voluntary and that I am free to refuse to participate or to withdraw from this workshop at any time, without prejudice.
- I understand that there are no risks associated with taking this questionnaire, and the intended benefit of the workshop will be the contribution to an improved understanding about the role of touch in the healing process of trauma and addiction with adolescents.
- I have read the above statements and have been informed of the details pertinent to my participation in the workshop. I agree to voluntarily participate in the above workshop.

Client Name: Signature: Date:

Parent Name: Signature: Date:

> **Discussion Questions**
>
> 1   Describe the importance of touch in child and adolescent development. Why might Movement and Dance Group Therapy be well-suited for the treatment of adolescent trauma?
> 2   As a group activity, play some music and move about the room and make contact with others in a way that is acceptable and comfortable for the group members (e.g., eye contact, high fives, and so forth). Do this activity three times, experimenting with different genres of music. Process the activity as a group.
> 3   Review the movement and dance group informed consent form and discuss the ways that the issues of touch were addressed in the document. In what ways could this consent form be adapted to use with a movement and dance group for younger children?

References

American Dance Therapy Association. (2016). *Code of ethics*. Retrieved on 14 November, 2016 from http://www.adta.org

Anda, R.F., Felitti, V.J., Bremner, J.D., Walker, J.D., Whitfield, C., Perry, B.D., & Giles, W.H. (2006). The enduring effects of abuse and related adverse experiences in childhood. *European Archives of Psychiatry and Clinical Neuroscience, 256(3)*, 174–186. Retrieved on 14 November, 2016 from: https://childtrauma.org/wp-content/uploads/2013/11/Anda_Perry_etal.pdf

Bowlby, J. (1988). *A secure base: Parent–child attachment and healthy human development*. London: Routledge.

Brody, V. (1997). *The dialog of touch: Developmental play therapy*. Northvale, NJ: Jason Aronson.

Cook, A., Spinazzola, J., Ford, J., Lanktree, C., Blaustein, M., Cloitre, M., DeRosa, R., Hubbard, R., Kagan, R., Liautaud, J., Mallah, K., Olafson, E., & van der Kolk, B. (2005). Complex trauma in children and adolescents. *Psychiatric Annals, 35(5)*, 390–398. Retrieved on 14 November, 2016 from: http://www.traumacenter.org/products/pdf_files/Complex_Child_Trauma.pdf

D'Andrea, W., Ford, J., Stolbach, B., Spinazzola, J., & van der Kolk, B.A. (2012). Understanding interpersonal trauma in children: Why we need a developmentally appropriate trauma diagnosis. *American Journal of Orthopsychiatry, 82(2)*, 187–200. Retrieved on 14 November, 2016 from: http://www.traumacenter.org/research/ajop_why_we_need_a_complex_trauma_dx.pdf

Elbrecht, C., & Antcliff, L. (2015). Being in touch: Healing developmental and attachment trauma at the Clay Field. *Children Australia, 40*, 209–220. Retrieved on 14 November, 2016 from: https://www.cambridge.org/core/journals/children-australia/article/being-in-touch-healing-developmental-and-attachment-trauma-at-the-clay-field/45E8DEA600EF4458643F52B53009E957

Field, T. (1999). American adolescents touch each other less and are more aggressive toward their peers as compared with French adolescents. *Adolescence, 34(136)*,

753–758. Retrieved on 14 November, 2016 from: http://europepmc.org/abstract/med/10730699

Field, T. (2002). Violence and touch deprivation in adolescents. *Adolescence, 37(148)*, 735–746.

Field, T. (2005). Touch deprivation and aggression against self among adolescents. In D.M. Stoff & E.J. Sussman (Eds.), *Developmental psychobiology of aggression* (pp. 117–140). New York: Cambridge University Press.

Field, T. (2014). *Touch* (2nd ed.). Cambridge, MA: MIT Press.

Green, E.J., & Myrick, A.C. (2014). Treating complex trauma in adolescents: A phase-based, integrative approach for play therapists. *International Journal of Play Therapy, 23(3)*, 131–145. Retrieved on 14 November, 2016 from: https://www.apa.org/pubs/journals/features/pla-a0036679.pdf

Green, E.J., Myrick, A.C., & Crenshaw, D.A. (2013). Toward secure attachment in adolescent relational development: Advancements from sandplay and expressive play-based interventions. *International Journal of Play Therapy, 22(2)*, 90–102. DOI:http://dx.doi.org/10.1037/a0032323

Halprin, A. (n.d.) Empowering creativity through movement, metaphor and dance. Promotion for workshop at The Tamalpa Institute. Retrieved on 29 January, 2017 from: http://tamalpa.org/programs/summer.html

Halprin, A. (2000). *Dance as a healing art: Returning to health with movement and imagery.* Mendocino, CA: LifeRhythm.

Jones, S.E. (1994). *The right touch: Understanding and using the language of physical contact.* Creskill, NJ: Hampton Press.

Kim, J., & Cicchetti, D. (2010). Longitudinal pathways linking child maltreatment, emotion regulation, peer relations, and psychopathology. *Journal of Child Psychology and Psychiatry, 51(6)*, 706–716. Retrieved on 14 November, 2016 from: https://www.ncbi.nlm.nih.gov/pmc/articles/PMC3397665/

LeFeber, M.M. (2014). Working with children using dance/movement therapy. In E.J. Green & A.A. Drewes (Eds.), *Integrating expressive arts and play therapy with children and adolescents* (pp. 125–147). Hoboken, NJ: Wiley.

Matherly, N. (2013). Navigating the dance of touch: An exploration into the use of touch in dance/movement therapy. *American Journal of Dance Therapy, 36*, 77–91. Retrieved on 14 November, 2016 from: http://link.springer.com/article/10.1007/s10465-013-9161-2

Milliken, R. (2008). Intervening in the cycle of addiction, violence, and shame: A dance/movement therapy group approach in a jail addictions program. *Journal of Groups in Addiction & Recovery, 3(1–2)*, 5–22. Retrieved on 14 November, 2016 from: http://www.tandfonline.com/doi/abs/10.1080/15560350802157346?src=recsys&journalCode=wgar20

Montagu, A. (1986). *Touching: The human significance of the skin* (3rd ed.). New York: Harper & Row.

National Association of Social Workers (2016). *Code of ethics.* Retrieved on 14 November, 2016 from: https://socialworkers.org/publications/code

Ogle, C.M., Rubin, D.C., Bernsten, D., & Siegler, I.C. (2013). The frequency and impact of exposure to potentially traumatic events over the life course. *Clinical Psychological Science, 1*, 426–434. Retrieved on 14 November, 2016 from: https://www.ncbi.nlm.nih.gov/pmc/articles/PMC3958943/

Pearce, C.M., Martin, G., & Wood, K. (1994). Significance of touch for perceptions of parenting and psychological adjustment among adolescents. *Journal of American Academy of Child and Adolescent Psychiatry, 34(2)*, 160–167. Retrieved on 14 November, 2016 from: http://www.academia.edu/4446127/The_Significance_of_Touch_for_Perceptions_of_Parenting_and_Psychological_Adjustment_among_Adolescents

Peifer, D.E. (2008). *Adolescent experiences of touch in psychotherapy.* (Doctoral dissertation). Available from ProQuest Dissertations and Theses database (UMI No. 3322264).

Perry, B. (2016). *Bonding and attachment in maltreated children: Consequences of emotional neglect in childhood.* Adapted in part from *Maltreated children: Experience, brain development and the next generation.* Manuscript in preparation. Retrieved on 14 November, 2016 from: https://childtrauma.org/wp-content/uploads/2014/01/Bonding-and-Attachment.pdf

Trickett, P.K., Negriff, S., Ji, J., & Peckins, M. (2011). Child maltreatment and adolescent development. *Journal of Research on Adolescence, 21(1)*, 3–20. Retrieved on 14 November, 2016 from: http://onlinelibrary.wiley.com/doi/10.1111/j.1532-7795.2010.00711.x/abstract

United States Association for Body Psychotherapy. (2007). *USABP code of ethics.* Retrieved on 14 November, 2016 from: http://usabp.org/about-us/usabp-code-of-ethics/

van der Kolk, B. (2005). Developmental trauma disorder. *Psychiatric Annals, 35(5)*, 401–408.

van der Kolk, B. (2014). *The body keeps the score.* London: Penguin, Random House.

van der Kolk, B. (2016). Commentary: The devastating effects of ignoring child maltreatment in psychiatry—A commentary on Teicher and Samson 2016. *Journal of Child Psychology and Psychiatry, 57*, 267–270. Retrieved on 14 November, 2016 from: http://onlinelibrary.wiley.com/doi/10.1111/jcpp.12540/abstract

Westland, G. (2011). Physical touch in psychotherapy: Why are we not touching more? *Body, Movement, and Dance in Psychotherapy, 6(1)*, 17–29. DOI:10.1080/17432979.2010.508597

Yamuna, S. (2013). Counseling adolescents. *Indian Journal of Pediatrics, 80(11)*, 949–958. Retrieved on 14 November, 2016 from: http://link.springer.com/article/10.1007/s12098-013-1104-x

Zur, O., & Nordmarken, N. (2016). *To touch or not to touch: Exploring the myth of prohibition on touch in psychotherapy and counseling.* Retrieved on 14 November, 2016 from: http://www.drzur.com/ethicsoftouch.html

11 The Emotion of Touch
Healing Reactive Attachment Disorder Through Child-Centered Play Therapy

Jenn Pereira and Sondra Smith-Adcock

> Sometimes, reaching out and taking someone's hand is the beginning of a journey. At other times, it is allowing another to take yours.
> Vera Nazarian, *The Perpetual Calendar of Inspiration*

Introduction

In Child-Centered Play Therapy (CCPT), the therapist allows the child to lead, creating a permissive space in which the child plays and interacts in ways that are meaningful to them. CCPT is consistent with the belief that children are innately capable of personal wisdom and growth when they are provided with a supportive and accepting environment (Axline, 1969; Landreth, 2012; Pereira & Smith-Adcock, 2011). During the therapeutic process, therapists often find themselves making clinical judgments and ethical decisions that involve responding to children's behavior without hindering the therapeutic journey. When children enter therapy with issues related to attachment difficulties or experiences of harmful touch in their caregiving relationships, the challenge of making clinical decisions about touch can be amplified. In this chapter, we explore issues related to the use of touch in CCPT. To illustrate the therapeutic value of touch and boundary setting, we present the case of Lela, a four-and-a-half-year-old child whose behavior is consistent with reactive attachment disorder.

Child-Centered Play Therapy

The tenets of Child-Centered Play Therapy (CCPT) (Axline, 1969; Landreth, 2012) convey the therapist's role as a partner rather than director in the child's journey. CCPT, drawn from the humanistic orientation of counseling, relies on the client and therapist forming a strong emotional connection and therapeutic relationship. Research related to CCPT has demonstrated its utility in helping children to overcome myriad issues such as physical, sexual, and emotional abuse, neglect, fears, adjustment issues, family concerns, and social and emotional problems (Bratton *et al.*, 2005). In CCPT, child clients are able to make important self-discoveries and positive strides in growth and development through their engagement with the therapist and the therapist's ability to develop a therapeutic milieu.

Touch in CCPT

Many scholars and practitioners consider the use of touch to be an essential element of human growth and development, and a profound method of human connection and communication. Decades of outcome research (Field, 1998, 2014; Jones & Glover, 2014; Milakovitch, 1993; Zur & Nordmarken, 2016) have shown that caring, physical forms of contact can improve client well-being and strengthen the therapeutic relationship. According to Zur and Nordmarken (2016), "there is great positive potential in forming a strong therapeutic bond and a vehicle for healing injuries created by early touch violations or lack of necessary touch" (p. 2).

In CCPT, because the child leads the process, touch is usually child-initiated (VanFleet et al., 2010). Because they are non-directive, CCPT therapists wait patiently for moments in which they can respond to the child in ways that foster nurturance, engagement, connection, and space for self-exploration. Although positive touch experiences are not planned as therapeutic activities, child-centered sessions are often full of opportunities to engage in appropriate and therapeutic touch. The child might initiate or request nurturance activities (holding hands, feeding, preparing meals, and caretaking behaviors), or invite the therapist to join in interactive play (painting the child's hands for a handprint or sword play). Touch may also arise during limit setting (limiting the child from unsafe climbing in the playroom) (Jernberg & Booth, 1999; Munns, 2000; VanFleet et al., 2010). Displays of aggressive play (sword fighting, good guys vs. bad guys, or competition games), while appropriate in CCPT for emotional expression, are also activities in which physical contact is likely and may provide opportunities for the therapist and the child to explore limits necessary for safety and emotional growth (Bennett et al., 2006).

In most of these situations, the touch between child and therapist is appropriate and acceptable and the therapist should respond empathically (VanFleet et al., 2010). As the play process unfolds, the therapist and child work through experiences as they arise, with the therapist attuned to opportunities to reflect the child's internal and external experience and struggles. Importantly, when these types of spontaneous touch between the child and therapist occur, the therapist determines what level of physical engagement would be most beneficial to the child (VanFleet et al., 2010). When dealing with issues of both therapist-initiated touch and responding to child-initiated touch, the child-centered therapist should be actively engaged in decision making that honors the child's experience and is purposeful in assessing the benefit or harm of current or foreseeable instances of touch.

Guidelines for the Ethical Use of Touch in CCPT

Children who have experienced maltreatment in the form of sexual or physical abuse can be confused about healthy versus unhealthy forms of touch (VanFleet *et al.*, 2010). In these cases, children may need modeling of appropriate touch (as presented in the case study that follows) within the therapeutic setting to remediate trauma and change maladaptive beliefs that were developed as a result of maltreatment (Gil, 1991; VanFleet *et al.*, 2010). One area of concern frequently seen is a child's lack of emotional and physical connection to self, others, and their environment. For example, a child who has been sexually abused may not tolerate physical closeness with others, while another child who has been sexually abused may show indiscriminate attachment, and seek inappropriate sexual contact. In other instances, such as when children have experienced neglect, touch may play an appropriate and necessary role in therapy and can assist clients in feeling nurtured, valued, and worthwhile. Therefore, decisions around engaging in touch in sessions would look very different for each of these situations.

When therapists sense or have direct knowledge that a child has endured negative touch experiences or a lack of engaging, caring touch, they may be eager to foster an environment of positive touch for which the child may not yet be ready. If children are rushed into touch in therapy, even with a supportive and attentive therapist, it can damage the fragile counseling relationship and cause further touch confusion. The therapist is, of course, vigilant regarding situations where boundaries around "appropriate touch" and purposeful lack of touch might be most helpful. In ethical practice, therapists work diligently to understand the child's history and provide a therapeutic environment that honors their experience. Therefore, it is imperative that therapists understand their own motivations for touching. Often, therapists will carry their own personal issues about touch into sessions (Courtney & Gray, 2014), due to their own touch history, societal perceptions, or strict training regarding touch. This discomfort may require that therapists engage in their own therapeutic process, receive supervision, or staff the case with a fellow therapist.

Given the issues outlined above, it is important for CCPT therapists to consider following a careful decision-making process about using touch and adhering to their professional code of ethics, such as the ethical code of the American Counseling Association (*ACA Code of Ethics*, 2014). To date, although some authors (McNeil-Haber, 2004) have offered guidelines for touch with children, there is very little literature on the use of touch for child-centered therapists to consider in their decision making. Therefore, the authors have created guiding questions for child-centered play therapists based upon the authors' extensive clinical experience and supervision of play therapists. These questions are an attempt to support therapists in understanding the process of therapist- and child-initiated touch. The authors acknowledge that the list is not comprehensive and is intended only as a beginning dialogue around the efficacy of touch in CCPT; we invite therapists to add to this list based on their own experiences.

Therapist-Initiated Touch

- In a therapeutic relationship that is child-led, when is therapist-initiated touch appropriate?
- What has the therapist intuited or observed that leads them to believe a specific touch may be therapeutic in that moment?
- What type(s) of touch are supportive of the child's therapeutic goals?
- How does the therapist assess and understand the child's reaction to touch?
- What is happening within the therapist that is causing a reaction of wanting to touch and be touched, or blocking touch in session?

Child-Initiated Touch

- What type of touch is the child seeking and what is the best way to respond?
- Is the child's touch assessed as a sign of a sexualized response pattern?
- Is the child's "requested touch" a search for connection, or reassurance?
- What physical, social, emotional, or safety need(s) is the child trying to meet?
- Is the child's seeking or avoiding touch from the therapist related to the child's cultural heritage?

The Ethics of Culture and Touch

As when working with any client, the therapist should be aware of the cultural values and heritage of the client's family system and how it can inform and impact treatment. When working with children, CCPT therapists should elicit from caregivers cultural considerations such as displays of affection, physical contact, and different parental styles of nurturance. This information can then be considered in understanding meaningful and appropriate physical contact with the child. For example, a therapist may be working with a child whose family does not engage in outward displays of affection or physical closeness. Engagement of this kind (e.g., hugging or hand holding to and from the play room) by the therapist may then be off-putting to the child and misinterpreted by the parents. Other families may have a culture that values a high level of physical contact, as in some Latin cultures, and a therapist who does not give affection may be misinterpreted as uncaring. Therefore, having a clear understanding of the cultural values related to touch is crucial.

Case of Lela

Presenting Problem

The case of Lela, a four-and-a-half-year-old girl, will be used to illustrate the use of touch in CCPT counseling sessions. For Lela, issues related to touch appeared to be consistent with a lack of positive, emotionally regulating touch from her early experiences with caregivers, and possibly hurtful or aggressive touch during her first years of life. Interplay between her fear of touching and being touched and engaging in aggressive touch were observed from the initial counseling session. Lela was brought to therapy due to her extensive behavioral issues at home with the Korean-American family who adopted her at age two. The orphanage from which she came, which was reportedly overcrowded with limited staff, had not been able to provide the family with much historical information. At intake, Lela's mother shared with me (Pereira) that Lela was aggressive toward her, but also clung to her upon leaving the house, did not speak to or make eye contact with anyone outside the family, was aggressive at home, and exhibited "unexplained" anger outbursts. Additionally, Lela routinely displayed little emotion other than anger and frustration, would not initiate or tolerate physical touch or nurturance, and rarely smiled or laughed. She also engaged in hurtful behaviors toward the family cat, and would horde food and small items belonging to others under her bed.

She became greatly distressed when away from her mother, and would not allow anyone to touch or comfort her in any way. If a situation arose where Lela was offered comfort, she became aggressive (i.e., hitting, shouting, kicking, or running away) or instantly dismissive (i.e., laughing loudly in the person's face, or turning her back and ignoring the gesture of comfort). Lela's mother reported that these behaviors had been happening since the adoption, and were steadily worsening.

Because of her young age and problems with emotional regulation, child-centered play therapy (CCPT) was an excellent fit for Lela due to its non-directive nature. CCPT would allow Lela to develop a sense of autonomy, to explore her environment on her own terms, and to begin to understand the connection between her emotions and behaviors. Her relationship with the therapist, a key component in CCPT, would help Lela begin to reconnect to others in a safe environment.

Diagnosis: Reactive Attachment Disorder

Following the intake interview, I considered Reactive Attachment Disorder (RAD) an appropriate diagnosis given the nature, background, time frame, and severity of Lela's behaviors. Lela met the criteria of RAD as characterized by the following symptoms. She displayed a "consistent pattern of inhibited, emotionally withdrawn behavior toward adult caregivers, manifested by both of the following criteria: The child rarely or minimally seeks comfort when distressed and the child rarely or minimally responds to comfort when distressed" (American Psychiatric Association, 2013, p. 265). Additionally, behavioral symptoms were also observed as "persistent social or emotional disturbance characterized by at least two of the following: Minimal social and emotional responsiveness to others; limited positive affect; episodes of unexplained irritability, sadness, or fearfulness that are evident even during nonthreatening interactions with adult caregivers" (p. 265). She also experienced a pattern of extremely insufficient care as evidenced by social neglect and deprivation, lack of having her basic needs met, and lack of comfort and affection from caring adults. An assumption in the diagnosis of RAD is that insufficient childcare is a precursor and impetus for the behaviors displayed. In consideration of the RAD criteria and diagnosis, the following treatment plan goals were created.

Treatment Goals

- Establish trust in others and engage in positive relationships.
- Build autonomy and positive sense-of-self, develop sense of safety in her environment.
- Facilitate healthy emotional and physical connections with her parents.
- Facilitate appropriate touch and healthy boundaries and provide responsive touch in the therapeutic environment.

During the course of therapy, these goals proved challenging due to Lela's pervasive distrust of others and lack of relationship-building skills. Lela's distrust was often evidenced in creating emotional and physical space between herself and others, acting out toward others, and displaying great discomfort with physical closeness, touch, and nurturance.

Touch and Informed Consent Considerations

While many people might consider children incapable of purposeful decision making, in CCPT it is helpful that they be included in the informed consent process along with their caregivers. While this discussion typically occurs at the outset of the therapeutic relationship, issues can arise throughout therapy that require revisiting informed consent—such as the use of touch in sessions. Due to Lela's struggle with attachment and discomfort with physical connection, it helped to sit with her parents and discuss the relevance of the use of touch in therapy.

Our previous discussions on RAD were revisited as were the importance of creating a safe environment, opportunities for emotional connection and trust, and the positive experience of physical contact. Lela's parents were informed that when opportunities arose, I would engage in physical contact such as touching Lela's hand, arm, shoulder, or head. I also let the parents know that as children progress in treatment, they often begin to initiate nurturance touch (i.e., feeding, pretending to be a baby needing care), and that I would capitalize on those moments to build positive touch experiences. During our conversations, it was also crucial to check in with the parents regarding any concerns about the use of touch, and maintain open communication. Keeping the parents informed of instances of touch also helped to keep them informed of emotional changes happening around attachment and connection.

Family Cultural Considerations

During this case, the opportunity arose to deal with the cultural aspects of touch brought by Lela's family. Lela's mother felt touch was important and she wanted to feel an emotional connection to Lela, but felt embarrassed by Lela's rejection of her. Lela's father, who described himself as "very traditional," did not see nurturing touch as an appropriate display of affection and care. He communicated that financial caretaking and engaging in learning activities were activities more consistent with his cultural beliefs. Navigating these cultural values successfully and providing Lela with experiences that met her emotional needs proved challenging at times. The family held very different cultural views than my own, which provided wonderful opportunities for us to discuss values and beliefs, helping me to better understand how I could best support the family.

Initial Phase: Recognizing and Responding to Issues of Touch

During the initial counseling session, Lela entered the office waiting room with her head tucked firmly under the back of her mother's shirt. She had severe issues surrounding attachment, ability to self-sooth or seek and accept comfort, and an aversion to physical touch and closeness. Lela refused to enter the playroom or acknowledge me (Pereira) in any way. It took two sessions of talking to her and reading children's books in the waiting room for Lela to emerge from under her mother's shirt. In order to make contact with her, I gently reflected her fear and need for safety. I made comments like:

> "Lela, you're really not sure what this is about, and that feels scary to you. It's so hard to meet new people. Even though you feel scared, I want you to know this is a safe place where kids come to see me, and we work on their worries and fears. In this safe place, I am here to help you, and I am not going to make you do anything you don't want to do, it's for you to decide what you'll do and how we'll play together."

Although personally I am very open to touch, I approached Lela in a friendly and warm, but physically reserved manner, because it was clear to me that she did not tolerate interactions or touch from strangers. On the third visit, Lela agreed to enter the playroom by nodding once when I asked if she wanted to join me. I let Lela know she could choose to have her mother come into session with us, or we could see her afterward, to which Lela let go of her mother and began to shove her away and swat at her. Lela then inched down the hallway to the playroom and went in. I felt the non-directive environment might be initially overwhelming to Lela, but that the importance of the relationship between therapist and client would create a space for therapeutic growth.

During the first month of weekly sessions, Lela avoided eye contact; she startled easily if I moved suddenly or made a loud noise, and frequently would slide along the walls dumping bins of toys on the floor as she went. Throughout the session she would open the door to see her mother (who sat in a chair outside the door), and then scream in her face or slam the door on her. There were many times during the initial two months of therapy that Lela looked fearful and uncertain; however, she seemed unable to soothe her fears by connecting with her parents or me as her therapist.

Lela's reaction to being in the playroom seemed to be one of tense anticipation. She was hypervigilant and watched me closely, seeming most comfortable when I sat cross-legged against the opposite wall (as demonstrated by her willingness to begin exploring the room and toys when I was very still). As I respected Lela's need for space, she became more comfortable, and we slowly began building our relationship. Over the next few sessions, as Lela explored I was able to sit in the center of the room and track her movements by turning slowly so as not to startle her. Providing a permissive space, combined with tracking her actions and reflecting her needs and concerns around safety, seemed to help Lela begin to see me as an ally and the playroom as a safe place.

As our sessions progressed through the third month together, Lela began to make eye contact and would allow me to move closer to her to see what she was doing and to hand her things she needed. Again, my insertions into her play were responsive with regard to her sense of safety and autonomy, and became more frequent as she increasingly tolerated my presence. At this point, she was still not verbally responding to my reflective statements (at times she would just look at me, at other times she would turn her back to me); however, she would whisper to herself.

Middle Phase: Recognizing and Responding to Issues of Touch

Throughout the initial three months, Lela refused to ask for help when she was unable to do something, which led to my making reflective statements such as, "You're still not sure you can trust me to help you. You just don't feel like you can ask me to help, it feels scary to you to need my help with that." After I made this comment to her one day, she threw the play-doh container at me and yelled, "Help." I opened the container and commented, "You've decided that maybe there are some things I can help you with; you trust me enough to help with the play-doh" and, rather than tossing it back to her, I put it into her hand, gently holding her hand in mine (Figure 11.1). I wanted to pair the ideas that I would always help her when asked and that the environment would stay safe for her, even if I were closer to her. This was an opportunity to introduce, in a simple but meaningful way, the idea that physical closeness and appropriate touch could be safe. Lela stared at me, but did not pull her hand away. She then rolled out the play-doh and handed me half so that I could play along.

Given her reaction, it seemed that Lela and I could now experience moments that included some nurturing touch. In keeping with CCPT, I wanted to follow

Figure 11.1 "The most beautiful things in the world cannot be seen or touched, they are felt with the heart." Antoine de Saint-Exupéry, *The Little Prince*.
Source: ©Depositphotos.com/Belchonock

Lela's lead in sessions; however, I also looked for opportunities to incorporate small instances of supportive, caring touch. These nurturing touch experiences could slowly begin to change her negative perceptions of life, and her sense of self in relationship to others. I spent time reviewing sessions (often through the use of videotape to which her parents had consented) for missed touch, nurturance, and engagement moments, helping me to identify opportunities when they arose in subsequent sessions. I also reviewed Lela's reactions to my reflections and interactions to gauge her comfort level and observe any progress made in our relationship.

One afternoon, Lela came into session and immediately began dumping all the play materials on the floor. As I sat in the center of the room, Lela went to the play kitchen, retrieved a plastic carving knife which she held near her leg, and slowly circled around behind me (which I was able to watch in a small mirror hanging in the room). When Lela was behind me, she raised her arm and jabbed the knife into the side of my neck. The blade, being soft rubber, immediately bent. When I turned to look at Lela, she had a look of fear and disappointment on her face. I reflected her need to hurt me to be sure she could keep herself safe, and reiterated that this was a safe place. As she stood and looked at me, I continued to reflect her fears that other people might hurt her, and that I might now be angry with her. While making these statements, I was mentally processing how I might respond next. Lela was still holding the knife as she listened to me, and I needed to think through what sort of response would be most beneficial to her and our relationship. I decided it was best to gently show her that her aggression was not necessary in our relationship.

In CCPT, limits are provided for safety, and would certainly be set for a child's purposeful act of aggression toward self or therapist. In this moment with Lela, I felt that in addition to the limit of her aggressive behavior, a corrective touch that communicated her safety would be therapeutically beneficial. Therefore, I slowly reached forward, gently cupped her hand in mine, and stated:

> "Lela, remember I said there were some things you can't do in here? One thing you can't do is hurt me. I am not for hurting and neither are you. You don't feel safe yet, you are scared and unsure and that's why you wanted to hurt me. I will not hurt you, Lela." I then stated, "You can play with any of the toys in your special room, and we will be safe together." Then, I smiled at her and let go of her hand. Lela stood for a few seconds looking at the floor so I commented again, "Lela, you can play with any of the other toys in the play room if you choose to, and I will play with you if you would like me to." She sat near me playing play-doh for the remainder of the session, glancing at me periodically. She then ran from the room when I told her our time was up for the day.

On the way to her car, for the first time, she glanced back at me as she walked, while I waved to her as I did each week.

The following two sessions were drastically different. Lela came into the playroom with me and did not want her mother sitting at the door. She spoke to me a few times, tersely telling me what she wanted to play with and what I should be doing, assigning me tasks to complete for her. These developments indicated that she might be open to more engagement. Then, in the second session following the knife incident, Lela took my hand briefly as we walked to the play room. She sat next to me on the floor and we bathed, dressed, and fed the baby dolls together. The following session, however, presented a significant challenge around the issue of touch. While playing with the baby dolls, Lela said she would be the baby and that I should feed her. She sat on a pillow while I fed her pretend food. She then wanted to sit in my lap and have me cradle her as I fed her water from the baby bottle. I was surprised at this request, but not wholly unprepared.

Final Phase: Recognizing and Responding to Issues of Touch

As our sessions progressed, I thought we might encounter a moment where she would request nurturing engagement that she may have missed as a small child. I had given thought to this intimate level of touch and caring and considered carefully the ethical principles related to nonmaleficence ("do no harm"), beneficence (promoting positive client change), and autonomy (allowing the client to choose their interactions) (Calmes *et al.*, 2013). I wanted to be sure that this type of touch, or this level of intimacy, would not contribute to unforeseen negative reactions. I wanted to be sure that any touch and nurturance would provide an example of safe, caring touch that might begin to heal her negative perceptions of connecting with others. Considering ethical practice, I also sought supervision from a play therapist colleague. I shared my decision-making model, and discussed Lela's progress and areas of concern. I decided that the benefit of the use of positive touch outweighed the concerns. Ultimately I did not want to create an environment in which Lela had asked for interpersonal connection that I had refused to provide.

> Therefore, when Lela made her request to be cradled like a baby, I followed along, saying to her, "You think it would feel nice to be the baby and have me take care of you." She crawled onto my lap, leaned back, and put the bottle in her mouth. I reflected to her that "Sometimes it's nice to be a baby; to feel safe and taken care of!" Then, which was quite extraordinary, she closed her eyes. We sat and rocked for several minutes, at which point she jumped up and began running around the room. I commented, "Even though it felt nice to be close to someone, being close for a long time might not feel really safe yet."

The following session, Lela came in and spent a good amount of the time ordering me around and yelling at me for "not doing things right." This seemed to be her way of reestablishing control and some distance between us in the playroom, which I reflected to her throughout the session. In the following session, she came in and had me read to her while she leaned on my shoulder. Over the next several months, many changes took place in session and at home. She began to smile and laugh periodically, verbalized some of her thoughts and worries, used some feeling words, showed care toward the family cat, sat in her mother's lap to read, and began asking for (brief) hugs at home.

Outcomes

As mentioned earlier, because of Lela's issues with emotional connection and physical touch, it was important to assist her parents in understanding the process of play therapy and the importance of my relationship with Lela. Because there is a great deal of stigma surrounding touch in therapy settings (Calmes et al., 2013), it was crucial that Lela's parents were well-informed throughout the counseling process. I worked to help Lela's parents match their use of touch at home with progress made in sessions. Interestingly, as Lela's ability to tolerate physical closeness and emotional connection grew, she began to also talk about things that made her happy, laughed more frequently, and acted silly. One day, she began saying "I love you" to the cat, and then to her parents and sister. Toward the end of treatment, sessions focused on building the bond between Mom and Lela. Lela's mother and I had met several times prior to her joining sessions, so I could begin teaching her ways to support Lela's development of autonomy and sense of self in session. I began to play a smaller role in sessions, moving off to the side, to allow them the opportunity to focus solely on each other in session. During this time, Lela was responsive and engaging toward her mother, allowing for and reciprocating nurturance. Lela's father was not able to participate in these joint play sessions; however, he began to engage in one-on-one play activities at home, which Lela talked positively about in sessions.

Closing Comments and Summary

Touch in therapy can be a daunting prospect for many therapists, clients, and caregivers, so much so that many therapists shy away from this aspect of connection. A personal decision-making model based on child-centered principles, informed consent around touch, understanding your own personal issues around touch, and engaging in appropriate supervision is critical. The case of Lela was used to illustrate the powerful healing properties of touch in CCPT when used with intent and transparency. Because of the powerful effect touch can have, as child-centered therapists we are always mindful of how and when we engage in touch in a way that honors children's emotional needs and autonomy.

Discussion Questions

1. With the child in the lead, what are your perceptions of the use of touch in therapy with young children? Think back to your upbringing: what were the messages around touch that you perceived? How might those impact you now? Is there professional development work you might need to do around this topic?
2. Responding reflectively to a client's aggressive actions can be challenging for therapists. Return to the incident detailing the client using a knife on the therapist. How might you have responded in that moment? How would you have felt personally? What do you think the child was feeling that led to that event and how do you process this as a therapist?
3. As therapists, it is imperative that we have a theory-driven decision-making model regarding the use of touch in therapy. What are the steps you currently use to make decisions regarding client nurturance and caregiving needs in a session?

References

American Counseling Association. (2014). *ACA Code of Ethics.* Alexandria, VA: Author. Retrieved on 14 November, 2016 from: http://www.counseling.org/resources/aca-code-of-ethics.pdf

American Psychiatric Association. (2013). *Diagnostic and statistical manual of mental disorders* (5th ed.). Washington, DC: Author.

Axline, V. (1969). *Play therapy.* Boston: Houghton-Mifflin.

Bennett, L., Shiner, S., & Ryan, S. (2006). Using Theraplay in shelter settings. *Journal of Psychosocial Nursing & Mental Health Services, 44(10)*, 38–48. Retrieved on 14 November, 2016 from: https://www.ncbi.nlm.nih.gov/pubmed/17063889

Bratton, S.C., Ray, D., Rhine, T., & Jones, L. (2005). The efficacy of play therapy with children: A meta-analytic review of treatment outcomes. *Professional Psychology: Research and Practice, 36(4)*, 376–390. DOI:10.1037/0735-7028.36.4.376

Calmes, S.A., Piazza, N.J., & Laux, J.M. (2013). The use of touch in counseling: An ethical decision-making model. *Counseling & Values, 58(1)*, 59–68. DOI:10.1002/j.2161-007X.2013.00025

Courtney, J.A., & Gray, S.W. (2014). A phenomenological inquiry into practitioner experiences of developmental play therapy: Implications for training in touch. *International Journal of Play Therapy, 23(2)*, 114–129. DOI:http://dx.doi.org/10.1037/a0036366

Field, T. (1998). Massage therapy effects. *American Psychologist, 53(12)*, 1270–1281.

Field, T. (2014). *Touch* (2nd ed.). Cambridge, MA: MIT Press.

Gil, E. (1991). *The healing power of play: Working with abused children.* New York: Guilford Press.

Jernberg, A.M., & Booth, P.B. (1999). *Theraplay: Helping parents and children build better relationships through attachment-based play* (2nd ed.). San Francisco: Jossey-Bass.

Jones, T., & Glover, L. (2014). Exploring the psychological processes underlying touch: Lessons from the Alexander Technique. *Clinical Psychology & Psychotherapy, 21*, 140–153. DOI:10.1002/cpp.1824

Landreth, G.L. (2012). *Play therapy: The art of the relationship* (2nd ed.). New York: Routledge.

McNeil-Haber, F.M. (2004). Ethical consideration in the use of nonerotic touch in psychotherapy with children. *Ethics & Behavior 14(2)*, 123–140. DOI:10.1207/s15327019eb1402_3

Milakovitch, J.C. (1993). Touching in psychotherapy: The differences between therapists who touch and those who do not. *Dissertation Abstracts International, 54(6-B)*, 3347.

Munns, E. (2000). Traditional family and group Theraplay. In E. Munns (Ed.), *Theraplay: Innovations in attachment-enhancing play therapy* (pp. 9–25). Northvale, NJ: Aronson.

Nazarian, V. (2010). *The perpetual calendar of inspiration: Old wisdom for a new world.* Highgate Center, VT: Norilana Books.

Pereira, J., & Smith-Adcock, S. (2011). Using a child-centered communication style for classroom management. *Action in Teacher Education, 33(3)*, 254–264.

VanFleet, R., Sywulak, A.E., & Sniscak, C.C. (2010). *Child-centered play therapy.* New York: Guilford Press.

Zur, O., & Nordmarken, N. (2016). *To touch or not to touch: Exploring the myth of prohibition on touch in psychotherapy and counseling.* Retrieved on 14 November, 2015 from: http://www.zurinstitute.com/touchintherapy.html

PART IV
Innovations and the Utilization of Touch with Children

12 The Role of Touch in Infant Mental Health

Strengthening the Parent–Infant Bond through Child Parent Psychotherapy

Maite Schenker, Veronica Castro, and Montserrat Casado-Kehoe

> There is no such thing as an infant, meaning, of course, that whenever one finds an infant one finds maternal care, and without maternal care there would be no infant.
> Donald Woods Winnicott, "The Theory of the Parent–Infant Relationship"

Introduction

Donald Winnicott, a highly respected pediatrician and psychoanalyst in the field of infant mental health, highlighted that we need to consider the importance of the parent–child relationship in the development of a child. Infants do not exist in isolation; we need to take into consideration their attachment to the primary caregiver. Of this relationship, touch is one of the key components in forming bonds, communication, security, and comfort between the primary caregiver and the infant. In fact, there is evidence that suggests that the sense of touch is the first to develop; the fetus being able to respond to touch as early as the second month of gestation (Duhn, 2010; O'Brien & Lynch, 2011). Heller (1997) described touch as the baby's *lifeline* that connects the infant and parent, with each nurturing experience of touch fostering a stronger tie. (Note, the terms "infant" or "baby" used throughout this chapter includes ages birth to three years old.)

Child Parent Psychotherapy (CPP)

Evidenced-based best practices in the field of Infant Mental Health dictate dyadic therapeutic modalities that involve joint parent–infant sessions (Tuters *et al.*, 2011; Cohen *et al.*, 1999; Lieberman *et al.*, 2006). Child Parent Psychotherapy (CPP) is a dyadic treatment approach developed by Alicia Lieberman and Patricia Van Horn, and has its origins in Infant–Parent Psychotherapy and also through the groundbreaking work of Selma Fraiberg (Fraiberg, 1977; Lieberman & Van Horn, 2005, 2008). CPP is a multitheoretical approach that integrates attachment, psychoanalytic, and trauma theory with intervention strategies derived from cognitive-behavioral and social learning therapies. The CPP therapist uses joint infant–parent sessions that are centered on the child's free play and spontaneous interactions. The therapist's role is to teach, facilitate, and support parents to develop strong attachment relationships with their infants. The therapist also facilitates the parents' understanding of the developmental and emotional meaning of the infant's behavior and promotes developmentally appropriate parenting practices through the use of play, language, physical activity, and nurturing touch and affection (Lieberman & Van Horn, 2008).

Lieberman and Van Horn (2008) acknowledged the importance of touch to an infant's healthy growth and development, and emphasized that the innermost feelings of love, intimacy, and safety are felt in the body and shared with others through physical contact. The CPP therapist encourages age-appropriate affection and *protective touch* between the parent and infant to build a sense of safety and to encourage loving and pleasurable experiences. The therapist might also educate parents about the power of physical contact with their infant; for example, the therapist may explain to a mother the positive benefits of picking up and holding her frightened baby, or of holding the baby on her lap when he's feeling upset and sad. Sometimes the infant shows physical affection in such subtle ways that the parent does not take notice. At such times, the therapist might bring this behavior to the parent's attention in order to facilitate the parent's attunement with her infant. The CPP therapist does not usually initiate physical contact with an infant, because, as Lieberman and Van Horn (2008) cautioned, parents might misinterpret the therapist's physical affection toward their baby as an attempt to displace them. However, many children may spontaneously hug, kiss, or lean against the therapist in sessions. In these situations, therapists are encouraged to use their clinical judgment based upon the needs of the infant or child in deciding how to best respond.

Parent–Infant Attachment

One cannot discuss parent–child relationships without acknowledging the contribution of British child psychiatrist John Bowlby. Bowlby's (1958) attachment theory is widely recognized and empirically supported. He concluded that a child's attachment to his caregiver/mother signifies the child's desire to obtain connection and contact with her during a stressful time. It is during these times that the "attachment behavioral system" is activated and children exhibit behaviors such as crying, clinging, or following their caregiver around in order to seek their proximity. Bowlby described the child's clinging response as having a survival value, which ensures that the infant is cared for by his mother and remains in close contact with her. According to Bowlby, the infant's response of extending his arms and legs in a way which is interpreted by the caregiver as a wish to be picked up can be seen in infants as young as four months old. He explained that clinging behaviors are especially apparent at bedtime or after a separation from the primary caregiver.

Some of the early studies that looked at the role of touch were conducted by Harlow (1958), and involved newborn monkeys that were separated from their mothers. One group was partnered with an inanimate cloth surrogate mother from which they could feed and an inanimate wire surrogate mother with no feeding capacity. The other group was assigned an inanimate cloth surrogate mother but their food could only be obtained from their inanimate wire surrogate mother. It became evident that the monkeys preferred the cloth mother. In addition, during frightening situations the monkeys consistently sought the cloth surrogate for comfort. Harlow's study provides one of the first empirical evidence of the role of interpersonal touch in social and emotional development and confirmed that the need for physical contact is as important as the need for food. Ainsworth conducted a longitudinal study in Kampala, Uganda, which enhanced our understanding of the importance of human touch in infant attachment. She found that Ganda babies, exhibiting behaviours indicative of a "secure" or healthy attachment with their caregivers, had experienced more physical contact during the early months of life than those children found to exhibit behaviors characteristic of an "insecure" attachment. Infants in the secure-attached group exhibited patterns of attachment behaviour found to be typical of their age, such as differential crying, differential smiling, and following exploration away from their mother as a secure base. Conversely, infants in the insecure-attached group demonstrated clinging behaviors, often cried, were fussy, and were unable to tolerate separation from their mothers at even a short distance.

Ganda infants who were held a lot by their caregivers and who did not spend long periods of time alone in their cribs were more likely to develop secure attachments (Ainsworth, 1967). Overall, research has indicated that attachment to the mother serves as a blueprint for future relationships in adolescence and adulthood, including romantic partners and spouses (Takeuchi *et al.*, 2010).

The Role of Touch in Child Development

Beyond the role of touch in promoting the development of a secure attachment of the infant to their caregiver, many researchers acknowledge the importance of touch in several other domains of the infant's life, including social, emotional, cognitive, communicative, and physical development. For an infant, touch is essential for survival. The use of touch ignites great activity in brain growth and development (Field, 2014). Feldman *et al.* (2010) wrote that numerous animal studies have demonstrated that maternal touch has a lifelong organizing effect on the infant's stress response system. The authors further advised that early maternal separation has been associated with long-term disruptions to the stress regulating system, resulting in increased baseline cortisol, altered patterns of cortisol reactivity, and disrupted recovery of the system following stress. Additionally, touch during periods of maternal deprivation buffers the negative effects of stress on the animal's physiological reactivity (Feldman *et al.*, 2010).

Touch also influences the infant–parent bond fostering attachment (see Figure 12.1). It regulates arousal levels in the infant, and has repercussions on development across domains. Hertenstein (2002) advised that touch can be used for communication of emotions as it can transmit the caregiver's thoughts and feelings to the infant. For example, if a mother is feeling angry, the way she holds and

Figure 12.1 Loving parent touch enhances secure attachment relationships.
Source: ©Shutterstock.com/Michaeljung

handles her baby will communicate to the infant her emotional state. In contrast, as Hertenstein explained, the second component of communication is the feelings, thoughts, and/or behaviors elicited in the infant as a result of the caregiver's touch. For example, the mother may elicit a negative reaction from the baby by touching him abruptly, regardless of how she may have been feeling at the time.

The Benefits of Infant Massage and Touch

Studies by Tiffany Field (2014) and her colleagues at the Touch Research Institute in Miami, Florida, show that the regular use of touch has benefits across the life span. Touch has been shown to not only lower cortisol levels but also to improve children's physical health. In addition, Field's work demonstrates that touch deprivation can lead to delayed growth in infants (Field, 2010). In one study Field treated human premature babies with massage for 15 minutes three times per day. She found that those infants who received the massages gained weight 47 percent faster than the control group of babies left in the incubators. Although these babies did not eat more than the controls, they still showed signs that their nervous systems were maturing more rapidly. They also became more active and more responsive to a face and rattle and were discharged from the hospital, on average, six days earlier (Barnett, 2005). In one sample of infants followed over the first year of life, Main and Stadtman (1981) found a significant relationship between the mother's aversion to physical contact with the infant in the first quarter of life, and displays of aggressiveness and anger in the infants (e.g., hitting the mother) in the last quarter of the first year. In addition, they found a significant correlation between maternal aversion to contact with the infant and displays of "odd behavior" by the infant (e.g., stereotypical movements, echolalia in their speech, hand-flapping, and hair-pulling) (Hertenstein, 2002). Significantly, Field (2002) advised that providing massage therapy to aggressive children revealed that they were able to increase norepinephrine and serotonin levels.

The Benefits of Touch to Caregivers

The benefits of touch transcend those experienced by the infant (Field, 2014). Research shows that the caregiver also gains a great deal from the experience (McGregor & Casey, 2012). O'Brien and Lynch (2011) summarized a number of studies which found that tactile interactions with their infants increases the mood levels of the mothers, as well as the emotional connection that parents feel with their babies. Other studies demonstrate that touch significantly reduces anxiety in pregnant women, the length of labor, and the degree of pain experienced (Barnett, 2005). In addition, Glover (1997), in a research study conducted with women suffering from postnatal depression, found that those who attended five weekly sessions of a massage class exhibited significant improvement in the quality of their interactions with their infants, including warmth and sensitivity. In later research, Neu (1999) found that the mothers described feeling intense connectedness with their infants and increased satisfaction in their roles as parents. All of these benefits experienced by the mothers will indirectly positively impact the infant, as improvement in the mother's mood, confidence in their parenting roles, and feelings of connection with their infants will all lead to increased parental bonds, and as Bowlby (1958) and Ainsworth (1967) would say, to a more secure attachment of the infant to their caregiver.

Ethical Considerations of Touch

Although we are very much aware of the many benefits of using touch in working with children, our field seems to see touch as an area that could potentially bring up unwanted accusations. In general, professional licensing boards do not condemn the use of touch with children, but it seems to be an area of controversy (Zur, 2015). Overall, there seems to be a lack of guidelines that define the use of appropriate, non-sexual touch or physical contact in therapy that is culturally respectful, for both infants and children. As a result, some therapists may refrain from incorporating touch that could have great therapeutic effects for infants, children, and parents. In Child Parent Psychotherapy, touch is seen as an adjunct to verbal therapy since the focus is on encouraging and facilitating the parents to provide caring touch to their infant—as do most infant models.

Case of Rebecca and Katrina

The following clinical case study will demonstrate how an infant mental health therapist integrates Child Parent Psychotherapy and the utilization of touch in the dyadic treatment of a young child with her mother. (This case was implemented by the chapter author, Castro.)

Family Background and Medical/Mental Health

Rebecca is a 25-year-old female, born in the United States, of Cuban descent. She was primarily raised by her maternal grandmother and was living with her during the course of therapy treatment. Rebecca explained that she was cared for by her grandmother because her mother "had no interest in raising a child." Her parents never married. Rebecca recalled her mother being affectionless, verbally abusive, and absent, and did not know her biological father. In spite of her grandmother playing such an important role in her life, Rebecca characterized her grandmother as very critical and verbally abusive. Rebecca was not working and on a disability pension due to a medical condition. She suffered from seizures and had a history of brain surgeries and hospitalizations. Due to her medical condition, she was not able to drive, her speech was somewhat slurred, the left side of her face was slightly distorted, and she walked with a small limp. Rebecca appeared to be of average intelligence, could perform daily living skills, and had completed some university credits in a local community college.

Rebecca's daughter, Katrina, was 30 months when they began treatment. According to Rebecca, Katrina was excessively clingy, always wanting to know where she was going, and was "disobedient." Reportedly, Rebecca had a brief affair with a man, who is currently married with children but did not want to be involved in Katrina's life. An additional issue that arose during the initial sessions was that Rebecca was about to undergo surgery to help with the seizures, and she wanted to prepare Katrina for her month-long stay in the hospital. Katrina presented as a typical 30-month-old girl, with no indication of developmental delays, and her anxiety toward her mother's health and the anticipated separation was to be expected.

Child Parent Psychotherapy Assessments

Due to Rebecca's impending hospitalization, the family was seen several times a week for the first month of treatment, instead of the typical once a week session. In this manner, the infant mental health and CPP series of assessments, which typically takes four sessions to complete, was done in a shorter span of time. The assessments included two structured interviews with Katrina's mother (i.e., the Working Model and the Family of Origin), the CROWELL observation between mother and child, which consists of a number of activities aimed at better understanding the parent–child relationship, in addition to the intake assessment and two measures, the Child Behavior Checklist (CBCL) and Parenting Stress Index (PSI).

Post-Assessment Conceptualized

Although Rebecca's original reason for bringing Katrina to treatment was to prepare her for Rebecca's long hospital stay, the assessment results suggested some attachment challenges. Of significance was an apparent lack of physical closeness and affection between mother and child. This was a significant observation as those from a Cuban cultural background commonly have a lot of physical touch between family members and friends. However, between Rebecca and Katrina there was virtually no observed displays of affection. Rebecca also presented with a flat affect and struggled to play with Katrina. She appeared not to know how to play or follow Katrina's lead, and often interrupted the play with her own ideas or criticism. As the therapist spent time with the family, it was noted that Rebecca never felt she could do anything to gain her family's love and approval. Rebecca reported that she was constantly ridiculed and criticized. Though she did not wish this upon her daughter, her "ghosts" from the past, unfortunately, were very much living within her relationship with Katrina. Rebecca was treating Katrina in a very similar fashion to how her mother and grandmother had treated her.

Treatment Plan

After Rebecca's return home from the hospital, the therapy then shifted to strengthen the attachment relationship between mother and child. Psycho-education on child development was provided to Rebecca in order to help her create realistic expectations of Katrina and to also develop age-appropriate behavior management skills. The importance of play with Katrina was highlighted with Rebecca in both psycho-educational sessions, as well as in weekly dyadic play sessions. This therapist used techniques such as "Speaking for Baby" (Carter *et al.*, 1991) to help Rebecca read Katrina's cues and emotions. (Speaking for Baby is a technique in which the therapist describes to a parent the baby's observed physical and emotional needs as if the baby was doing the talking.) Individual sessions with Rebecca were also used to give her the opportunity to explore her own emotions and reactions toward Katrina, and to further explore her own relationships with her mother and grandmother.

Initial Phase

Given Rebecca's medical circumstances, the first month of treatment did not focus on these attachment issues. Instead, it consisted of preparing Katrina for her mother's absence. The therapist used play to help explain in child-friendly terms to Katrina what to expect when her mother went into the hospital. Katrina's guardian in her mother's absence was Rebecca's grandmother. The grandmother was informed of the importance of keeping Katrina's school routine consistent and to maintain routine phone calls with Rebecca on a daily basis (due to the delicacy of the surgery, visitations were not allowed). In addition, Katrina was provided with transitional objects, photos, and drawings in order to help her with the separation.

After Rebecca returned home from the hospital, dyadic sessions were slow during the initial and middle stages of therapy (first eight months). Rebecca struggled greatly with providing emotional and physical comfort to Katrina and only seemed to understand criticism as a form of love. Although Rebecca was aware of how that criticism had hurt her growing up, she could not see that she was creating a similar relationship with her daughter. Rebecca interpreted her daughter's clinginess and lack of "obedience" as Katrina misbehaving "on purpose to bother me." Her play periods with Katrina were brief, as she at first could only handle five to ten minutes of play before she became uncomfortable, and then would talk to the therapist, usually to complain about Katrina's behaviors. This was very challenging as this therapist wanted to validate Rebecca's stress and concerns, but did not want to indulge her constant negative output on Katrina. When Rebecca was asked, "What has gone right today?" or to point out anything positive Katrina had done, Rebecca replied, "Nothing."

The therapist used Speaking for Baby to let Mom know when Katrina was seeking a hug or a comforting touch, which produced no response from Rebecca. This was usually during a time when Katrina's negative behaviors (e.g., whining, tantrum, sadness) were perceived by her mother as "bad behaviors" instead of understanding her needs (e.g., wanting assurance, love, or security, or expressing anxiety, fear, or anger). However, there were moments when Rebecca would briefly touch Katrina on the shoulder or hair. Typically, these were at times when both mother and child were in a good mood and were having a positive interaction. During such moments, this therapist reinforced to Rebecca the importance of communicating love, enjoyment, and security to Katrina.

Although selectively done in CPP, this therapist also carefully modeled certain behaviors, such as touch, for Mom. During individual sessions when Rebecca shared difficult memories or anger, this therapist would often briefly touch her shoulder or arm. These touches were accepted by Rebecca and sometimes she would begin to cry. She was never "cared for" in this manner by her caregivers and touch, therefore, become a powerful tool within the therapy. As time went on, the therapist continued to selectively initiate touch during moments of difficult emotions (e.g., anger, sadness, frustration, stress). In order to focus and anchor Rebecca in the therapy moment, this therapist would sometimes gently squeeze Rebecca's knees if playing on the floor, touch her shoulder, or pat her arm. This therapist also began doing the same thing with Katrina, in order to provide caring touch modeling for Rebecca, in addition to using Speaking for Baby to talk directly to Mom. This therapist used touch, play, and the acceptance of emotions without judgment to help Rebecca and Katrina feel safe in a caring atmosphere, and to help Rebecca see the benefits she would gain from developing that kind of relationship with her daughter.

Process Example of a Session during the First Eight Months

Rebecca came into a session frustrated and was ignoring and not talking to Katrina. This therapist noted, "You seem upset, Mom," but Rebecca failed to acknowledge any feelings and went on with her usual complaints about Katrina's "attitude," and indicated that she "cannot take it anymore." Katrina sat silently in the playroom with her head down and eyes watering. This therapist first held Mom's hands and reflected, "You do so much to help your family, and you have a weight on your shoulder. It must be so stressful, frustrating at times. Especially when no one can see all the hard work you do."

The therapist then gently squeezed her shoulder very briefly. Mom took a deep breath and stared at the therapist and then at Katrina. The therapist then used Speaking for Baby, "Mommy, I don't want you to be upset with me. I care about you." Katrina cried and looked at her Mom. The therapist continued, "Mommy, I need a hug. I want to make sure we are all okay." Rebecca did not respond. Katrina stared at Mom. Mom instead said, "Let's just play." The therapist then said to Katrina, "It looks like Mom is okay. She is ready and is okay with playing." Katrina accepted this interpretation and began to play with Mom. Rebecca was not ready to give of herself emotionally nor physically yet.

Therapy Progression after Eight Months

After eight months of treatment, some progress was observed by the therapist. During individual sessions, Rebecca accepted the "possibility" that just like she felt she couldn't do anything right and nothing was ever good enough to gain the love and acceptance she craved from her family, that "maybe" she understood why "Katrina might get that same idea from her great-grandma and sometimes me." During dyadic sessions, Rebecca's play with Katrina increased from 10 to 30 minutes per session. Rebecca was more frequently able to follow Katrina's lead, give affection during moments of "good behavior," and began to respond better to Katrina's cues and needs. However, this was still a great struggle for Rebecca.

Turning Point in Treatment

A pivotal moment in therapy occurred when Rebecca and Katrina were playing a game of catch, with made-up rules by Katrina. Rebecca struggled with following Katrina's rules and complained that they did not make sense. After hearing Mom's complaints, Katrina cried, dropped the ball, and began to tantrum. The therapist intervened at this point and first reflected Katrina's feelings by saying, "I'm so upset and sad because I really want to play my ball game with my rules." The therapist repeated different versions of the same phrase to validate Katrina's emotions, and also to help Rebecca understand why Katrina was so upset. She stopped her tantrum and crying and then stared at her mother.

This therapist then used Speaking for Baby and said, "Mommy, I really need a hug right now to feel that it is all okay, and that you are not mad at me." Rebecca was frozen, as giving physical affection—especially during what she considered a negative behavior—was very difficult for her. However, after a few seconds (which felt like an eternity to the therapist and probably to Katrina), she hugged Katrina, lightly rubbed her back, and then Katrina sat on her lap. Rebecca stopped the embrace, but allowed Katrina to sit on her lap and gently patted her hair. She looked at the therapist with trepidation, to which the therapist responded with a short nod and a brief smile. Rebecca then validated Katrina's feelings: "I know you were mad, but I just didn't understand the game. Let's try again." Katrina laughed and the game was resumed. Later Rebecca told the therapist with a smile, "You're good! It worked!"

Case Reflections

Hispanic Cultural Considerations Regarding Touch

It is a common understanding that Hispanics show affection primarily through touching (Schneider & Patterson, 2010). For example, in the Cuban culture (the same as the therapist's in this case example), greetings among friends and family members are done with kisses on the cheek and high use of affectionate touch. In raising children, it is taught and expected for children to be affectionate in their greetings with others. What stood out, therefore, in this case presentation, was that the family who were also from a Cuban background were observed to have limited touch and affection amongst each other. Early on in treatment, the therapist noticed the disconnection and lack of affectionate touch between the mother and her young child. Clinically speaking, the lack of the observed affection between them underscored some of the underlying attachment issues that Rebecca, the mother, and her young child were experiencing. At the same time, it highlighted the intergenerational familial patterns since Rebecca did not receive affection from her mother or grandmother growing up. In this case, disconnection in family dysfunctional dynamics, and perhaps the mother's special needs, overruled traditional familial cultural patterns regarding touch.

Therapist Challenges and Countertransference

This therapist [Castro] found this case to be very challenging. It was very difficult at times to be sympathetic or even to like Mom especially when she would withhold affection when Katrina needed it the most. At such times I desired to go to Katrina's rescue and meet her emotional and physical needs. However, it was recognizing these feelings of countertransference that helped this therapist gain more empathy for Rebecca. She seemed to benefit from the therapeutic alliance with me and I used the relationship as a springboard to help strengthen her relationship with Katrina.

Rebecca and Katrina participated in dyadic therapy for a period of two years. During this time, as Katrina matured, she developed a somewhat better understanding of her mother's health issues. She was aware when mother needed to go for hospital visits and the family had a consistent plan for preparing Katrina. Katrina and her mother were able to better label and express their own emotions through words and gestures. All of the above helped reduce Katrina's anxiety surrounding her mother's health and separations. Rebecca reported being more connected to Katrina as evidenced by her words and increase of physical affections. Although progress was made, Rebecca continued to struggle with dealing with negative emotions and being available to meet Katrina's emotional needs. It was easier for her to focus on the negative behaviors and get lost in them. However, she made constant efforts to gain insight, and it was apparent that she loved her daughter. She attended treatment on a consistent basis, even when she reported no improvements. Toward the end of treatment, Rebecca also agreed to seek her own individual therapy and psychiatric care to help her deal with her own depression and past traumas.

Conclusion

In working with infants, play and interpersonal touch are the medium that facilitates communication, fosters attachment, and strengthens bonds. Child Parent Psychotherapy facilitates dyadic family sessions where parents learn to strengthen their relationships with their infants and young children. In these sessions, playful engagement is free, spontaneous, and developmentally appropriate, and parents learn how to be attuned to their infants and young children's needs and emotions through the use of playful interactions and safe and nurturing touch.

Discussion Questions

1   Describe Child Parent Psychotherapy, its theoretical roots, and treatment modality.
2   What are the benefits of touch to the infant? To the caregiver?
3   In the case study highlighted in this chapter, discuss with a colleague why culture was important. Describe your experience of touch within your own family/culture. Does culture make a difference in how we interpret the interpersonal touch of others?

References

Ainsworth, M. (1967). *Infancy in Uganda: Infant care and the growth of love.* Baltimore, MD: Johns Hopkins University Press.

Barnett, L. (2005). Keep in touch: The importance of touch in infant development. *Infant Observation, 8(2),* 115–123. Retrieved on 13 November, 2016 from: http://www.tandfonline.com/doi/abs/10.1080/13698030500171530?journalCode=riob20

Bowlby, J. (1958). The nature of the child's tie to his mother. *International Journal of Psycho-Analysis, 39,* 350–373. Retrieved on 13 November, 2016 from: http://expert-nurse.com/yahoo_site_admin/assets/docs/The_Nature_of_the_Childs_Tie_to_His_Mother_-_John_Bowlby.123173702.pdf

Carter, S.L., Osofsky, J.D., Hann, D.M. (1991). Speaking for the baby: A therapeutic intervention with adolescent mothers and their infants. *Infant Mental Health Journal, 12(4),* 291–301. Retrieved on 14 November, 2016 from: http://www.mhfamilypsychology.com/docs/Speaking%20for%20the%20Baby%20(Sheena%20et%20al,%201991).pdf

Cohen, N., Muir, E., Parker, C., Brown, M., Lojkasek, M., Muir, R., & Barwick, M. (1999). Watch, wait, and wonder: Testing the effectiveness of a new approach to mother-infant psychotherapy. *Infant Mental Health Journal, 20(4),* 429–451. Retrieved 13 November, 2016 from: http://onlinelibrary.wiley.com/doi/10.1002/(SICI)1097-0355(199924)20:4%3C429::AID-IMHJ5%3E3.0.CO;2-Q/epdf

Duhn, L. (2010). The importance of touch in the development of attachment. *Advances in Neonatal Care, 10(6),* 294–300. DOI:10.1097/ANC.0b013e318fd2263

Feldman, R., Singer M., & Zagoory, O. (2010). Touch attenuates infants' physiological reactivity to stress. *Developmental Science, 13(2),* 271–278. DOI:10.1111/j.1467-7687.2009.00890.x

Field, T. (2002). Infants' need for touch. *Human Development, 45,* 100–103. DOI:10.1159/000048156

Field, T. (2010). Touch for socioemotional and physical well-being: A review. *Developmental Review, 30,* 367–383. Retrieved on 13 November, 2016 from: http://www.sciencedirect.com/science/article/pii/S0273229711000025

Field, T. (2014). *Touch* (2nd ed.). Cambridge, MA: MIT Press.

Fraiberg, S. (1977). *Every child's birthright: In defense of mothering.* New York: Basic Books.

Glover, V. (1997). Maternal stress or anxiety in pregnancy and emotional development of the child. *British Journal of Psychiatry, 171,* 105–106. Retrieved on 13 November, 2016 from: http://bjp.rcpsych.org/content/171/2/105

Harlow, H. (1958). The nature of love. *American Psychologist, 13,* 673–685. Retrieved on 13 November, 2016 from: http://psychclassics.yorku.ca/Harlow/love.htm

Heller, S. (1997). *The vital touch: How intimate contact with your baby leads to happier, healthier development.* New York: Henry Holt.

Hertenstein, M. (2002). Touch: Its communicative functions in infancy. *Human Development, 45(2),* 70–94. Retrieved on 13 November, 2016 from: http://citeseerx.ist.psu.edu/viewdoc/download?doi=10.1.1.484.2478&rep=rep1&type=pdf

Lieberman, A., & Van Horn, P. (2005). *Don't hit my mommy!: A manual for child-parent psychotherapy for young witnesses of family violence.* Washington, DC: Zero to Three Press.

Lieberman, A., & Van Horn, P. (2008). *Psychotherapy with infants and young children: Repairing the effects of stress and trauma on early attachment.* New York: Guilford Press.

Lieberman, A., Ghosh-Ippen, C., & Van Horn, P. (2006). Child-parent psychotherapy: Six-month follow-up of a randomized controlled trial. *Journal of the American Academy of Child and Adolescent Psychiatry, 45,* 913–918. DOI:10.1097/01.chi.0000222784.03735

McGregor J., & Casey J. (2012). Enhancing parent–infant bonding using kangaroo care: A structured review. *Evidence Based Midwifery, 10(2),* 50–56. Retrieved on 13 November, 2016 from: https://www.researchgate.net/publication/225309074_Enhancing_parent-infant_bonding_using_kangaroo_care_A_structured_review

Main, M., & Stadtman, J. (1981). Infant response to rejection of physical contact by the mother. *Journal of the American Academy of Child Psychiatry, 20,* 292–307. Retrieved on 13 November, 2016 from: http://dx.doi.org/10.1016/S0002-7138(09)60990-0

Neu, M. (1999). Parents' perception of skin-to-skin care with their pre-term infants requiring assisted ventilation. *Journal of Obstetric, Gynecologic, and Neonatal Nursing, 28(2),* 157–164. DOI:10.1111/j.1552-6909.1999.tb01980.x

O'Brien, M., & Lynch, H. (2011). Exploring the role of touch in the first year of life: Mothers' perspectives of tactile interactions with their infants. *British Journal of Occupational Therapy, 74(3),* 129–136. DOI:10.4276/030802211X12996065859247

Schneider, E.F., & Patterson, P.P. (2010, December). You've got that magic touch: Integrating the sense of touch into early childhood services. *Young Exceptional Children, 13(5),* 17–27. DOI:10.1177/1096250610384706

Takeuchi, M., Miyaoka, H., Tomoda, A., Suzuki, M., Liu Q., & Kitamura, T. (2010). The effect of interpersonal touch during childhood on adult attachment and depression: A neglected area of family and developmental psychology? *Journal of Child and Family Studies, 19,* 109–117. DOI:10.1007/s10826-009-9290-x

Tuters, E., Doulis, S., & Yabsley, S. (2011). Challenges working with infants and their families: Symptoms and meanings—Two approaches of infant-parent psychotherapy. *Infant Mental Health Journal, 32(6),* 632–649. DOI:10.1002/imhj.20323

Winnicott, D. W. (1960). The theory of the parent infant relationship. *International Journal of Psycho-Analysis, 41,* 585–595. Retrieved on 29 January, 2017 from: http://icpla.edu/wp-content/uploads/2012/10/Winnicott-D.-The-Theory-of-the-Parent-Infant-Relationship-IJPA-Vol.-41-pps.-585-595.pdf

Zur, O. (2015). *Ethical and legal aspects of touch in psychotherapy.* Retrieved on 13 November, 2016 from: http://www.zurinstitute.com/ethicsoftouch.html

13 The Utilization of Touch and StoryPlay® in Preschool Bereavement Groups

Amy Davis King and Danielle Woods

> Children can never get enough hugs and safe touching ... Touch can be one of the most powerful tools available to help a child learn to be safe and to trust life again.
>
> Helen Fitzgerald, *The Grieving Child*

Introduction

This chapter presents an eight-week bereavement support and psycho-educational group designed by author, Davis King to address the specific needs of preschoolers; and then authors Woods and Davis King facilitated the group together. The theoretical approaches used for the groups were based upon Worden's (2009) four tasks of grieving, and the StoryPlay® model (Mills, 2015). Worden's model, which is task oriented rather than linear, adapts very well to the needs of preschoolers. The ethical considerations of safe touch are highlighted in relationship to child-initiated touch with therapists, child-to-child touch, and child-with-caregiver touch. This group took place within the context of a larger organization that offers grief support for families.

Grief and Children

The tasks of grieving, as outlined by Worden (2009), remain the same no matter the age group. However, because young children grieve differently than adults, parents and professionals often do not know how to help them, thinking they are too young to understand, or question whether they even have the capacity to process grief (Crenshaw & Lee, 2010). We now know that if you are "old enough to love, you are old enough to mourn" (Wolfelt, 2013, last para.), and preschoolers, of course, consistently demonstrate their ability to attach and love. Young children tend to live in the present moment, and also have a shorter time frame for handling difficult emotions, so their reactions and comprehensions don't fit into the traditional framework of what processing grief means. They may express aggression and may not cry or appear sad. If they do express sadness, it may be for a very brief moment, and then they may shift the conversation by asking, "What can I play with now?" They also may not spend much time in processing memories of their loved one, or they may experience much of their memories in sensory, rather than verbal, ways. For example, children may rarely talk about their loved one, but may insist on hugging the loved one's shirt for comfort. For these reasons, a StoryPlay® perspective, with its play-based and indirect approach and a focus on sensory systems, proved helpful.

Worden's Four Tasks of Grieving

Worden (2009) described the four tasks of grieving as: (1) accepting the reality of the loss, (2) experiencing the pain of the grief, (3) adjusting to an environment in which the deceased is missing, and (4) relocating the deceased in one's life and moving on. These tasks were one of the guiding frameworks for the organization of the bereavement groups, and were adapted specifically for use with preschoolers. For young children who have little understanding of the permanency of death, the working through of these tasks is not quick, easy, or linear. A clinical question arises: "What *do* preschoolers bring to a group such as this?" They are often dealing with emotional and behavioral changes such as fear of abandonment, regression to an earlier stage of development, and expressions of anger (Fitzgerald, 2003; Silverman, 2000). They also have concrete and magical thinking, sometimes believing the power of their thoughts can cause bad things such as the death of the loved one.

StoryPlay®

The second guiding framework for the preschool bereavement groups was the resiliency-focused StoryPlay® model of play therapy developed by Joyce C. Mills, PhD. With the taproot being founded on the principles of Milton H. Erickson, StoryPlay® integrates the neural importance and key components of metaphor, story, and creativity, as well as transcultural healing philosophies and nature resources (Mills, 2011; Courtney & Mills, 2016). In StoryPlay®, utilizing what the client brings to the session is key. Lankton (2004) defined utilization as "making use of common understandings and behaviors that clients bring to the office so that these may be part of the motivation or reinforcements of therapy" (p. 107).

Children need to create a narrative for the healing process and, because of their immaturity, preschoolers have difficulty putting this narrative together (Lieberman & Van Horn, 2011). The right-brain involvement of metaphor, play, and story (Mills & Crowley, 2014) helps children embrace a narrative, which then helps them move through the tasks of their grief. The utilization of story is a natural vehicle for expression for children—in their worlds they are accustomed to hearing stories, seeing stories through their favorite shows or movies, and telling stories in their world of make-believe. The power of story in general can be interpersonal and intrapersonal, and is a cross-cultural medium of expression. Nafisi (2014) wrote,

> Stories are not mere flights of fantasy or instruments of political power and control. They link us to our past, provide us with critical insight into the present and enable us to envision our lives not just as they are, but as they should be or might become. Imaginative knowledge is not something you have today and discard. It is a way of perceiving the world and relating to it.
>
> (p. 3)

How fitting then, is the power of story and imaginative knowledge to assist preschoolers in their grieving process. They strive to remain linked to their precious memories of their loved ones, make sense of current confusing life changes and emotions, and move forward into a future that is not as it *should* be, but holds hope in what it might become.

The StoryPlay® model of therapy embraces and highly utilizes the power of story. Mills (2011) advocated, "Stories and metaphors convey a message and idea in an indirect yet paradoxically more meaningful way; bypassing resistance and opening the doorway to receptive communication" (p. 12). She further advised that an essential root of StoryPlay® is the "sharing of personal life experiences as a therapeutic medium through which a child can explore new ways of seeing obstacles, problems, and developing creative solutions" (p. 12). Within the context of a bereavement group, a StoryPlay® practitioner may utilize this power of story through storytelling metaphors. Artistic metaphors (specific drawing activities) or StoryCrafts (which are described later in this chapter) are also integrated.

Ethical Considerations of Touch in Grief and StoryPlay® Groups

Leading experts in the field of child bereavement often speak to the importance of touch as a healing tool. As Wolfelt (2001) so poignantly wrote, "Physical touch is one of humanity's most healing gifts" (p. 31). Whether to touch or not in therapy has a long history of ethical discussion (Aquino & Lee, 2000). As touch for the preschool developmental period is so important, one wonders if withholding appropriate touch is detrimental to the healing process. Courtney and Gray (2014) discussed the use of touch as a core principle in helping child clients in Developmental Play Therapy. McGuirk (2012) advised that touch as intimate process can bring about healing and also reduce stress. And according to van der Kolk (2014), "The most natural way that we humans calm down our stress is by being touched, hugged and rocked. This helps with excessive arousal and makes us feel intact, safe, protected, and in charge" (p. 217). Joyce Mills (March 17, 2016, personal communication), addressed the StoryPlay® philosophy on therapeutic attunement and wrote the following, "Touch is viewed as a responsive element to a client's individual needs in the moment. Additionally, neuroscience currently teaches us that the brain has the ability to change by the introduction of new experiences (Doidge, 2007; Siegel, 2012). Keeping in line with these concepts, a gentle touch of reassurance offered to a child who has known harshness or is dealing with physical pain from an illness can evoke new neural pathways of comfort."

Some authors argue that the prohibition of touch is more about protecting the therapist than providing the necessary tools for healing (Zur & Nordmarken, 2016). In their paper on touch, Aquino and Lee (2000) noted that child-initiated touch can be part of the therapeutic process for the child, and denial of a hug when one is asked can increase a child's stress. They also offered guidelines to make touch safe for the child and the practitioner, which included using a co-therapist, teaching boundaries, and informed consent. For the group model discussed in this chapter, using co-therapists and discussion with parents about the group process, including hugging, helped reduce concerns about touch.

Preschool Bereavement Group

Children in the groups were ages three to five years old, all of whom had had a family member die. Some of the deaths were expected due to illness, and some were unexpected due to an accident or purposeful injury. Caregivers ranged in age and gender from a newly widowed young mother to grandparents taking over care after the death. A group for the children and a group for the parents or caregivers each met separately over eight weeks, but gathered together for a closing ritual at the end of each session. The groups also met jointly in week six for a memento sharing experience, which will be detailed later.

Adult Group

The adult group's purpose was to offer support to bereaved caregivers and to help them understand the experience and needs of the preschool-aged grieving process. Helping adults use the word "died," along with preparing them for questions from their children, was part of the adult group process. The group therapy philosophy modeled cultural acceptance of different beliefs about what happens after death, which gave family members permission to grieve in their own way.

Children's Group

The children's group began with a talking circle experience, with children sharing energetic touch with each other as well as with group facilitators, as they were seated close together in a circle on the floor. The circle thus becomes a living metaphor of the concept of entering the child's world. Facilitators sat on the floor amongst the children, not *above* them in a chair, thus demonstrating "to be conscious of the *circle of children*" (Berryman, 1995, p. 33). Each group session children's group, Suzie said that she remembered her older sibling being angry with her brother, who was ill. She stated, "My big sister hit my little brother and then he went away and died." Suzie was able to share this same perception of the death during the memento sharing exercise, and the grandmother lovingly embraced her as Suzie sat on her lap. This had a profound impact on the grandparents' understanding of her grief and how they related to her.

This case example demonstrated the importance of StoryPlay® theoretical concepts:

- *Utilization:* Following the power of the memento sharing session, Suzie's grandparents were able to utilize her understanding of her sibling's death to shift how they related to her.
- *Limbic Attunement:* It was the power of Suzie's heart-felt sharing of her memento, and the eye contact she made with her grandparents while sharing, that helped the grandparents accept that the child had a different understanding of the death than they did.
- *Healing Power of Touch:* Suzie was able to feel emotionally safe to share her memento and understanding of the death by feeling her grandparents' supportive, energetic, and warm physical touch.

Case of John

John's brother died in a car accident while his mother was driving, and the father was outside of the car and observed the accident. John was also in the car, but was unharmed. The child who died was rushed to the hospital following the accident with the rest of the family. The family spent a good deal of time waiting at the hospital and ultimately the brother died. The parents were, of course, very traumatized by this experience. They expressed concern to their adult group leader that John would develop a fear of hospitals, doctors, and such like. During the memento sharing session, John sat on his mom's lap and shared his perception of that time at the hospital. He remembered it as the place where they "gave him a hamburger," and therefore did not associate the hospital as a trauma trigger. The memento he chose, his brother's baseball team shirt, displayed to his parents that he remained connected to his brother in remembering him and the connection they had before the accident. Following the conclusion of the group, the authors heard from the family that they were expecting another child. Since the memento sharing session had helped the parents understand that John was not afraid of doctors and hospitals, they invited John to attend some of the prenatal doctor appointments.

This case example demonstrated the following key concepts:

- *Developmental Stages:* the parents were able to accept John's developmental understanding and perception of the events surrounding the accident.

Figure 13.1 Nature representations of "Dead" (left) and "Alive" (right) are shown in this collage. (Photo used with permission from Amy Davis King.)

- **Limbic Attunement:** It was only after the parents gained a deeper understanding and a felt-sense of John's experience, which occurred during the memento sharing, that the parents were able to shift their perception. This paved the way for them to share new, affirming emotional experiences as a family, such as attending the mother's prenatal appointments together.
- **Healing Power of Touch:** John felt emotionally safe as he was held in his mother's arms and shared his feelings.

StoryCrafts

Creating StoryCrafts with children is another way to expand the storytelling metaphor into physical form through artistic expression. These creative activities inspire healing, motivation, self-empowerment, positive problem-solving skills, and a reconnection to an inner core of resilience. StoryCrafts differ from art therapy activities in that they are always connected to a therapeutic metaphorical story (Mills, 2015). For these young group members, stories offered a metaphor, in the safe and familiar form of a story, to begin to understand death, what being dead and gone means, and that the dead person is not coming back. A different craft or activity was offered during each weekly session following the circle time. Any craft or directed activity was offered in the spirit of the Ericksonian principles of utilization and entering the children's world—and they were free to choose their level of participation.

The "Dead and Alive Collage" StoryCraft was offered during a group session (Figure 13.1).

Dead and Alive Collage

Rationale for Craft

Preschool children often have difficulty cognitively understanding the concept of dead and alive, and especially, the permanency of death.

Step One: The book *Lifetimes* (Mellonie, 1983) was read during circle time.

Step Two: The children were then invited to a safe outside environment to collect items from nature, which were *dead* or *alive* (dead leaf, rock, dried seed pod, a live leaf, or flower).

Step Three: Once the items were collected, the children were given poster paper and glue to create a collage of these items, grouped according to dead or alive.

Step Four: Children shared their creation with other group members, facilitators, or caregivers at the end of the session. Sharing helped them connect to a new understanding of death.

Step Five: Children could take home their craft to strengthen the concepts of dead and alive.

Non-Directive Group Play Therapy

Following the activity, the group moved to an open play period. As in a child-centered play therapy room, toys were offered in different categories. This allowed children opportunities to choose and work through different emotional themes through the availability of nurturing, make-believe, and creative toys, among other items. During open play, children often made use of touch in a nurturing way with each other—playing house, giving a hug, or pretending to tuck someone into bed. If the children were working through power, control, or anger themes, such as using the bop bag, facilitators worked one-on-one with the child to carefully monitor the activity for safety, making sure no negative touch was directed toward other children. The therapist's monitoring for safety is consistent with the Association for Play Therapy's guidelines regarding touch in play therapy groups (APT, 2015, p. 3).

Closing "Hand-Hug" Ceremony

All weekly group sessions closed with coming together of children and adults in a circle. A candle was lit and all held hands and sang a song. At this time, we also passed a hand-hug around the circle. A child was invited to start the hug, and would gently squeeze the hand of the person on his or her right, who squeezed the hand of the next person, and so on, until the hug came full circle. "Passing the hug" is a gentle, but intentional use of interpersonal touch to facilitate a positive closing experience of connection each week. Some adults took the opportunity to get hugs from others or hug their children when the song ended.

Summary

From the standpoint of Ericksonian utilization (Lankton, 2004), the StoryPlay® model (Mills, 2015), and the developmental needs of preschoolers, touch, as described, met the needs of these young children in ways that facilitated moving forward in their tasks of grieving (Worden, 2009). Supporting touch interactions—child-initiated with therapists, child-to-child, child with caregiver, and caregivers with each other—helped children, caregivers, and therapists to create a nurturing healing environment. As highlighted in this chapter, ethical guidelines were set in place to ensure touch was used in safe and approriate ways.

Discussion Questions and Exercise

1 Reflecting on Worden's four tasks of mourning, discuss the potential impediments to successfully navigating these tasks of grieving for preschool and younger children.
2 How would you embrace the Ericksonian and StoryPlay® concept of utilization with these young group members, especially in regards to the varied dynamics of touch in group sessions?
3 With your colleagues, role play a children's bereavement group memento sharing exercise. Choose two facilitators and four others to play preschool-aged children. Using an available object, have each "child" share about their object. Practice the group experiential two ways: First by sharing the memento *without* touch, and then sharing again *with* touch (such as a hand hold) as offered by the designated "facilitator." Process experiences.

References

Aquino, A.T., & Lee, S.S. (2000). The use of nonerotic touch with children: Ethical and developmental considerations. *Journal of Psychotherapy in Independent Practice, 1(3)*, 17–30. DOI:10.1300/J288v01n03_02
Association for Play Therapy. (2015). *Paper on touch: Clinical, professional, and ethical issues*. Retrieved on 15 January, 2016 from: http://c.ymcdn.com/sites/www.a4pt.org/resource/resmgr/Publications/Paper_On_Touch_2015.pdf
Berryman, J. (1995). *Teaching godly play: The Sunday morning handbook*. Nashville, TN: Abingdon Press.
Courtney, J.A., & Gray, S. (2014). A phenomenological inquiry into practitioner experiences of developmental play therapy: Implications for training in touch. *International Journal of Play Therapy, 23(2)*, 114–129. DOI:10.1037/a0036366

Courtney, J.A., & Mills, J. C. (2016). Utilizing the metaphor of nature as co-therapist in StoryPlay®. *Play Therapy*, *11(1)*, 18–21.

Crenshaw, D.A., & Lee, J. (2010). Disenfranchised grief of children. In N.B Webb (Ed.), *Helping bereaved children: A handbook for practitioners* (4th ed., pp. 91–106). New York: Guilford Press.

Doidge, N. (2007). *The brain that changes itself.* New York: Penguin Books.

First People of North America and Canada—Turtle Island. (n.d.). Retrieved on 14 November, 2016 from: www.firstpeople.us

Fitzgerald, H. (2003). *The grieving child: A parent's guide* (Fireside ed.). New York: Simon & Schuster.

Gilligan, S. (2012). *Generative trance: The experience of creative flow.* Bancyfelin, UK: Crown House.

Lankton, S. (2004). *Assembling Ericksonian therapy: The collected papers of Stephen Lankton.* Phoenix, AZ: Zeig, Tucker, & Theisen.

Lieberman, A., & Van Horn, P. (2011) *Psychotherapy with infants and young children: Repairing the effects of stress and trauma on early attachment.* New York: Guilford Press.

McGuirk J. (2012). *The place of touch in counseling and psychotherapy and the potential for healing within the therapeutic relationship.* Irish Association for Humanistic and Integrative Psychology. Retrieved on 8 December, 2015 from: http://iahip.org/inside-out/issue-68-autumn-2012/the-place-of-touch-in-counselling-and-psychotherapy-and-the-potential-for-healing-within-the-therapeutic-relationship

Mellonie, B. (1983) *Lifetimes, the beautiful way to explain death to children.* New York: Bantam Books.

Mills, J.C. (2011). *StoryPlay® foundations training manual.* Phoenix, AZ: Imaginal Press.

Mills, J.C. (2015). *StoryPlay®: A narrative play therapy approach.* In D.A. Crenshaw & A.L. Stewart (Eds.), *Play therapy: A comprehensive guide to theory and practice* (pp. 171–185). New York: Guilford Press.

Mills, J.C., & Crowley, R.J. (2014). *Therapeutic metaphors for children and the child within* (2nd ed.). New York: Routledge.

Nafisi, A. (2014). *The republic of imagination: America in three books.* New York: Viking Press.

Siegel, D.J. (2012). *The developing mind* (2nd ed.). New York: Guilford Press.

Silverman, P. (2000). *Never too young to know: Death in children's lives.* New York: Oxford University Press.

van der Kolk, B. (2014). *The body keeps the score: Brain, mind and body in the healing of trauma.* New York: Penguin Books.

Wolfelt, A. (2001). *Healing a grieving child's heart.* Ft. Collins, CO: Companion Press.

Wolfelt, A. (2013). *Helping infants and toddlers when someone dies.* Retrieved on 8 December, 2015 from: http://griefwords.com

Worden, J. (2009). *Grief counseling and grief therapy: A handbook for the mental health practitioner* (4th ed.). New York: Springer Publishing Company.

Zur, O., & Nordmarken, N. (2016). *To touch or not to touch: Rethinking the prohibition on touch in psychotherapy and counseling.* Retrieved on 8 December, 2015 from: http://www.zurinstitute.com/touchintherapy.html

14 The Ethics of Touch with Canines as Co-Therapist with Children

Bonnie Martin and Janus Moncur

When an eighty-five-pound mammal licks your tears away, then tries to sit on your lap, it's hard to feel sad.

Kristan Higgins, *In Your Dreams*

Introduction

A little-known fact: Sigmund Freud had his own therapy dog, a chow chow named Jofi, who hung around the office during therapy sessions. Freud came to the conclusion that the dog had a relaxing effect on himself and his patients (Fine, 2010; Wilkes, 2009). In the 1960s, Boris Levinson championed the use of Animal Assisted Therapy (AAT) in a therapeutic setting as a therapy technique long before his colleagues and the industry accepted the practice (Fine, 2010; Wilkes, 2009). Today, the most well-known use of trained therapy animals is found in settings including hospitals, nursing homes, hospice care, geriatric centers, schools, psychiatric hospitals, and rehabilitation and veterans' centers. This activity is considered Animal Assisted Activities (AAA), which typically consists of visitations and *non-goal* driven activities (Chandler, 2012; Chandler et al., 2010; Delta Society, 2004; Fine, 2010). AAT, on the other hand, is a *goal-directed* intervention in which the animal often takes on the role of a co-therapist that can be paired with most other therapeutic interventions that the therapist already practices (Fine, 2010). Additionally, according to Chandler (2012): "The therapist's orchestrated interactions between the client and the therapy animal ... are a vital component to the success of therapy" (p. 166).

When AAT is combined with play therapy, it is labeled as Animal Assisted Play Therapy™ (AAPT™) (VanFleet & Faa-Thompson, 2015), and play therapy used specifically with canines was labeled by VanFleet and Coltea (2012) as Canine Assisted Play Therapy (CAPT). Risë VanFleet is noted as the leading expert and researcher in AAPT™ (Crenshaw, 2012), and she offers a comprehensive certification program that prepares play therapists to utilize animals therapeutically in their work with children (refer to playfulpooch.org). VanFleet (2008) defined AAPT™ as the utilization of animals in play therapy, "in which appropriately trained therapists and animals engage with children and families primarily through systematic play interventions, with the goal of improving children's developmental and psychosocial health as well as the animal's well-being" (p. 19).

Positive Benefits of AAT and Touch with Canines

It has long been shown that the therapeutic benefits of animal–human interaction included social memory, attachment, positive maternal behavior, reflection, unconditional positive regard, authenticity, empathy, acceptance, relaxation, slowed heart rate, and decreased aggressive behavior (Chandler *et al.*, 2010; Crenshaw, 2012; Fine, 2010; Parish-Plass, 2008; van de Kolk, 2014; VanFleet, 2008; VanFleet & Coltea, 2012). At times, during a session, clients may greatly benefit from appropriate nurturing physical contact and therapy dogs can work as a surrogate to provide therapeutic touch. It is common for children, in particular, to cling to a stuffed animal for comfort. As Chandler (2012) pointed out, the advantage of a canine co-therapist over a stuffed toy is that "the animal responds in kind with affectionate behaviors that reinforce the therapeutic benefits of the touch" (p. 168).

A key component in the positive benefits from AAT is the release of the "feel good" hormone, oxytocin (OT), (Beetz *et al.*, 2012; Fine, 2010; Handlin *et al.*, 2011; Miller *et al.*, 2009; Odendaal & Meintjes, 2003). Interaction with dogs significantly increased oxytocin levels, as well as other hormones including dopamine (Odendaal & Meintjes, 2003; VanFleet & Coltea, 2012). Beetz *et al.* (2012) wrote that oxytocin is released in response to eye contact and also "via pleasant tactile interactions which seem to play a major role for the OT-mediated decrease of stress levels. OT effects may be triggered in response to single meetings with animals" (p. 12). Interactions with dogs increased the oxytocin levels particularly for women and lowered the stress hormone cortisol, more so than other stress reducing interventions, such as reading. This reaction may be due to the maternal inclinations of women (Beetz *et al.*, 2012; Fine, 2010; Miller *et al.*, 2009).

Canines and the Therapeutic Alliance

Therapists are taught to provide a non-judgmental and accepting stance. A child-client's experience with adults may have been hurtful, hopeless, and dangerous. For these children, getting emotionally or physically close to another human often triggers fear of harm and resistance to the therapeutic alliance. Play with a canine co-therapist can break down those barriers and facilitate the therapeutic relationship. Van der Kolk (2014) wrote, "In the past two decades it has become widely recognized that when adults or children are too skittish or shut down to derive comfort from human beings, relationships with other mammals can help" (p. 80). Thus, for some children, the only positive, comforting, and dependable relationship they might have ever experienced was with their pets (Wilkes, 2009).

The perception of a canine co-therapist as also a pet member of a loving family, sets the therapeutic stage of familiar intimacy which could generate a quicker therapeutic alliance and increased frequency of positive touch interactions between child and canine in the play therapy setting (Martin, 2012). When a dog is present, clients often view the therapist as friendly, safe, and secure (VanFleet, 2008). Adding the assistance of a trained therapy dog that has the "right temperament" (VanFleet & Faa-Thompson, 2015, p. 204) can help to gain the trust and attention of children, thus allowing children to feel more comfortable when sharing and developing new skills.

Ethics of Touch in Therapy with Canines

The inclusion of a canine in therapy provides unique opportunities for touch interactions to occur encompassing child-initiated touch to the canine *and* canine-initiated touch to the child, thus broadening the potential for ethical issues to emerge. Therapists may need assistance when applying ethics to specific cases and resolving any ethical problems that may arise in AAT. It is important for the therapist to remember that even the most loving, trained dog is still an animal. The therapist's first ethical obligation is to keep the client safe. This obligation extends to include the safety of the canines too. With this in mind, the ethical guidelines listed below are summarized and adapted from the following sources (APT, 2015; Delta Society, 2004; Lawrence & Kurpius, 2000; Seymour & Rubin, 2006; VanFleet, 2008; VanFleet & Faa-Thompson, 2015; Webb, 2011), and can assist the therapist with ethical decision making involving touch with children and canines.

- Therapists need training in a recognized animal assisted therapy program that addresses the ethical considerations of touch between children and canines.
- The canine co-therapist also needs extensive training specifically with children. VanFleet and Faa-Thompson (2015, p. 205) highlighted that "The dog must also be trained to a significant degree, learning many skills and cues that can be used creatively by children."
- Therapists should include an informed consent that specifies the inclusion of canines in therapy and addresses the therapeutic variable of touch between the child and canine.
- The child and parent need to be educated on the appropriate interactions of touch between the child and canine. The child specifically is taught how to pick up on the cues of the canine, and the therapist is trained to monitor all interactions.
- The therapist takes responsibility for prevention and handling of acts of aggression—either by the child to the dog, or the dog to the child.
- The child's history and any trauma related to touch must be assessed.
- Therapists need to be sensitive to the cultural views of clients about animals. For example, Webb (2011) advised that most Jamaicans believe that animals should be kept outdoors and "do not consider them as 'indoor pets'," and that "many Muslims consider dogs to be unclean" (p. 349).

- Therapists need to be aware of any countertransferences (VanFleet & Faa-Thompson, 2015) related to touch that may emerge during canine-assisted sessions.
- Therapists must document any significant incidents involving touch during the sessions, as well as undertake consultation from peers and legal counsel regarding any ethical issues.
- Malpractice insurance that includes the canine's involvement must be secured.

Ethics, Touch, and Safety between Children and Canines

A therapeutic relationship cannot happen when the client feels unsafe. Whether from a negative experience with a pet or from the child's perception of potential harm, the animal's presence may produce a fear response in the child. One example would be a child who experiences sensory processing problems, such as a sensitivity to noise (i.e., dog bark), tactile sensations (i.e., dog drool or fur), or odors. Therefore, certain precautions need to be implemented to avoid any potential ethical dilemmas and to provide and facilitate a corrective experience environment for the client. This can occur through proper intake procedures and assessment, and discussions with the parents and child about the inclusion of the canine in sessions. This will establish a baseline for the gradual inclusion of the canine that is based upon the child's comfort level. Additionally, for a child who has been known to hurt animals, ethical touch in play with canines can be taught and monitored by the therapist in sessions. This process may facilitate open discussions related to setting boundaries and respect of pets and people at home. Aggressive or sexual touch by any party in therapy sessions is always unethical.

It is also important to know how the animal responds to touch and to protect the well-being of the canine by setting limits to inappropriate touch initiated by a child. The therapist must be educated to read and understand the sometimes subtle body language and various stress indicators and know the canine's typical fear reactions (VanFleet & Faa-Thompson, 2015). Neck hugging, directly staring into the canine's eyes, and approaching a canine directly head-on could be interpreted as aggressive acts to a canine. Many signals, such as lip licking and tail wagging, may indicate very different emotions or moods for the canine depending on the situation. For example, in the canine, lip licking can indicate hunger, stress, discomfort, or be a calming signal (Rugaas, 2006).

Ethical treatment ensures that the therapist uses this knowledge to set boundaries prior to an incident and ensures safe touch in the therapy room for all participants. For instance, the child-client may choose the stethoscope as a play prop and want to initiate an "inspection" of the therapy dog's body, including the genital area. The play therapist intervenes by setting a limit and advising that "This is the dog's private body part," and then gives an alternative by stating, "Let's choose another area to check out. What do you think?"

Ethical Touch with Canines When Using Non-Directive Play Therapy

The therapist's professional ethics requires that the clinician choose a treatment that is effective and appropriate to meet the client's treatment goals. In doing so, the play therapist may implement play therapy techniques from a directive or non-directive approach (Landreth, 2012; VanFleet & Coltea, 2012; VanFleet & Faa-Thompson, 2015). Likewise, the canine co-therapist, in therapeutic play, may take an active or passive role. Non-directive methods involve allowing the child to take the lead and to interact naturally with the canine. The client may want to speak to the canine from afar, to play separately from the canine, or to make the canine an active participant in role play (i.e., dress him up as a character, "doctor" him, etc.). The pretense is that the child intuitively knows what is needed to establish emotional healing through self-directed play. Research conducted by Thompson, Mustaine, and Weaver in 2008, is cited in Thompson (2009) as the first known controlled study about non-directive play therapy with dogs. Thompson (2009) highlighted the study outcomes:

> In the presence of the dog, children in the study showed an improvement in mood and affect, an increased ability to engage in thematic play, and more readily established rapport. They also exhibited a decrease in aggressive behavior and play disruptions. Another interesting finding was when children with PTSD disclosed their abuse for the first time, it was always in the presence of the therapy dog.
>
> (p. 207)

The therapist also needs to teach the child how to pick up on the cues of the canine co-therapist. By sitting on the floor next to the canine co-therapist, the clinician can monitor for safety and reflect attuned touch interactions. For example, if the play therapist observes the canine turning away from the child when touched, the therapist may make statements such as, "Noodle [the therapy dog] is saying he doesn't like his eyes covered. Noodle likes when you rub behind his ears best. Here let me show you." The touch is safe, ethical, and monitored.

The duty to maximize the individual's rights to make his or her own decisions is an ethical concern in all types of mental health treatment. Mastery and autonomy in an indirect play therapy animal-assisted session allows the child ample freedom, within limits of safety, to explore and experience his or her world. This can be provided by allowing the child to have control over a situation through choices: for example, to touch (petting) the canine or not, to approach or avoid, to initiate a trick, or to allow the animal a nap. The following is a vignette of autonomy and touch with a canine co-therapist. (Note, all identifying information in all the vignettes presented in this chapter has been changed to protect confidentiality.)

Vignette A: Case of Sally

> A 5-year-old girl, Sally, tried to dress Noodle into a pair of dog pajamas. However, she puts Noodle's back legs in first and finds that the front legs won't bend in the direction she needs to finish the job. The clinician monitored Noodle's stress level and gave positive feedback both to him and to the client: "Noodle, you are being very patient. And, Sally, you are working hard to find out how Noodle's pajamas can fit him." Sally subsequently took Noodle's hind legs out of the pajamas and started from the front where she found success in being able to dress him completely. Sally smiled broadly and stated, "There!" Her feeling of mastery and empowerment were apparent and tangible. The touch was necessary for the activity and demonstrated the ethics of client autonomy.

Ethical Touch with Canines When Using Directive Play Therapy

In directive play therapy with canines, the therapist chooses goal-directed activities for the client's play that can "facilitate the clients' work toward particular therapeutic goals" (VanFleet & Faa-Thompson, 2015, p. 209). Touch can occur in numerous directive activities such as reading books, playing games, doing tricks, rewarding behavior change, identifying social skills, and modeling emotional regulation. The following vignette process recording is an example of a therapist's directive verbalization during a play session:

Vignette B: Case of Cara

> **Case Background**: A 4-year-old girl, Cara, came to therapy due to "fussing about bedtime." The treatment goals were emotional regulation and improved bedtime compliance. During the second session, the therapist sat with her and the canine co-therapist to explore the nighttime problem and to read a book about bedtimes that the therapist chose. Prior to reading the book, Cara was petting the canine co-therapist (Noodle) as they sat together on the floor. The following is an excerpt of the encounter.
>
> THERAPIST: "How does it feel when you pet him?"
> CARA: "Soft. He likes me."
> THERAPIST: "Yes, he likes that you are feeling calm and petting him softly. Do you know what a calm feeling is?"
> CARA: "Quiet."
> THERAPIST: "Yes. You know that calm is a quiet feeling. How do you think Noodle is feeling?"
> CARA: "Quiet."
> THERAPIST: "Yes he feels quiet. You can put your hand right here [on dog's side] and feel how calm he is." (Cara puts a hand on Noodle's side).

"You are feeling calm, and Noodle feels calm. How do you feel when it's time to go to bed?"
CARA: "I don't like to go to bed."
THERAPIST: "Oh, you don't want to go to bed. You feel angry about going to bed. That is the fussy and angry feeling, not the calm or quiet feeling. Noodle doesn't want to go to bed sometimes. He wants to play. Sometimes I have to tell him it is time for bed so that he gets a good sleep and doesn't get sick. Would you like to see how Noodle goes to bed?" (Cara nods her head "yes.")
THERAPIST: "Okay. Noodle, it is time for bed. Go to bed." (Noodle goes to his dog bed arranged in the playroom and lies down.) "Would you like to pet Noodle one more time and tell him he did a good job going to bed?"
CARA: (Cara nods and pets Noodle and he licks her on the arm. She smiles and looks at the therapist.)
THERAPIST: "He's feeling calm and likes you. Do you think you could go to bed at night and be calm?" (Cara nods.) You know how to go to bed quietly, without a fuss, and stay calm just like Noodle. Noodle can play tomorrow, and you can play after your bedtime. Now let's read this special book I picked out for you."

The mother reported that Cara was successful six days out of seven when going to bed the next week. The ethical use of canine-assisted touch was highlighted when the child petted Noodle and also when he licked her arm. The touch anchored the demonstration of positive bedtime behavior.

Ethics of Touch with Traumatized Children

Other ethical concerns regarding touch may also arise with the traumatized client. The attachment relationship and therapeutic alliance are often a slow process for traumatized children who often find it difficult to trust or connect with human beings. Consequently, they may be resistant to the therapist's attempts to establish trust and rapport. However, they are often willing to develop a relationship with other mammals, namely dogs and horses (van der Kolk, 2014).

The canine co-therapist can assist in overcoming the challenge of mistrust and resistance and can act as a bridge to facilitate the therapeutic relationship between therapist and child. At the same time, the child's emotional health and self-regulation can improve through the sensory experience of touch.

Much like the sucking of a thumb or the rubbing of a favorite stuffed animal's ears, when the child pets the therapy-canine the stroking rhythm can help anchor him or her and soothe distress. The rhythmic touch of petting or grooming the canine co-therapist can help a child decrease anxiety so that the stress response is not triggered during the process of recovery (Chandler, 2012). However, touch during play therapy sessions with canines can trigger trauma-related hurtful memories and feelings. This can happen when children externalize their trauma onto the canine co-therapist. Goodyear-Brown (2010) indicated that play props help children have a tangible vehicle to externalize their trauma experience. One form of communicating their inner trauma state is when children use a toy as a perpetrator symbol (e.g., a snake, a two-headed monster, etc.). Like toys, the canine co-therapist could also represent a perpetrator symbol which can trigger a repressed trauma memory.

The following vignette demonstrates this point in work with a child client, Ben, where the disclosure of sexual abuse was revealed through the relationship developed with the canine.

Vignette C: Case of Ben

> *Six-year-old Ben was referred to therapy due to symptoms of tantrums, attention problems, somatic complaints, and sensory problems. During the initial assessment, Ben's mother stated that her son had never been an abuse victim. Ben developed a quick rapport with Noodle, the canine co-therapist, and by the third session he chose to draw a picture of himself and Noodle together. The therapist was concerned when viewing the drawing because it appeared that Noodle was being depicted as a possible sexual perpetrator, yet very much loved (see Figure 14.1 and note the heart above Noodle's head in the drawing).*
>
> *When finished with the drawing, Ben took a long look at the picture and said, "Noodle's licking me." Ben added that he was feeling "tickled" in the picture. His affect became more subdued, and he asked if we could brush Noodle's hair. Ben and the therapist sat with Noodle and he brushed the dog in silence. At the end of the grooming, Ben shared that the picture was "like what happened with my dad." Ben then disclosed being sexually abused by his father, and that as part of the sexual abuse ritual his father would finish the abuse by stroking his hair. The therapist then took the appropriate actions and steps to report the abuse, and Noodle continued to play a central role in the healing process in therapy with Ben.*
>
> *In the drawing (Figure 14.1), Noodle became an externalized, safe symbol for the perpetrator in the child's trauma experience. The picture revealed a beloved image of Noodle ("father") who victimized him, and yet one the child cared enough for that he would groom the perpetrator in the end. This vignette example speaks volumes about the synergy of the ethical use of touch in play therapy with canines.*

Systematic Desensitization as Adapted to Canine-Assisted Therapy

A systematic desensitization approach includes gradual exposure, regulation of emotion, and shaping behavior that may assist the client with fear abatement (Garber, 2015). As in the case vignette described below, systematic desensitization may be helpful with some traumatized clients as a means to facilitate safe

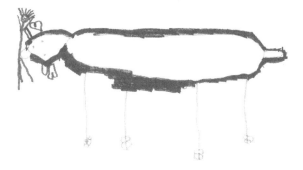

Figure 14.1 Noodle depicted as sexual predator yet very much loved. (Drawing used with permission.)

and appropriate human–animal therapeutic touch. Systematic desensitization is first introduced by teaching clients some relaxation techniques (Garber, 2015). Next, the relaxation techniques are combined with imagined situations that include the feared object (in this case a canine)—all of which is sensitively guided by the therapist.

When the client is ready, the next step involves viewing pictures of the feared subject (canines). Eventually, through the guidance of the therapist, the client will use the learned relaxation techniques in actual exposure to the feared object (in this case with a trained canine co-therapist). Once touch is initiated, the canine co-therapist, as facilitated by the therapist, can gain a relationship with the client that may break down barriers to establish healthy emotional expression. The safe sensory experience of touch with a canine can encourage new emotional and cognitive healing.

Vignette D: Case of Julie

> *The following vignette demonstrates canine-assisted therapy with a 15-year-old traumatized female, Julie, receiving inpatient treatment for substance abuse. During a therapy session, she disclosed to her clinician early childhood sexual abuse that had been perpetrated by a close family member through the use of the family dog. This trauma resulted in Julie developing an intense fear and dislike of dogs. The clinician then worked with Julie utilizing a systematic desensitization intervention and taught Julie relaxation techniques to utilize when the fear of dogs arose. Additionally, with Julie's consent, the clinician contacted a reputable canine-assisted therapy organization for further help. Several pictures of therapy-canines were sent to the clinician for Julie to view and choose a therapy dog to meet. She selected a pair of Pomeranian therapy dogs because she liked their non-threatening "teddy-bear" appearance.*

The following account describes a brief highlight of the systematic desensitization process with the Pomeranian therapy canines, Mack and Jack (see Figure 14.2), and the certified AAT therapist (also a licensed clinical social worker) who was assigned to assist in this case:

> *The smaller, more sensitive dog, Mack, and the AAT therapist first met Julie outdoors at a park so Julie would not feel trapped, and that provided her with a sense of safety. Julie's clinician accompanied her to this first session. The AAT therapist and Mack sat at a distance from Julie, so Julie could advance at her own pace. Julie was able to sit near Mack and the AAT therapist while Mack was held with his back to Julie. However, she did not initiate touch or eye contact with Mack during this first meeting.*
>
> *During the second meeting with Mack, the AAT therapist and Julie met together indoors in a large open area of the treatment center, which felt safe to Julie. At this time, Julie reached out to touch Mack's back and began to pet him; she stated, "He is so soft." After the initial contact of touch was accomplished by Julie, future sessions progressed to include the second canine co-therapist, Jack. The AAT therapist observed a tender moment when Mack sat at Julie's feet and they quietly gazed at*

Figure 14.2 Therapy canines Jack and Mack. (Photo used with permission from Margaret Malinowski.)

each other. Over time, Julie would ask to meet with "the boys" (as she liked to call them) rather than attend fun activities with her peers. This behavior indicated the success and termination point of the AAT. After these sessions, Julie was able to face her fears and reportedly became strong enough to face her abuser in a court of law.

Summary

Children and animals naturally know how to play. In play therapy with canines, child clients can develop trust and rapport with the canine co-therapist. Therapeutic touch with canines in play therapy becomes a tool for emotional healing, as well as presenting unique ethical challenges related to touch. Therefore, AAT therapists have an ethical duty to prioritize the physical and emotional safety of their child-clients and of their animal partners. This chapter also demonstrated how a systematic desensitization approach with therapy canines can be successfully implemented. Additionally, as deemed therapeutically appropriate, practitioners can contact organizations to inquire about certified therapy canines and therapists who might assist in the therapy process (such as the case example with therapy canines Mack and Jack). Canines can be trained and vetted through the certification process of Pet Partners (formerly Delta Society, refer to Petpartners.org), Therapy Dogs International (TDI), or Canine-Assisted Therapy, Inc. (CAT), among others.

Discussion Questions

1. Conduct an Internet search to locate where one can discover more information about AAA, AAT, AAPT™, CAPT and other sources that therapeutically use animals. Next, search for programs that specifically offer training certifications for canines (TDI, CAT, Pet Partners, etc.). Compare and contrast the different programs for all searches.
2. What are some of the ethical issues that therapists must consider when working with a canine co-therapist: For the therapist? For the child-client? For parents? For the canine co-therapist?
3. With a partner, discuss the following questions: How do interactions with canines benefit humans? Why do humans sometimes trust canines more than people? Tell a story about a personal interaction that you have had with a canine (or another animal, a horse, cat, etc.).

References

Association for Play Therapy (APT). (2015). *Paper on touch: Clinical, professional, and ethical issues*. Retrieved on 29 November, 2015 from: http://c.ymcdn.com/sites/www.a4pt.org/resource/resmgr/Publications/Paper_On_Touch_2015.pdf

Beetz, A., Uvnäs-Moberg, K., Julius, H., & Kotrschal, K. (2012). Psychosocial and psychophysiological effects of human-animal interactions: The possible role of oxytocin. *Frontiers in Psychology, 3(234)*, 1–13. DOI:10.3389/fpsyg.2012.00234

Chandler, C.K. (2012). *Animal assisted therapy in counseling*. New York: Routledge.

Chandler, C.K., Portrie-Bethke, T.L., Bario Minton, C.A., Fernando, D.M., & O'Callaghan, D. M. (2010, October). Matching animal-assisted therapy techniques and intentions with counseling guiding theories. *Journal of Mental Health Counseling, 32*, 354–374. DOI:10.17744/mehc.32.4.u72lt21740103538

Crenshaw, D.A. (2012). Secrets told to Ivy: Animal-assisted play therapy in a residential treatment facility. *Play Therapy, 7(2)*, 6–9.

Delta Society. (2004). *Team training course manual: A Delta Society program for animal-assisted activities and therapy*. Bellevue, WA: Author.

Fine, A. (2010). *Handbook on animal-assisted therapy: Theoretical foundations and guidelines for practice* (3rd ed.). London: Academic Press.

Garber, B.D. (2015). Cognitive-behavioral methods in high-conflict divorce: Systematic desensitization adapted to parent-child reunification interventions. *Family Court Review, 53(1)*, 96–112. DOI:10.1111/fcre.12133

Goodyear-Brown, P. (2010). *Play therapy with traumatized children: A prescriptive approach*. Hoboken, NJ: Wiley & Sons.

Handlin, L., Hydbring-Sandberg, E., Nilsson, A., Ejdeback, M., Jansson, A., & Uvnäs-Moberg, K. (2011). Short-term interaction between dogs and their owners: Effects of oxytocin, cortisol, insulin and heart rate. *Anthrozoos, 24(3)*, 301–315. DOI:https://doi.org/10.2752/175303711x13045914865385

Higgins, K. (2014). *In your dreams*. Toronto, Canada: Harlequin Enterprises.

Landreth, G. (2012). *Play therapy: The art of the relationship* (3rd ed.). New York: Routledge. DOI:10.4324/9780203835159

Lawrence, G., & Kurpius, S. (2000). Legal and ethical issues involved when counseling minors in non-school settings. *Journal of Counseling and Development, 78*, 130–136. DOI:10.1002/j.1556-6676.2000.tb02570.x

Martin, B. (2012). *Pet assisted play therapy (PAPT): The theory and dynamics of PAPT— Your pet assistant can be much more than a friendly visitor*. New Port Richey, FL: Author.

Miller, S.C., Kennedy, C., DeVoe, D., Hickey, M., Nelson, T., & Kogan, L. (2009). An examination of changes in oxytocin levels in men and women before and after interaction with a bonded dog. *Anthrozoos, 22(1)*, 31–42. DOI:10.2752/175303708x390455

Odendaal, J.S.J., & Meintjes R.A. (2003). Neurophysiological correlates of affiliative behavior between humans and dogs. *Veterinary Journal, 165(3)*, 296–301. DOI:10.1016/S1090-0233(02)00237-X

Parish-Plass, N. (2008). Animal-assisted therapy with children suffering from insecure attachment due to abuse and neglect: A method to lower the risk of intergenerational transmission of abuse? *Clinical Child Psychology & Psychiatry, 13(1)*, 7–30. DOI:10.1177/1359104507086338Clin

Rugaas, T. (2006). *On talking terms with dogs: Calming signals* (2nd ed.). Wenatchee, WA: Dogwise Pub.

Seymour, J.W., & Rubin, L. (2006). Principles, principals, and process (P3): A model for play therapy ethics problem solving. *International Journal of Play Therapy, 15(2)*, 101–123. DOI:10.1037/h0088917

Thompson, M.J. (2009). Animal-assisted play therapy: Canines as co-therapists. In G.R. Walz, J.C. Bleuer, & R.K. Yep (Eds.), *Compelling counseling interventions* (pp. 199–209).Alexandria, VA: American Counseling Association.

van der Kolk, B. (2014). *The body keeps the score: Brain, mind, and body in the healing of trauma.* New York: Penguin Group.

VanFleet, R. (2008). *Play therapy with kids and canines: Benefits for children's developmental and psychosocial health.* Sarasota, FL: Professional Resource Press.

VanFleet, R., & Coltea, C. (2012). Helping children with ASD through canine-assisted play therapy. In L. Gallo-Lopez & L.C. Rubin (Eds.), *Play-based interventions for children and adolescents with autism spectrum disorders* (pp. 39–72). New York: Routledge.

VanFleet, R., & Faa-Thompson, T. (2015). Animal assisted play therapy. In D.A. Crenshaw & A.L. Stewart (Eds.), *Play therapy: A comprehensive guide to theory and practice* (pp. 201–214). New York: Guilford Press.

Webb, N.B. (2011). *Social work practice with children* (3rd ed.). New York: Guilford Press.

Wilkes, J. (2009). *The role of companion animals in counseling and psychology: Discovering their use in the therapeutic process.* Springfield, IL: Charles C. Thomas.

15 Teaching Positive Touch

A Child-to-Child Massage Model for the Classroom

David Palmer and Jean Barlow

> The future of a nation that is either touch-starved or full of affection and aliveness, depends on one thing—our children.
>
> Mariana Caplan, *Untouched: The Need for Genuine Affection in an Impersonal World*

> My daughter has loved the classroom massage program from day-one. To tell the truth I didn't know what to make of it at first, I knew I would personally like it, but I wasn't too sure my daughter would be keen on other children (outside her friendship circle) touching her ... but to my surprise she does not have any issues with this, and better, she absolutely loves it! She says it calms her down and relaxes her, but the benefits are beyond her words. At home she is always very keen to teach us how to do it [the massage activities], then she asks for us to practice on her, and by the end of a session we're all happy, calm, and relaxed. She has been practicing positive touch at school for around a year now, and if she identifies someone feeling a bit tense or under the weather, she will happily volunteer her wisdom with 10 minutes of positive touch—and I must say it does wonders for us all!
>
> Mother of a second-grader in the "A Child to Child Kind & Caring Hands" school program

Overview

Touch is not optional. Developmentally we know that positive touch is essential for the emotional and psychophysical health of children (Bowlby, 1988; Field, 2010, 2014). There is also a growing body of evidence that lack of positive touch in the early years has lasting effects on the ability of adults to maintain good physical health and successful interpersonal relationships (Field, 2010). Yet social fears of inappropriate touching between children and adults have reached new heights, resulting in more laws and regulations defining inappropriate touch in health care and educational settings (Carlson, 2006). The primary impact of these policies has, more often than not, been to expand prohibitions around touch (Carlson, 2006). Concerns around child-to-child touch and safety have likewise intensified. However, the answer is not to prohibit all touch, but rather to encourage and teach appropriate or positive touch.

Most children learn appropriate touch in the family. However, as they become increasingly autonomous and begin to navigate the social world outside of the family, children become more uncertain about the social norms related to touch. Societal norms may teach children how not to touch others or be touched by others, but not how to provide or share touch appropriately.

The child-to-child massage movement (peer massage) in primary schools fills this void by teaching children simple positive touch routines in a safe and structured context. Peer massage is a developmental strategy designed to continue the important role touch has in promoting healthy biophysical integration, self-regulation, interoception, a sense of self-worth, and an ability to master the environment (Barlow, 2012; Boyatzis *et al.*, 2000). Peer massage also teaches essential social skills, such as empathy and respect, while setting clear boundaries and behavioral norms related to asking for and receiving positive touch (Barlow, 2012). While not intended as a therapeutic intervention per se, peer massage can also be viewed as a preventative strategy in that it can help to mitigate some of the negative effects of touch deprivation or touch abuse (Blair, 2012). Finally, peer massage also creates a positive social and emotional learning environment (see Figure 15.1), aiding the absorption and retention of academic material in the classroom framed with clear ethical standards (Cowley, 2005).

The Physiology of Touch

Positive touch triggers two physiological responses that immediately provide a calming experience for children. Treatment with massage is linked to oxytocin release in both sexes (Uvnäs-Moberg *et al.*, 2005). Oxytocin is an important mediator for reducing cortisol levels and blood pressure, increasing the perception of well-being and the ability for friendly interaction while decreasing

Figure 15.1 Children practicing child-to-child massage in the classroom. (Used with permission from Thea Blair, *Calm, Focused and Friendly.*)

levels of anxiety and perception of pain (Uvnäs-Moberg, 2003; Field, 2014). Additionally, moderate pressure massage stimulates a parasympathetic nervous system (PNS) response, which activates the internal rest and recovery functions, and reduces sympathetic nervous system activity, the body's stress response system (Diego & Field, 2009). According to Diego and Field (2009) "Inasmuch as PNS function can profoundly affect neuroendocrine function, psychological outcomes, immune function and growth and development; the increase in PNS activity elicited by massage therapy may explain the diverse benefits documented for massage therapy" (p. 637).

History of Child Massage in Schools

Structured touch in the classroom is a relatively new phenomenon. The first well-documented attempt to introduce a program in the United States was developed in 1980 by Jeanne St. John for the Santa Cruz (CA) County Office of Education. St. John (1987) created an approach called Physical Response Education System (PRES) based on touching select sequences of acupressure points on clothed and generally seated children. Originally targeted at special needs children and classrooms, the touch routines were performed by professional acupressurists and trained volunteers in two pilot studies. Although this was an adult-to-child program, the success of the intervention was dramatic with 74 percent of children showing improvement in the areas of health, sensory-motor, cognitive/communication, and social/emotional development (St. John, 1987). Despite the training of more than 20,000 clinicians, educators, parents, and volunteers and presentations at hundreds of state, national, and international conferences in all fields of education and health, within ten years most PRES programs had been abandoned. According to St. John, "Schools lost all funding for staff training and lost their nerve regarding touch about the same time" (St. John, J., personal communication, March 8, 2012).

The next model that brought positive touch routines to the classroom was developed at Axelsons Institute in Sweden in 1996. This new approach, called Peaceful Touch, differed from the PRES program in two significant ways. First, it eliminated virtually all adult-to-child touch in favor of structured touch between children. Second, the touch routines in the Axelsons program were far simpler than the acupressure point systems created by PRES, thus making it easy to train children. Today, according to Axelsons Institute (2015), "more than 10,000 trained teachers affect 300,000 students, from pre-schoolers to teens, on a regular basis" in Sweden.

Axelsons' Peaceful Touch model encouraged the worldwide development of numerous other programs, most notably the Massage in Schools Programme (MISP), which debuted in London in 2000. Within five years this program, which incorporated both movement and massage, had spread throughout the United Kingdom and Ireland, as well as affiliate programs in 30 countries around the world (Massage in Schools Association, n.d.).

In 2007, one of the first MISP trainers in the United Kingdom, Jean Barlow (co-author on this chapter), designed a Child-2-Child Kind and Caring Hands (AC2C) program (Barlow, 2007) to specifically focus on peer massage (without a movement component) as a way to address the social and emotional development of children, promote mental health resilience, and improve student success. The following program description details the AC2C program and is documented in Barlow (2012).

Ethical Standards and Safety in a Child-2-Child Massage Program (AC2C)

A successful peer massage program requires a classroom where every child feels safe. Ethical issues around the delivery and practice of the AC2C program are formally addressed in each school's Safeguarding Policy document. Individual children who have been identified as having special educational or additional needs will also have a mandated Education, Health, and Care (EHC) plan. Each EHC plan is approved by all the parents and informs them that positive touch will be included within the curriculum and the school will respect each child's choice to participate or not. Teachers agree to no adult-to-child touch unless the child is unable to learn the program without assistance. In those cases, there is legal documentation stating that a named adult will assist in the work.

In the classroom it is the responsibility of the teacher to generate the structure necessary to ensure each child's sense of security. That is done by first, carefully creating a positive context and then, implementing the program in incremental stages. The most important safeguard in the classroom is asking the children every day whether or not they wish to participate in the peer touch session and encouraging them to recognize that, just as they sometimes need times when they are very active and noisy, so they also need times when they are quiet and reflective. Not taking part in the kinesthetic work means that they are taking time for quiet thought and thus still participating in the session in a different way, sitting quietly while others around them follow the routine. This normalizes opting out of the activity and maintains a quiet, respectful environment for the repetition of the sequences.

Teaching children positive touch in a supervised classroom environment is itself an inherent safeguard against inappropriate or abusive touch between children. Learning and practicing positive touch develops knowledge and understanding of what is respectful "safe touch" and promotes the skills to ask for and receive permission for touch. This makes it a very powerful protection tool for children, especially on the playground and in unsupervised environments beyond the school or home.

Practitioner and Teacher Training in a Child-2-Child Massage Program (AC2C)

All teachers and practitioners are required to attend a one-day practitioner training course that is also open to parents, school administrators, therapists, health workers, group leaders, volunteers, and any other interested school personnel. This training begins with the learning theory that underpins the program and details the anticipated benefits and outcomes. Then the instructor models the implementation steps in the classroom (as described in the next section) with the participants taking the role of the pupils. Course participants are also taught games and activities as icebreakers and invited to be creative in their use of the strokes and making up routines.

A second day-long training, the coordinator course, is for school board members, consultants, therapists, health professionals, and any others who will have responsibility for coordinating the program in their educational setting or area. Since each educational district and school is unique, the participants have the opportunity to consider and discuss implementation issues that might arise in their particular context, such as parental concerns, cultural appropriateness, special types of child difficulties, and age groups.

Typical AC2C Program Content

The AC2C program is a five-minute, interactive, positive-touch activity between children that involves simple massage strokes first practiced and performed on the hand, then the back, head, and shoulders, in teacher-directed routines. These sequences can be carried out in pairs, groups, circles, chains, or even on oneself (see Figure 15.2). Children are positioned in chairs or on the carpet either facing each other (for the hand) or one behind the other (for the shoulders, back, and head). Children are partnered initially by the teacher using the standard classroom methods (such as alphabetical order or friendships) then later randomly

Figure 15.2 Children start a day of learning with a hand massage. (Used with permission from Jean Barlow.)

each week using student suggestions (such as hair or eye color or birthdate). The random partnership process breaks down interpersonal barriers and promotes friendships and new communication skills. Children with any special needs participate alongside their classmates with teachers providing special support as needed to ensure full participation. Teachers check that each partner is comfortable and that there is enough space to perform the activities.

Children can also choose not to take part and instead sit quietly in reflection with no judgment. Allowing each child to choose whether or not to participate in the touch activities is critical to affirming their control over their bodies and they still benefit from the atmosphere of calm and stillness. For the same reason, each session begins by the giver asking permission of the receiver with such questions as: "Please may I massage your hand?" or "Is it okay if I touch your hand?" The children are then asked to shake hands and the one giving the strokes must put both his or her hands over the single hand of the receiver, beginning the structured touch experience. The routines begin after each pair agrees who shall be first to "give" and who will "receive."

The children learn the strokes quickly from visual prompts and by listening to and watching the teacher and each other and soon gain confidence delivering the strokes. At the same time, the students are encouraged to talk about the activities as they practice by telling each other what they think and feel about each stroke. If there is a stroke a child does not like, the receiver can ask for it to be omitted and substitute another stroke or "still" or "resting" hands. Over time, children become more discriminating in their likes and dislikes, perhaps requesting that the fingers be more together, or apart, using two hands or one at a time, pressing more firmly or gently. There is a quiet dialogue between partners that ensures the receiver always enjoys the routine.

For the shoulder, back, and head sequence the strokes are assembled into two standard routines: Animals and Solar System. The children follow the routine from their white board, computer, or DVD in the classroom, so that all the children are working on the same activities at the same time. Children use pats, kneading, and soothing strokes named after animals, or planets and stars that each have individual music to keep the routine identifiable. As the strokes change so does the background music, enabling children with their back to the screen to keep pace. At the end of the routine there is a short time to discuss the experience and then the partners change roles. Children improve eye contact while giving feedback face-to-face and learning the hand routine. Teachers and students can also improvise new routines in conjunction with current topics of study.

Benefits of the Peer Massage Program

Although research in peer massage is still in its infancy, there is a group of ten studies from the United Kingdom that used various methodologies to examine the Massage in Schools Programmes between 2001 and 2012 (Massage in Schools Programme, 2015). In aggregate, these studies show that the main benefits of the program were:

- Improved calmness and concentration
- Increased self-confidence and self-esteem
- Children feel happier and more relaxed
- Increased awareness of the body and signs of stress and anxiety
- Improved social skills with a greater number of relationships and friendships with peers and adults
- A reduction in aggressive behavior and bullying
- A more positive attitude and greater engagement with learning
- Improved ability to work in groups and independently
- Greater creativity and problem solving.

The next sections will examine many of these outcomes more closely and include research from additional sources.

Self-Awareness of Calming Sensations

According to Uvnäs-Moberg (2003), "Touch ... appears to be one of the strongest sources of input to the calm and connection system" (p. 13). This is probably why studies (McLennan *et al.*, 2011; Simons, 2011) have consistently demonstrated that massage is a reliable way to reduce anxiety and calm pupils in the classroom. Atkinson (2014) reported that while doing peer massage children are learning conscious relaxation and the benefits of refreshing the mind and body, which is an essential life skill. Children also learn best when they feel valued, have a sense of self-esteem, and feel happy—which can be accomplished by learning life skills in the classroom. Neurophysiological calming through structured touch in a safe environment allows children time to explore their inner world of sensations (interoception) undistracted from the pressure of accomplishment. Receiving a massage is "being" time during which children are encouraged to notice and report on their subjective experience.

Empowerment and Self-Esteem

Increasing children's self-awareness of internal sensations and feelings means that they can make informed choices about what they want and need. The predictability of a structured touch routine helps children learn that they have the ability to profoundly regulate their own physiology through touch (van der Kolk, 2014) and provides individual children a sense of autonomy and control.

In all peer massage programs children are given a daily choice about participating in the session. It helps pupils to develop a voice and understanding that they have rights with responsibilities. Children learn to link their spoken words with actions, thoughts, and feelings that they are experiencing during the peer touch session. They report feeling more confident talking to other children and speaking out in class (McLennan et al., 2011) and, in turn, enhancing their self-esteem (Simons, 2011).

As they develop ownership of their bodies on a daily basis, they become empowered to accept or refuse touch, develop social skills, respond appropriately to their partner, and participate in joint problem solving. A peer massage program allows the class to engage in an ongoing conversation that enhances overall touch literacy and provides each child with an opportunity to articulate and understand the difference between appropriate and inappropriate touch and to become responsible for self-protection or safeguarding. Morgan (2011) advised that peer massage "provides an opportunity to promote positive attitudes within the classroom and to interact through touch co-operatively at a level rarely seen in today's environment" (p. 150).

Empathy and Positive Touch

Positive touch in the classroom naturally releases oxytocin, which promotes calmness, interpersonal empathy, and trust (Bartz et al., 2010). In a review of oxytocin and social affiliation in humans, Feldman (2012) details how oxytocin and other "neurohormonal substrates play an important and mutually-influencing role in the formation and maintenance of affiliative bonds" (p. 388), including those of close friends. Empathy and attachment undergird critical social affiliations. As Rosenthal (1993) wrote: "For the child there is both an emotional and cognitive necessity for friendship. And the child, who for whatever reasons is friendless, is 'at risk' both emotionally and educationally" (p. 112).

Relieving social stress through peer massage can be a potent methodology for eliminating all forms of bullying in the classroom (Blair, 2012; Davis, 2010; Marsh, 2011). With a greater sense of belonging, a child's confidence grows and the child is more likely to reach his or her potential, be creative, and resilient. These key ideas are a central feature of "attachment theory," mainly developed by Bowlby (1988). More recent writers, notably Boyatzis et al. (2000), suggested that children are best served by nurturing methods that promote a sense of acceptance, respect, and predictability, which are seen as essential for emotional growth in young children and are all characteristic of child-to-child classroom massage.

Positive Peer Relationships

Over the course of the ten years of implementation of the AC2C initiative with different classes and ages of children in a variety of educational settings, children reported having more friends after they started doing the program. The evidence of improved social cohesion was striking in the AC2C program in Cambridgeshire,

Figure 15.3 A classroom sharing structured touch activities. (Used with permission from Thea Blair, *Calm, Focused and Friendly*.)

England, in two primary schools (Barlow, 2015; "Cambridgeshire primary school," 2015). After just one month of regularly experiencing the routines every day, in one school every class showed an increase in the numbers of children who said that they were playing with more children after participating in the program. The research found that 69 percent of students improved their peer interactions. In the second school the overall increase was 64 percent. Other studies (McLennan, *et al.*, 2011; Simons, 2011; MacIntyre *et al.*, 2010) reported similar results.

A peer massage program that emphasizes positive communication by asking permission, giving feedback, and thanking as part of the work promotes respectful understanding of one another and allows children to swiftly bond. Without these social bonds, learning suffers. According to Bester (2001), "As much as 29% of the variance in academic achievement can be explained by social isolation making it an important variable when academic achievement is predicted at primary school level" (p. 1).

Academic Focus

A calm classroom directly affects the learning experiences of children (Cowley, 2005). Children who are not stressed and feel confident are able to be creative and achieve higher academic attainment (Figure 15.3). Schools with peer massage programs found improvements in concentration and on task behavior (McLennan *et al.*, 2011; Woolfson *et al.*, 2005) along with a greater engagement with learning (Simons, 2011). Even a simple touch on the arm can increase motivation to participate in learning (Guéguen, 2004). When the AC2C program came to an underperforming school in Cambridgeshire, United Kingdom, within six months the academic performance was elevated to the degree that a "special measures" designation was no longer required ("Cambridgeshire primary school," 2015).

Case Vignettes of Classroom AC2C Implementation
Vignette A: Case of Jeremy

> In a school in Salford, UK, a boy named Jeremy, aged 10 years, was experiencing social isolation from his classmates. After the AC2C program was introduced, his teacher assigned a partner to Jeremy and taught the massage routines to the pair. The two boys demonstrated the routines to the rest of the class and Jeremy soon became the class expert in performing the massage strokes. Jeremy suggested that children who had no friends during recess could ask student volunteers from his class to become "Positive Touch Buddies!" and involve them in the kinesthetic activities. Jeremy succeeded in making his class and school more socially inclusive for not only himself but for all the students.

Vignette B: Case of Michael

> In a North Manchester, UK, school for special needs children, twelve boys were all diagnosed as having autistic spectrum disorder. One child, Michael, an elective mute, found it difficult to participate with others in his class. He joined the class in September, at which time the school introduced the AC2C program. Initially Michael sat in a way that isolated him from others in the room. However, after only a few weeks he began to be curious about taking part in the peer massage. The teacher invited him to work with two other boys to make a row allowing Michael to choose where in the row he wanted to stand or sit. After this experience, for the first time he began to talk in class. After the Christmas holidays two visitors from the United States, who were making a film about the work, came into the classroom to talk to the boys. He volunteered to say how it made him feel and said, on camera, "It makes me feel nice and calm and relaxed!"

Summary

There is a second "digital" revolution brewing in our schools, this one not utilizing computers but rather the hands and fingers of young children. Instead of focusing on virtual relationships and communication, peer massage in elementary schools helps children learn how to master real-life interpersonal skills and communication. In the process, children also learn to monitor their subjective emotional states and build self-awareness, self-esteem, and self-control. Peer massage builds competency in touch awareness and skills, setting the stage for adolescent and adult interpersonal relationships that are built upon a strong touch-positive foundation.

The reader is encouraged to hear directly from the children, teachers, parents, and administrators profiled in the 34-minute documentary *Calm, Focused and Friendly*, produced by Peaceful Hands founder Thea Blair and available at https://youtu.be/OUrFpuAXuZU. Blair visited Jean Barlow in 2013 and filmed various AC2C programs in the United Kingdom. A one-minute clip of just children talking about their experience can be found at http://tinyurl.com/gqkusxr

---

Discussion Questions

Together with a colleague discuss the following questions:

1. Imagine that you have been certified as a Peer Massage Trainer, and then outline the barriers that you would have to overcome in introducing peer massage to a local elementary school system.
2. What are the advantages and disadvantages of teaching touch literacy in a therapeutic context versus peer massage in the classroom?
3. Reflect on your comfort level for teaching child-to-child massage in the classroom.

References

Atkinson, M. (2014). *Once upon a touch ... story massage for children*. London: Singing Dragon.

Axelsons Institute. (2015). *Peaceful touch*. Retrieved on 16 November, 2016 from: http://axelsons.com/peaceful-touch

Barlow, J. (2007). *Practitioner's handbook*. Bolton, UK: Author.

Barlow, J. (2012). Peer massage in the classroom. *International Perspectives on Inclusive Education*, 2, 237–249. DOI:10.1108/S1479-3636(2012)0000002018

Barlow (2015). *Can peer massage in schools help children with their emotional wellbeing?* Retrieved on 16 November, 2016 from: http://www.achild2child.uk/.

Bartz, J., Zaki, J., Bolger, N., Hollander, E., Ludwig, N., Kolevzon, A., & Ochsner, K. (2010). Oxytocin selectively improves empathic accuracy. *Psychological Science*, 21(10), 1426–1428. DOI:10.1177/0956797610383439

Bester, G. (2001). Social isolation: A learning obstacle in the primary school. *South African Journal of Education*, 21(4), 331–335. Retrieved on 16 November 2016 from: http://www.ajol.info/index.php/saje/article/view/24924

Blair, T. (2012). *From bullying to belonging: How peer massage relieves social stress*. Retrieved on 16 November, 2016 from: http://www.waldorftoday.com/2012/10/from-bullying-to-belonging-how-peer-massage-relieves-social-stress/

Bowlby, J. (1988). *A secure base: Parent-child attachment and healthy human development*. New York: Basic Books.

Boyatzis, R.E., Goleman, D., & Rhee, K. (2000). Clustering competence in emotional intelligence: Insights from the emotional competence inventory (EICs). In R. Bar-On & J.D.A. Parker (Eds.), *Handbook of emotional intelligence* (pp. 343–362). San Francisco: Jossey-Bass.

Cambridgeshire primary school out of school out of special measures after pupils started massaging each other. (2015). *Cambridge News*, May 14. Retrieved on 16 November, 2016 from: http://tinyurl.com/jal7qv9

Caplan, M. (1998). *Untouched: The need for genuine affection in an impersonal world*. Prescott, AZ: Hohm Press.

Carlson, F. (2006). *Essential touch: Meeting the needs of young children*. Washington, DC: National Association for the Education of Young Children.

Cowley, S. (2005). *Letting the buggers be creative*. London: Continuum.

Davis, D. (2010). *An evaluation of the effectiveness of peer massage in one primary school*. Retrieved on 16 November, 2016 from: http://misa.org.uk/research/worcester/

Diego, M.A., & Field, T. (2009). Moderate pressure massage elicits a parasympathetic nervous system response. *International Journal of Neuroscience*, *119*, 630–638. DOI:10.1080/00207450802329605

Feldman R. (2012). Oxytocin and social affiliation in humans. *Human Behavior*, *61(3)*, 380–391. DOI:10.1016/j.yhbeh.2012.01.008

Field, T. (2010). Touch for socioemotional and physical well-being: A review. *Developmental Review*, *30(4)*, 367–383. DOI:10.1016/j.dr.2011.01.001

Field, T. (2014). *Touch* (2nd ed.). Cambridge, MA: MIT Press.

Guéguen, N. (2004). Nonverbal encouragement of participation in a course: The effect of touching. *Social Psychology of Education*, *7*, 89–98. DOI:10.1023/B:SPOE.0000010691.30834.14

MacIntyre, H., Colwell, J., & Ota, C. (2010). *Moving against the grain?* Retrieved on 16 November, 2016 from: http://misa.org.uk/research/brighton/

McLennan, J., Bateman, P., Pringle, P., & Smith, M. (2011). *An evaluation of MISP in 5 schools in Nottinghamshire*. Retrieved on 16 November, 2016 from: http://misa.org.uk/research/nottingham/

Marsh, L. (2011). Evaluation of the massage in schools program in one primary school. *Educational Psychology in Practice: Theory, Research and Practice in Educational Psychology*, *27(2)*, 133–142. DOI:10.1080/02667363.2011.567092

Massage in School Association. (n.d.) Retrieved on 16 November, 2016 from: http://massageinschools.com/

Massage in Schools Programme (MISP) (2015). *Massage in Schools Programme Research 2001–2012*. Retrieved on 16 November, 2016 from http://misa.org.uk/research/National Education Association.

Morgan, J. (2011). *Children's experiences of a massage in schools programme: A thematic analysis* (Masters thesis/dissertation). Retrieved on 16 November, 2016 from: http://aut.researchgateway.ac.nz/bitstream/handle/10292/3439/MorganJ.pdf?sequence=3/

Rosenthal, H. (1993). Friendship groups: An approach to helping friendless children. *Educational Psychology in Practice*, *9*, 112–120. DOI:10.1080/0266736930090208

Simons, M. (2011). *Massage in Schools Programme (MISP): Evaluation in Northamptonshire TaMHS Project*. Retrieved on 16 November, 2016 from: http://misa.org.uk/research/north-hants/

St. John, J. (1987). *High tech touch: Acupressure in the schools*. Novato, CA: Academic Therapy Publications.
Uvnäs-Moberg, K. (2003). *The oxytocin factor: Tapping the hormone of calm, love, and healing*. London: Pinter & Martin.
Uvnäs-Moberg, K., Ingemar, A., & Magnusson, D. (2005). The psychobiology of emotions: The role of the oxytocinergic system. *International Journal of Behavioural Medicine, 12(2)*, 59–65. DOI:10.1207/s15327558ijbm1202_3
van der Kolk, B. (2014). *The body keeps the score*. New York: Penguin Group.
Woolfson, R., Campbell, L., & Banks, M. (2005). The Renfrewshire "massage in schools" programme (MISP): An evaluation of its impact in a primary school. Retrieved on 16 November, 2016 from: http://massageinschools.com/why-massage-in-schools/research-articles/

Part V

Toward the Development of Core Competencies Supporting the Ethics of Touch in Child Counseling and Play Therapy

16 Core Competencies and Recommendations Supporting the Ethics of Touch in Child Counseling and Play Therapy

Susan W. Gray, Janet A. Courtney, and Robert D. Nolan

> I will not follow where the path may lead, but I will go where there is no path, and I will leave a trail.
>
> Muriel Strode, *Wind-Wafted Wild Flowers*

Introduction

Looking to the ethics of competent practice and the growing number of specialized therapies aimed at working with children, the therapeutic landscape is beginning to shift away from a no-touch approach to one of paying more attention to when and how touch encounters happen in therapy with children. Unfortunately, many practitioners from different professional fields of practice remain uncertain or confused about touch when working with children and their families (Lynch & Garrett, 2010). In these instances, adapting a strict "no touch" approach seems to be the more comfortable solution. The practice reality is that young children do not participate in the more traditional forms of talking therapy by having a quiet, reflective conversation sitting in a chair across from the therapist. They are on the move and touch will inevitably happen.

While most professionals would agree that touch in clinical practice is of the utmost importance to address, very little guidance on the topic can be found in the literature. As we have seen, touch does happen between the practitioner and the child but, as Hunter and Struve (1998) observe, the thought of "even discussing the topic of touch is anxiety producing for many clinicians" (p. xiii). This concern impacts practitioners internationally (Thomas & Jephcott, 2011). For example, in a study of social workers in Ireland, participants expressed reservations about even taking part in a study examining touch in practice (Lynch & Garrett, 2010).

Clearly, understanding the role of touch in therapeutic practice with children is a complex and multidimensional process. Practitioners are called upon to integrate multifaceted knowledge of the child's development, the different interrelated systems affecting the child (see Figure 16.1), and what is relevant from client-centered, psychodynamic, humanistic, attachment, and social learning theories.

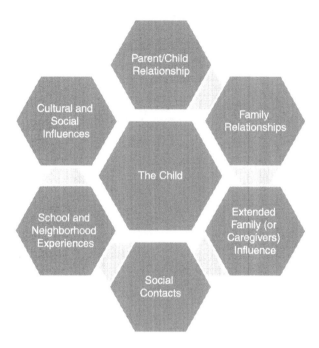

Figure 16.1 The interrelated systems affecting the child.

In that split second when touch occurs between the practitioner and the child, the psychological processes at work in three key areas of relationship—that is, between self and significant other people, past and present experience, and inner and outer reality—must be assessed in order to understand what is happening (Brearley, 1991). See Figure 16.2.

Taking what is known about the child, the different theories of development and the interconnections between personal and environmental factors, and ultimately translating them into practice suggests a number of core practice competencies revolving around touch when working with children.

The core practice competencies are aspirational in their intent in that they are intended to facilitate the practitioner's continued systematic development and to help advance a high level of practice. These core competencies are not intended to be mandatory or exhaustive and are primarily applicable to professional situations revolving around touch. The fundamental goal of these core competencies is to promote proficiency when the therapist is confronted with touch issues in practice.

5 Clinical Competencies in Touch

Taken together, the chapters in this book propose a number of practice competencies that define the core knowledge, values, and skills for the use of touch in

Figure 16.2 Psychological processes at work in the child's relationships when touch occurs.

therapy. The notion of "ability" is central to these competencies or what practitioners need to know and are able to do when challenged by touch issues in practice. The components of these competencies all share a commonality insofar as they contribute to the effective use of touch. You will note that each competency has a brief descriptor, which is then elaborated in a couple of sentences. Framed around Bloom's taxonomy (Anderson & Krathwohl, 2001), the competency then goes on to suggest specific practice behaviors that are listed as bullet points and understood to comprise the essence of the competency. To further support touch practices, a table follows each competency offering suggestions for reflective discussion and/or activities around how to get started learning these skills. Again, each competency is operationalized by the practice behaviors or the skills of doing. These touch competencies set the stage for establishing a clear set of expectations for knowing about and using touch in practice.

In sum, the aim of these touch competencies is to suggest a core foundation to ensure practitioners have a body of knowledge and a range of clinical practice skills in order to sensitively, effectively, and appropriately respond to the dignity and needs of the child across a variety of practice settings. They can be incorporated into formal educational curricula, training seminars or workshops, and the practice models and approaches reviewed in this book. When learning any practice skill, we assume the practitioner will use supervision and consultation, when needed. Advanced training in a specific area leading to certification may also be incorporated with the competencies in order to further develop touch skills in child counseling and play therapy.

We now turn to the touch competencies.

Touch Competency 1: Demonstrate Ethical and Professional Behaviors in Child Counseling and Play Therapy

Practitioners understand their professional code of ethics as well as risk management standards related to touch and boundaries. Practitioners understand frameworks of ethical decision-making and how to apply them to situations surrounding touch that may arise in clinical practice with children (and their families.) Practitioners understand relevant policies, laws, and regulations that impact clinical practice within their own agencies and institutions, and at the local, state, and federal levels. Practitioners:

- Make ethical decisions by applying the profession's code of ethics related to boundaries relevant to touch in the practitioner's field of study.
- Apply ethical frameworks of decision making and risk management standards.
- Adhere to agency and institutional policies, and local, state, and federal laws and regulations surrounding touch.
- Use supervision, consultation, and seek legal counsel, when necessary, to guide ethical behaviors regarding touch.

Table 16.1 Suggested activities to support learning and practice in Touch Competency 1.

Demonstrate Ethical and Professional Behaviors in Child Counseling and Play Therapy

- Read your professional code of ethics related to boundaries, such as the National Association of Social Workers Code of Ethics (2008), and discuss with a colleague or supervisor how they apply to your practice setting.
- Review and discuss with a colleague varied ethical frameworks of decision making or risk management standards related to touch practices, and identify how they relate to your own use of touch in therapy with children.
- Review agency and institutional policies, and local, state, and federal laws and regulations surrounding touch and consider how they apply to your touch-oriented practice.
- Develop a list of questions for your supervisor (or consultant) about how to deal with potential (or actual) ethical concerns regarding touch.

Touch Competency 2: Engage Touch Practices in Child Counseling and Play Therapy

Practitioners understand the historical perspectives and current societal attitudes and perceptions related to touch. In order to interact more effectively with children and their families, practitioners know the multicultural and religious norms related to client family backgrounds, the child's developmental needs related to touch (beginning with birth, pre-school, school-aged, pre-adolescent, to adolescents), as well as healthy childhood sexual development. Practitioners understand the process of translating current research, including the positive benefits and harmful effects, of touch in practice. Practitioners:

- Apply and communicate understanding of the importance of historical perspectives, and current societal attitudes and perceptions related to touch practices.
- Relate the understanding of children's developmental needs and healthy sexuality development to touch in child counseling and play therapy.
- Communicate and apply understanding of the importance of cultural and religious norms regarding touch.
- Apply knowledge of current, available research into touch practices including the positive benefits of touch and the negative consequences related to the absence of touch.

Table 16.2 Suggested activities to support learning and practice in Touch Competency 2.

Engage Touch Practices in Child Counseling and Play Therapy

- Examine available historical writings related to touch and identify key ideas to inform your own touch practice.
- Review children's developmental needs related to touch and healthy childhood sexuality and discuss with a colleague and/or your supervisor how they apply to your clinical practice.
- Interview someone from a cultural or religious background commonly seen in your setting about touch practices and discuss with your supervisor or colleague how the insights you gathered apply to your touch practice. For example, in some cultures touching the head is frowned upon or considered inappropriate.
- Participate in a group discussion with other colleagues aimed at exchanging ideas around ways to enhance understanding of cultural and religious norms; include in this discussion ways to develop your awareness of personal biases regarding touch.
- Read the most current research about touch including the positive benefits of touch and the detrimental effects related to the absence of touch. To get started, consider reviewing advances in the field of neurobiology and how this informs the understanding of touch in the developing child.

Touch Competency 3: Assess Touch Practices with Children and Their Families

Practitioners understand the context of the child and his or her presenting situation and the impact of varying mediating factors on clinical decision making. Practitioners understand the varied needs of children and their family based upon diagnoses and problem areas. Practitioners understand the differences in child-initiated touch, therapist-initiated touch, unintentional touch, and how to competently assess these situations. Practitioners understand professional best practice guidelines, and know the appropriate clinical skills to sensitively, effectively, and critically evaluate the in-the-moment challenges that occur in therapy, and the ways to provide respectful touch appropriate to the needs of the child. Practitioners understand how to create a sense of safety, set appropriate boundaries, and implement alternative actions with aggressive and negative behavior and the use of child restraint as a last resort. Practitioners understand when touch may be contraindicated and how to set appropriate physical boundaries as needed. Practitioners:

- Engage in processes to assess touch in clinical practice to collect and organize data that takes into account the context of the child's background and related multidimensional mediating factors.
- Develop appropriate touch intervention strategies based on the critical assessment of problem areas, the child's diagnosis, guidelines for best practices, and the values and preferences of the client and his or her family.
- Assess alternative actions to deal with negative touch behaviors with a consideration of using child restraint measures for safety and protection as a last resort.

Table 16.3 Suggested activities to support learning and practice in Touch Competency 3.

Assess Touch Practices with Children and Their Families

- Select a case situation from your practice experience and discuss with your supervisor or colleague the varied mediating factors that impact touch issues in work with children.
- Based on your case review, discuss with your supervisor or colleague how to go about assessing for the best intervention. (Note that if you do not have case experience, ask your supervisor or colleague to share case experiences.)
- Review with a colleague or your supervisor what assessment information you would need in order to provide a therapeutic response to a child's aggressive or negative behaviors related to touch.
- Looking back to your case experience(s) with a particular child, role play with a colleague how you would go about establishing boundaries related to touch.

Touch Competency 4: Intervene in Touch Practices with Children and Their Families

Practitioners understand basic treatment methods regarding children's experiences of touch and know when referrals to other child specialists and/or programs are necessary. They know the signs and indicators of child abuse and the protocols for reporting child abuse (emotional/psychological, physical, sexual, or neglect). Practitioners know the skills necessary to help children develop touch awareness by teaching them, through developmentally appropriate methods, about body ownership and appropriate personal space boundaries with peers and others. Practitioners know how to educate parents and/or caregivers about a child's developmental needs related to touch, about healthy childhood sexuality development, and understanding personal space boundaries and body ownership. Practitioners know how to guide parents about positive discipline alternatives. Practitioners understand how to critically evaluate this knowledge in order to effectively intervene with clients, and are able to educate parents about the positive and hurtful effects of touch. Practitioners:

- Apply knowledge of developmentally appropriate child assessment methods related to touch in practice in order to make appropriate referrals based upon the outcomes of those assessments, as necessary.
- Apply knowledge of the basic indicators and signs of child abuse to an intervention plan.
- Apply knowledge of agency, institutional policies, and local, state, and federal laws to effectively intervene in situations of child abuse (emotional/psychological, physical, sexual, or neglect).
- Set appropriate boundaries in sessions with child clients, as necessary.
- Apply knowledge of developmentally appropriate ways to provide psychoeducation to children about body ownership and personal space boundaries.
- Translate knowledge of child development, the positive and harmful effects of touch, positive discipline, and personal space boundaries to parents and caregivers.

Touch Competency 5: Advance Professional Self-Awareness Related to Touch

Practitioners understand the importance of self-awareness regarding touch and personal space boundaries for themselves. As well, practitioners understand their own cultural, religious, and familial norms and biases related to touch. Practitioners understand the potential countertransferences that could emerge related to touch and how these personal reactions influence professional judgment and behavior. Practitioners also understand the value of self-care.

Table 16.4 Suggested activities to support learning and practice in Touch Competency 4.

Intervene in Touch Practices with Children and Their Families

- Select a developmentally appropriate touch-based intervention and review with your supervisor or consultant the types of situations when a child (and his or her family) may also need a referral for further assistance.
- Review your agency policies and identify how you would go about reporting inappropriate touch and child abuse; alternatively, look into local, state, and federal policies, laws, and regulations.
- Select a recent research article reporting recent interventions related to touch and discuss these findings with a colleague. Hint: you might consider looking into the field of neuroscience and the emerging understandings related to touch.
- Interview at least five to eight parents of children whom you know as friends or neighbors and ask what form of (positive) discipline they use; join with a colleague who has also conducted five to eight similar parent interviews and determine what seems to be the most common form of positive child discipline methods. Compare these discipline methods with those seen in child abuse situations.
- Select any one of the case vignettes in the book related to a child who has been sexually abused and, together with a colleague, practice developmentally appropriate ways to teach this child about personal space boundaries and body ownership. Alternatively, imagine the child in this vignette has been assigned to you and engages in inappropriate boundary behaviors and, together again with your colleague, practice how you would intervene around setting appropriate boundaries.

Practitioners understand the distinction between the child's needs regarding touch as separate from their own needs. Practitioners:

- Demonstrate self-awareness regarding comfort and discomfort concerning personal space boundaries with clients in practice.
- Use reflection, self-awareness, and self-regulation to manage personal biases related to touch and to maintain professionalism in practice.
- Recognize the link between countertransferences and personal history, and reactions related to touch.
- Use reflective-oriented supervision and/or consultation to identify personal issues and take action, as needed, for self-care.
- Recognize their own personal biases and cultural, religious, and family norms related to touch.

Table 16.5 Suggested activities to support learning and practice in Touch Competency 5.

Advance Professional Self-Awareness Related to Touch

- Attend an experiential training program with a colleague that focuses on an exploration of one's own personal space boundaries and together discuss what you (and your colleague) learned.
- Expanding on your reflections around attending an experiential training program, quietly reflect on potential countertransference(s) that may have arisen and record them in a personal journal; set some time aside to develop an action plan for self-care. Consider reviewing your plans with your supervisor, consultant, or a colleague.
- Keep a personal journal for one or two weeks noting those times you are uncomfortable with a touch-oriented exchange with a client, and include in your reflection when would be the "best time" to reflect on personal biases and who you might check-in with when these uncomfortable occasions occur. Include in your reflection your own cultural, religious, and family norms related to touch.
- Make a list of ways to continue professional development and how to maintain professionalism in clinical practice.
- Together with a colleague develop a list of reasons why self-care is important in touch-oriented child counseling when working with a child and his or her family.

Touch Competencies Summary

As we begin to know more about the use of touch, it is incumbent upon the practitioner to seek new and creative ways to engage in and to organize this knowledge. The five core touch competencies offered here move in that direction and challenge practitioners to progress even further to develop what is currently known about the use of touch in child counseling and play therapy. The knowledge explosion in neurobiology, for instance, has profound implications for the use of touch.

However, touch practices are only part of the knowledge base that practitioners need. The work around touch with children and their families does not take place in a vacuum but in a larger organizational and legislative context. Additional areas essential to providing competent counseling and play therapy include not only understanding the tasks of the professional around touch within the context of his or her own agency or private practice but also taking into account the roles and tasks of other professionals who are contributing to the promotion of the welfare of the child and their practice perspective. In this respect, it is also important to consider the impact of the larger practice arena such as agencies, organizations, and the legislature, which can also influence outcomes for children.

Some cautions are in order. The proposed touch competencies, comprised of knowledge, values, and skills, should be considered as a beginning understanding and not the "final word" on the use of touch. The suggested practice behaviors are intended to capture the essence of the competency. A number of learning activities are recommended as a way to measure these learning outcomes. These touch competencies are envisioned to provide practitioners with a basic framework that defines effective and sound practice in child counseling and play therapy. The body of knowledge available to those who struggle with touch practice is continuing to evolve but what we currently know is far and away greater than what could be called upon in the past. The practice guidance found in these core competences has been developed to help practitioners, supervisors, administrators, educators, and trainers who have the responsibility for responding to the needs of the most vulnerable child and to ensure that these children do not suffer further disadvantage. Knowledge is continually being updated and we anticipate important developments will take place over the next few years. Therefore, it is incumbent on all professionals to be continually alert to new developments.

Taking the Book With You

The authors recall a highly controversial incident that happened a few years ago when a youngster was expelled from school because he had hugged his teacher in a way that made her feel uncomfortable. The teacher claimed the student had hugged her after she had previously asked him not to touch her. From the student's point of view, it was an innocent hug. In fact, his family identified themselves as "the huggers"—most likely stemming from a cultural orientation toward a lot of hugging. Additionally, this behavior was considered to be a part of family dynamics over many generations. This scenario could easily happen between a practitioner and his or her client, or even between a school counselor and a student in a school hallway.

When this scenario is presented at workshops, it stirs up a heated debate with practitioners on both sides—some are concerned about the possibility of the youngster feeling rejected while others strongly believe the child wrongly crossed a boundary. Even seemingly simple forms of touch, such as holding hands, kindles deep emotional feelings very quickly (Courtney & Gray, 2011, 2014). For a variety of reasons, there are a number of practitioners who acknowledge the positive benefits of providing a caring touch that responds to the needs of the child in therapy, while others see it as highly controversial (Association for Play Therapy, 2015; Aquino & Lee, 2000; Brody, 1997; Courtney & Gray, 2014; Field, 2014; Lynch & Garrett, 2010; McNeil-Haber, 2004; Booth & Jernberg, 2010; Zur & Nordmarken, 2016). Unfortunately, there is little information available to guide the practitioner's full consideration of the multifaceted components of touch in child counseling or play therapy.

Touch in practice can be professionally demanding and sometimes personally stressful. Each new client, regardless of similarities to other clients, is unique. Each practitioner is unique. Each situation is unique and constantly evolves. Our culture, the client's culture, and so many other contexts can influence what we see and how we see it. Further, the demands and stresses presented in each situation may intensify when the client's history includes child abuse, neglect, and/or family violence. Second-guessing difficult boundary decisions related to touch can be overwhelming and plays a role in the tendency to rationalize questionable decisions. All of us can, and sometimes do, overlook something important, make mistakes about decisions related to touch or not to touch in practice, or reach a conclusion that is wrong or even misguided.

Practitioners are called upon to remain alert to how these issues may affect them personally and, when appropriate, consider when to seek peer or other personal support, and undertake relevant education, training, supervision, and/or consultation. We recognize that each practitioner is solely responsible for his or her work and strives to "do the right thing" guided by adhering to ethical standards of practice and following licensing requirements or applicable laws. Looking back on the ideas presented in the book and the insights gained from the various case studies and vignettes presented, we conclude with a summary of recommendations around touch in child counseling and play therapy. Keep in mind that this is not intended to be a comprehensive list, but a working document. As more research is completed and touch-oriented practices with children continue to evolve, we anticipate this list can be added to and improved upon. The recommendations are listed in Table 16.6.

Table 16.6 Recommendations supporting the ethics of touch in child counseling and play therapy.

A Beginning Foundation

Ethical Considerations

- Any sexual contact or inappropriate touching of a child is ethically and morally wrong. When working with children, the "slippery slope" argument as addressed in the literature related to adults is not the primary dynamic between the practitioner and child, nor are the actions against them the same. The inappropriate touching of a child is an egregious violation of ethics constituting a felony that puts the practitioner at severe legal risk including incarceration and being branded a pedophile.
- Practitioners should never touch a child if they are uncomfortable with the touch, sexually aroused, angry, or frustrated.
- Never touch vulnerable areas of a child such as chest, stomach, thighs, trunk area, genitals, or buttocks. As well, never touch a child's legs above the knee; most acceptable areas include the hands, arms, or shoulders.

Self-Awareness

- Practitioners are aware of their own countertransference(s) regarding touch. Additionally, transference issues beginning with the child are also considered.
- Practitioners are cognizant of the positive benefits of touch as well as being aware of situations in which touch may be contraindicated.
- Touch should never be a "secret" within a session.
- Practitioners will know that rejecting a child's reach or desire for a hug (appropriate touch) could potentially cause emotional harm to a child. However, the context of the presenting problem (e.g., sexualized behaviors) may require that therapeutic boundaries be set regarding a child's need for touch.
- Practitioners need to be clear about what type of hug they are comfortable providing and this may vary depending on the developmental level of the child and relevant contextual issues. Some practitioners are only comfortable with side-by-side hugs, and may teach this to the children they work with.

Education, Training, Supervision, and Consultation

- Practitioners who use a touch-based therapy approach must receive advanced education, training, supervision and/or consultation especially when working with children who have been harmed or traumatized by touch.
- Practitioners seek supervision or consultation regarding questionable touch issues that may arise in sessions with children.
- Practitioners document occurrences of touch and adhere to risk management, agency, and institutional policies required for such documentation.
- Practitioners are aware of the most recent literature and research related to touch.

Considerations of Touch in Therapy

- Touch is considered when it meets treatment goals and the individual needs of the child, and not the needs of the practitioner. This includes being attuned to the child's verbal and nonverbal cues regarding touch.
- Practitioners are aware of all the different types of touch that can occur within sessions (e.g., therapist-initiated touch versus child-initiated touch).
- Use informed consent to advise parents or caretakers regarding the treatment goals and if touch is included as a part of therapy. Practitioners will provide examples about different types of touch to parents that can happen in sessions with the child.
- Practitioners are aware of applicable institutional policies regarding touch as well as any local, state, or federal regulations, and seek legal consultation as appropriate.
- Practitioners understand the differences in the developmental needs of children related to touch and how this may change based upon the context and mediating factors that influence the presenting problems.
- Never tickle a child.

- Practitioners assess when a child may need additional referrals; for example, children who have touch sensitivities may need a referral to an occupational therapist.

Special Considerations in the Counseling Relationship with the Child

- Practitioners are attentive to power differentials in the practitioner–child relationship.
- The practitioner considers the range of mediating factors that can affect the child in counseling and play therapy.
- The practitioner is aware of cultural differences related to touch and the proximity of personal space boundaries.
- As a rule of thumb, always ask a child's permission before initiating touch. For example, without pressure of expectation and in respect that the child can say "no," ask, "Could we shake hands to say we agree to work on your new behavior?" If the child gives an affirmative answer, consider this as an indication that the child agrees to the touch.
- Practitioners monitor a child's reactions and responses before, during, and after a touch interaction; for example, if a child initially accepted and permitted the practitioner to hold his or her hand, then it is the practitioner's responsibility to be attuned to the child's cues for when the holding must be released.
- Acknowledge accidental forms of touch, "Oops, my arm just knocked yours." As well, practitioners take note of excessive incidences of "accidental" touch from a child as this could be a clinical issue to address.
- Physical restraint of a child should only be implemented after all other measures have been exhausted, and only to provide safety for the child. Practitioners need to be aware of protocols regarding restraint.
- Practitioners are vigilant regarding touch including situations of physical or sexual abuse so as not to retraumatize a child. Practitioners are especially mindful of quick body movements and space proximity in relationship to the child.

Concluding Comments

There is a distinction between touch practices with children and when working with adults. This book has focused primarily on the question, "How can we go about effectively addressing the myriad of dynamics that surround ethical issues of touch in clinical practice with children?" Reflecting back on the earlier touch incident described in this chapter between the young student and his teacher where the student was expelled, imagine that this boy was your client. Ask yourself what you would do in a situation like this. As a part of your answer, we hope you will take this book with you and consider the core touch competencies aimed at learning and the professional development necessary for successful decision-making practices, along with our beginning recommendations supporting the ethics of touch in child counseling and play therapy. Overall, we hope this book will start a conversation for you.

References

Anderson, L.W., & Krathwohl, D.R. (2001). *A taxonomy for learning, teaching, and assessing: A revision of Bloom's taxonomy of educational objectives*. New York: Longman.

Aquino, A.T., & Lee, S.S. (2000). The use of nonerotic touch with children ethical and developmental considerations. *Journal of Psychotherapy in Independent Practice, 1(3)*, 17–30. DOI:10.1300/J288v01n03_02

Association for Play Therapy (APT). (2015). *Paper on touch: Clinical, professional, & ethical issues*. Retrieved on 10 November, 2016 from: http://c.ymcdn.com/sites/www.a4pt.org/resource/resmgr/Publications/Paper_On_Touch_2015.pdf

Booth, P.B., & Jernbern, A.M. (2010). *Theraplay®: Helping parents and children build better relationships through attachment-based play* (3rd ed.). San Francisco: Jossey-Bass.

Brearley, G. (1991). *Counseling and social work*. Buckingham: Open University Press.

Brody, V.A. (1997). *The dialogue of touch: Developmental play therapy* (2nd ed.). Northvale, NJ: Jason Aronson.

Courtney, J.A., & Gray, S.W. (2011). Perspectives of a child therapist as revealed through an image illustrated by the therapist. *Art Therapy: Journal of the American Art Therapy Association, 8(23)*, 132–139. DOI:10.1080/07421656.2011.599719

Courtney, J.A., & Gray, S.W. (2014). A phenomenological inquiry into practitioner experiences of developmental play therapy: Implications for training in touch. *International Journal of Play Therapy, 23(2)*, 114–129. DOI:http://dx.doi.org/10.1037/a0036366

Field, T. (2014). *Touch* (2nd ed.). Cambridge, MA: MIT Press.

Hunter, M., & Struve, J. (1998). *The ethical use of touch in psychotherapy*. Thousand Oaks, CA: Sage.

Lynch, R., & Garrett, P.M. (2010). "More than words": Touch practices in child and family social work. *Child & Family Social Work, 15*, 389–398. DOI:10.1111/j.1365-2206.2010.00686.x

McNeil-Haber, F.M. (2004). Ethical considerations in the use of nonerotic touch with children. *Ethics and Behavior, 14*, 123–140. DOI:10.1207/s15327019eb1402_3

Thomas, J., & Jephcott, M. (2011, Winter). Touch is a "hot topic". *The Journal of the International and UK Societies of Play and Creative Arts Therapies, 5*.

Strode, M. (1903). Wind-wafted wild flowers. *The Open Court, 17 (8)*, 505. Retrieved on 30 January, 2017 from: http://opensiuc.lib.siu.edu/do/search/?q=muriel%20strode&start=0&context=1068461

Zur, O., & Nordmarken, N. (2016). *To touch or not to touch: Exploring the myth of prohibition on touch in psychotherapy and counseling*. Retrieved on 10 November, 2016 from: http://www.zurinstitute.com/touchintherapy.html

Index

abuse and neglect, working with children impacted by 91–103; boundaries and clear guidelines 96–8; brain images 95; case 99–101; child abuse and trauma 91–3; competence 98–9; cortisol fluctuations 95; discussion questions 101; ethical considerations 95–6; neglect and absence of touch 95; power dynamics 97; "third ear" 99; touch and working with traumatized clients 93–5; vignette 93, 94, 96

abused infant, teenage mother and *see* Firstplay® infant massage storytelling

ADHD (Attention Deficit Hyperactivity Disorder) children in a school setting, use of touch in Theraplay® with 63–72; ADHD and school children 64; calming touch 66–7; case 68–72; commonly used approaches to work with ADHD children 64–5; community-appropriate touch 67; discussion questions 72; engaging touch 66; ethical considerations 67–8; Head Start programs 63; importance of touch in therapy 65; Marschak Interaction Method 69; nurturing touch 66; structuring touch 66; Theraplay® (attachment-based play therapy) 64–5; touch and Theraplay® 65–7

adolescent trauma, healing of 134–46; adolescents, touch, and professional ethics 138–9; Attachment Theory 135; complex relational trauma in adolescents 136–7; dance/movement therapy 137–8; "developmental trauma" 136; discussion questions 146; facilitator cultural considerations, countertransference, and self-care 143; metaphors 141; movement and dance therapy group session example 139–43; post-traumatic stress disorder 136; sample movement and dance group informed consent 144–5; touch deprivation and negative touch 135–6

Adverse Childhood Experiences (ACE) longitudinal study 136

aggressive young children, ethical use of touch and nurturing-restraint in play therapy with 120–31; aggressive behaviors in children and the ethical use of restraint 122; aggressive behavior in young children 120–1; case 125–9; consent for use of nurturing-restraint for young children under 6 years of age 130–1; co-regulation 124; discussion questions 131; ethical considerations regarding the use of touch 121–2; ethical considerations in the use of physical restraint 122–3; importance of reflective supervision for recognizing countertransference and projection 129; importance of touch in child development and healing 121; issue brought to supervision 126; nurturing-restraint approach 123–4; reflective supervision 125; reflective supervision session excerpts 127–8; vignettes 13–4

Ainsworth, M. 169
Allen, T. 98
ambidextrous ethical dilemma 18
American Dance Therapy Association (ADTA) 139
American Psychological Association (APA) 139
Anda, R.F. 136

Animal Assisted Activities (AAA) 189
Animal Assisted Play Therapy™ (AAPT™) 189
Animal Assisted Therapy (AAT) 189
Aquino, A.T. 80, 85, 41, 181
Aristotle 5, 9
Association for Play Therapy (APT) 110, 139
Atkinson, M. 208
Attachment Theory 135
Attention Deficit Hyperactivity Disorder (ADHD) 10, 137
autism *see* DIRFloortime®, touching autism through
Autism Spectrum Disorder (ASD) 10, 76

Baby Tree Hug© 51–2, 54, 57–9
Badenoch, B. 7, 37, 52
Barkley, R.A. 65
Barlow, Jean 202, 205
bereavement groups, preschool *see* StoryPlay®, utilization of touch and (in preschool bereavement groups)
Bester, G. 210
Bonet, Norma 120
Bowen, Murray 51
Bowlby, J. 7, 37, 50, 63, 166, 169, 209
Boyatzis, R.E. 209
brain science of nurturing touch 35–9
Bredy, T.W. 107
Bremner, J.D. 136
Brody, Viola 6, 35, 48, 50, 136
Brown, R.E. 107
Brown, Stuart 48
Buddhist monks 5
Buscaglia, Leo 120

calming touch 66–7
Campos, R. 79
Canine Assisted Play Therapy (CAPT) 189
Canine-Assisted Therapy, Inc. (CAT) 199
canines as co-therapist with children, ethics of touch with 189–99; Animal Assisted Activities 189; Animal Assisted Therapy 189; canines and the therapeutic alliance 190–1; discussion questions 199; ethical touch with canines when using directive play therapy 194–5; ethical touch with canines when using non-directive play therapy 193–4; ethics, touch, and safety between children and canines 192; ethics of touch in therapy with canines 191–2; ethics of touch with traumatized children 195–6; positive benefits of AAT and touch with canines 190; systematic desensitization as adapted to canine-assisted therapy 196–9; vignette 194
Caplan, Mariana 202
caring touch, oxytocin and 7–8
Carlson, F. 4
Carlson, M. 95
Casado-Kehoe, Montserrat 165
Casenhiser, D.M. 78
Castro, Veronica 165
Chandler, C.K. 190
"change agent," parents as 51–2
Chhahbria, R. 78
Child Behavior Checklist (CBCL) 171
Child-Centered Play Therapy (CCPT), healing Reactive Attachment Disorder (RAD) through 149–60; case 152–60; Child-Centered Play Therapy 149–52; diagnosis 153–4; discussion questions, 160; ethics of culture and touch 152; family cultural considerations 155; final phase 158–9; guidelines for ethical use of touch in CCPT 151–2; informed consent considerations 154; initial phase 155–6; middle phase 156–8; outcomes 159–60; touch in CCPT 150; treatment goals, 154
child-initiated touch 9
Child Parent Psychotherapy (CPP) 165; *see also* infant mental health, role of touch in
child-to-child massage model for the classroom *see* teaching positive touch (child-to-child massage model for the classroom)
Child-2-Child Massage Program (AC2C) 205
circle of children 181
civil suits 24
client's needs 41
Coltea, C. 189
community-appropriate touch 67
Cooke, Kristina 120
core competencies and recommendations 217–30; advance professional self-awareness related to touch 223–5; assess touch practices 222; clinical

competencies in touch 218–25; demonstrate ethical and professional behaviors 220; engage touch practices 221; interrelated systems affecting the child 218; intervene in touch practices 223; recommendations 227–9; touch competencies summary 225–6; *see also* ethical and risk-management issues
corrective touch experiences *see* Firstplay® infant massage storytelling
cortisol 7; fluctuations 95; hurtful touch and 8
countertransference: adolescent trauma and 143; autism and 84–5; domestic violence and 116; infant mental health, role of touch in 174–7; reactions 12
Courtney, Janet A. 3, 48, 217
Cozolino, L. 64
Crenshaw, D.A. 138
C-tactile fibers 36, 45
culture 12, 15, 67, 80, 95, 116, 123, 143, 152, 174; cultural norms 12

dance/movement therapy (DMT) 137–8
Dawson, G. 82
Denworth, L. 5
Developmental Play Therapy (DPT) 6, 11, 41–2, 49, 136
"developmental trauma" 136
Dick, B. 65
Diego, M. 107
Diego, M.A. 204
Diorio, J. 108
DIRFloortime®, touching autism through 76–86; approach 77–8; autism spectrum disorder 76; case 81–4; countertransferences and cultural considerations 84–5; culture, role of 80–1; discussion questions 86; ethical considerations of touch 80; evidence-based practice 78; foundational milestones 77; functional, emotional, and developmental goals 78; parent's role 78–9; post-case discussion and the role of touch in treatment; symbolic mothering 85; touch in working with children on the autism spectrum 79
discussion questions: abuse and neglect, working with children impacted by 101; ADHD children in a school setting, use of touch in Theraplay® with 72; adolescent trauma, healing of 146; aggressive young children, ethical use of touch and nurturing-restraint in play therapy with 131; canines as co-therapist with children, ethics of touch with 199; Child-Centered Play Therapy, healing Reactive Attachment Disorder through 160; DIRFloortime®, touching autism through 86; domestic violence, redefining touch for children exposed to 117; ethical and risk-management issues 28; Firstplay® Infant Massage Storytelling 60; infant mental health, role of touch in 175; neurobiology of touch 46; overview 15; StoryPlay®, utilization of touch and (in preschool bereavement groups) 187; teaching positive touch (child-to-child massage model for the classroom) 212
disgruntled clients 23
domestic violence (DV), redefining touch for children exposed to 106–17; case 110–6; clinical implications 116–17; corrective and reparative touch 55, 112–3; countertransference and cultural considerations 116; discussion questions 117; empirical support for the use of touch following traumatic events 108–10; empirical support for the use of touch in psychotherapy 107; ethical considerations of touch 115–16; ethical rationale for utilizing a touch-based intervention 111; impact of domestic violence on children and the importance of touch 107–8; informed consent and assessment 111; Kinesthetic Storytelling® 106, 113; theoretical and research base 106–10
"do no harm" principles 122
Drehobl, K.F. 55
Drose, L.A. 109
Duhn, L. 85

Earls, F. 95
electroencephalogram (EEG) 48
Emerson, Ralph Waldo 217
emotion of touch *see* Child-Centered Play Therapy, healing Reactive Attachment Disorder through
engaging touch 66
Ericksonian-based storytelling 52
ethical and risk-management issues 18–28; ambidextrous ethical dilemma 18;

boundaries in clinical work, concept of 18–22; civil suits 24; consulting colleagues and supervisors 25–6; discussion questions 28; disgruntled clients 23; documenting and evaluating 27–8; ethical and legal risks 22–4; ethical and risk-management guidelines 24–8; licensing boards 23; malpractice 23–4; obtaining legal consultation 27; obtaining proper informed consent 26; potentially helpful touch in a clinical context, view of 20–1; procedural standard of care 25; reviewing appropriate literature 27; reviewing regulations, laws, standards of practice, and policies 26; reviewing relevant ethical standards 26; sexualized touch 25; *see also* core competencies and recommendations

ethical considerations: abuse and neglect, children impacted by 95–6; aggressive young children and 121–2; canines as co-therapist with children 191–2; DIRFloortime®, touching autism through 80; domestic violence, children exposed to 115–16; in grief and StoryPlay® groups 180–1; infant mental health, role of touch in 169–170; use of touch in Theraplay® 67–8

evidence-based practice (EBP) 78

Faa-Thompson, T. 191
Feldman, R. 167, 209
Feldstein, M. 19
Felitti, V.J. 136
Field, T. 107, 109, 135, 168, 204
Filial Therapy 51–2
Finklehor, D. 93
Firstplay® Infant Massage Storytelling 48–60; case 55–6; case implementation 56–60; corrective touch with a teenage mother and her abused infant (case) 55; Ericksonian-based storytelling and StoryPlay® 52; ethical touch, implementing of 54–5; family play therapy and intergenerational family systems theory 51; Filial Therapy (parents as "change agent") 51–2; FirstPlay Therapy® 49–52; harmful effects of touch in infancy 53; infant mental health and attachment 50–51;

mindfulness 52–3; modern attachment theory 50; multigenerational transmission process 51; role of touch in Developmental Play Therapy 49–50; training and the ethics of touch 53–5

Fitzgerald, Helen 178
Fredrick II 5
Fuhr, M.G. 55
Fuller, D. K. 117
functional, emotional, and developmental goals (FEDLs) 78

Ganda infants 167
"Gandhi neurons" 7
Garland, T. 43
Garrett, P.M. 3
Gartrell, N. 19
Gaskill, R.L. 65
Gibb, R. 106
Gil, E. 55
Giles, W.H. 136
Gillette, C.S. 109
Gilligan, Stephen 183
Glover, V. 169
Goleman, D. 209
Golly, Carol 134
Goodyear-Brown, P. 195
Gray, S. 180, 217
Green, E.J. 138
Greenspan, Stanley 77
Gregan, Audrey 76
grief 178–9
Grobbel, Roxanne 120
group therapy: preschool 181–2; adolescents 139–43
Guerney, Bernard 51
Guerney, Louise 51–2

Halprin, Anna 134
Harlow, H. 106, 166
Hart, S. 109
Head Start programs 63
healing touch *see* abuse and neglect, working with children impacted by
Heath, S. 65
Heller, S. 165
Herenstein, M.J. 79
Herman, S. 19
Hernandez-Reif, M. 107, 109
Hertenstein, M. 167
Higgins, Kristan 189

Index

Hippocrates 5, 19
Hispanic cultural considerations regarding touch 174
Hodgson, P. 65
Hunter, M. 107, 217
Hurricane Andrew 109
hurtful touch, cortisol and 8
hypothalamic-pituitary-adrenal (HPA) stress reactions 108

infant massage 50, 168–9
infant massage storytelling *see* Firstplay® infant massage storytelling
infant mental health, role of touch in 165–75; benefits of infant massage and touch 168–9; benefits of touch to caregivers 169; case 170–4; case reflections 174–5; Child Parent Psychotherapy 165–6; discussion questions 175; ethical considerations of touch 169–170; family background 179; Ganda infants 167; Hispanic cultural considerations regarding touch 174; parent–infant attachment 166–7; post-assessment conceptualized 171; protective touch 166; role of touch in child development 167–8; therapist challenges and countertransference 174–7; treatment plan 171–4
interoception 37–8
interpersonal neurobiology 45

Jean, A. 65
Jennings, S. 79, 80
Jernberg Ann 63
Jesus 5

Kaiser, E.M. 109
Keats, John 18
Keltner, D. 63
Kestly, T.A. 65
Kinesthetic Storytelling® 106, 113
King, Amy Davis 178
Kolb, B. 106
Krizek, C. 99
Kuhn, C. 109

Lal, R. 78
Landreth, Gary 6
Lawry, S.S. 93
Lee, A.W. 107
Lee, S.S. 41, 80, 85, 181

LeFeber, M.M. 137
licensing boards 23
Lieberman, Alicia 165
Linden, D. J. 53
Liu, D. 108
Localio, R. 19
Lynch, H. 169
Lynch, R. 3

Maddigan, B. 65
Magic Rainbow Hug© 113–4
Main, M. 169
malpractice, evidence of 23–4
Marschak Interaction Method (MIM) 69
Martin, Bonnie 189
Martin, G. 135
massage 98, 109, 135, 169; vignette 97
Massage in Schools Programme (MISP) 204
McNeil-Haber, F.M. 122, 128, 129
McWilliam-Burton, T. 65
Meaney, M.J. 107, 108
mediating factors and the context of touch related to ethical practice 8–13; child and family cultural norms 12; child and family problems 10–11; child and family religious norms 12; child-initiated touch 9; child's developmental stage 11; child's diagnosis 10; developmental phase of therapy 11; practitioner–child unintended touch 10; practitioner-initiated touch 9–10; practitioner's examination of countertransferences 12–13; practitioner's experience level 11; practitioner's gender 11–12; type of therapeutic modality 11; type of therapy session 11
memento sharing 182–3
mental health, infant *see* infant mental health, role of touch in
Mills, Joyce 52, 179
mirror neurons 7, 37, 45
Mister Rogers 76
Moncur, Janus 189
Montagu, A. 5, 12, 80, 106
Morgan, J. 209
movement and dance therapy group *see* adolescent trauma, healing of
multigenerational transmission process 51
Muslims 12
Myrick, A.C. 138

Nafisi, A. 180
National Association of Social Workers (NASW): Code of Ethics 26, 98, 139; Insurance Trust 19
Nazarian, Vera 149
negative touch 135–6
Neu, M. 169
neural systems 37
neurobiology of touch 35–46; brain–mind–body connection, therapeutic relationship and 39; brain science of nurturing touch 35–9; case presentation 42–4; C-tactile fibers 36, 45; Developmental Play Therapy 41–2; discussion questions 46; emotional touch 36; ethical and clinical considerations of nurturing touch 40–1; implications 40; interoception 37–8; interpersonal neurobiology 45; mirror neurons 7, 37, 45; neural systems 37; neuroplasticity 38–9; Neurosequential Model (Perry) 42; nurturing touch 40; right-brain credibility 39; role of oxytocin in relationships 7, 36–7, 45, 65, 136, 190, 203, 209
neuroplasticity 38–9
Neurosequential Model (Perry) 42
New Testament, people in 5
Nolan, Robert D. 217
Nopmaneejumruslers, K. 78
Nordmarken, N. 139
Nowakowski-Sims, Eva 76
nurturing touch 40; corrective experience of 55; demonstration of 128; distortion of 110; experiences 156–7; family cultural considerations 55; first-play activities 51; lack of 101, 135; need for 113, 115; symbolic mothering and 85; Theraplay® 66

O'Brien, M. 169
O'Connor, K.J. 83
Olarte, S. 19
organ touch 5
Orthodox Jews 12
overview (touch related to professional ethical and clinical practice with children) 3–15; bio-psychosocial-cultural (and spiritual) paradigm shift 7; cortisol and hurtful touch 8; discussion questions 15; feeling dialogue of touch 5–6; "Gandhi neurons" 7; high-profile child sexual abuse cases 4; historical context of touch 5; "love' hormone 7; mediating factors in action (responses) 13–14; mediating factors and the context of touch related to ethical practice 8–13; mind-body connection 7; organ touch 5; oxytocin and caring touch 7–8; Practical Wisdom 9; professional context of the problem of touch related to children 3–5; relevance of advances in neuroscience to touch in clinical practice 6–8; relevance of touch in clinical practice 8–13
oxytocin (OT) 190, 203; caring touch and 7–8; role of in relationships 36–7

Pajareya, K. 78
Palmer, David 202
Panksepp, J. 65
Papadimos, T.J. 108
parasympathetic nervous system (PNS) response 204
parent–infant bond see infant mental health, role of touch in
Parenting Stress Index (PSI) 171
Patton, Stacy 116
Peaceful Touch 204
Pearce, C.M. 135
Peifer, D.E. 135, 138
Pereira, Jenn 149
Perry, B.D. 42, 50, 53, 55, 121, 136
Physical Response Education System (PRES) 204
Pilarz, K. 78
playful hand game 9
Pope, K. 19
Porges, S.W. 37
post-traumatic stress disorder (PTSD) 136, 144
Practical Wisdom 9
preschool bereavement groups see StoryPlay®, utilization of touch and (in preschool bereavement groups)
procedural standard of care 25

Quintino, O. 109

Raasch, Andrea 91
Radey, Melissa 106
Rainbow Hug© imagery 53
Ramachandran, V. S. 7
Rawat, Prem 52

Reactive Attachment Disorder *see* Child-Centered Play Therapy, healing Reactive Attachment Disorder through
Reamer, Frederic G. 18
recommendations *see* core competencies and recommendations
reflective supervision session *see* aggressive young children, ethical use of touch and nurturing-restraint in play therapy with
religious norms 12
Rentz, E.A. 78
Rhee, K. 209
Riccelli, Daniela 134
right-brain credibility 39
risk-management issues *see* ethical and risk-management issues
Rosenthal, H. 209

Sale, K. 99
Satir, Virginia 91
Schaefer, C.E. 83
Schanberg, S. 109
Scharlepp, Rachel 106
Schenker, Maite 165
Schore, A.N. 7, 12, 39, 50, 56
Schore, J.R. 50
Semi-Structured Observation of Parent-Child Interactions 111
Sensory Processing Disorder (SPD) 10, 42; case 42–5
sexual abuse, cases and vignettes 93–4, 96, 99, 196–7
sexualized touch 25
sexual misconduct, prelude to 18
Shanker, S.G. 78
Siegel, D.J. 64
Singer M. 167
Siu, Angela F. Y. 63
Smith, Mark 134
Smith-Adcock, Sondra 149
Snelgrove, C. 65
Spinazzola, J. 109
Stack, D. 65
Stadtman, J. 169
Stammers, Lynn 35
state licensing boards 23
Stawicki, S. 108
Stern, D.N. 48
Stieben, J. 78
St. John, J. 204
St. John, K. 65

Stoicea, N. 108
StoryPlay®, utilization of touch and (in preschool bereavement groups) 178–87; adult group 181; cases 183–4, 184–5; children's group 181–2; circle of children 181; closing "hand-hug" ceremony 186–7; discussion questions 187; ethical considerations of touch in grief and StoryPlay® groups 180–1; four tasks of grieving (Worden) 179; grief and children 178–9; memento sharing 182–3; non-directive group play therapy 186; preschool bereavement group 181; StoryCrafts 185–7; utilizing touch 182
Strozier, A. 99
structuring touch 66
Struve, J. 107, 217
Sutriasa, Shakti 91
symbolic mothering 85
Szalavitz, M. 121

Tai Chi 99
Tannenbaum, B. 108
teaching positive touch (child-to-child massage model for the classroom) 202–12; academic focus 210–11; benefits of the peer massage program 207–11; case vignettes 211; Child-2-Child Massage Program 205, 206; discussion questions 212; empathy and positive touch 209; empowerment and self-esteem 208–9; ethical standards 205; history of child massage in schools 204–7; Massage in Schools Programme 204; overview 202–3; parasympathetic nervous system response 204; Peaceful Touch 204; physiology of touch 203–4; positive peer relationships 209–10; self-awareness of calming sensations 208
Theraplay® *see* ADHD children in a school setting, use of touch in Theraplay® with
Therapy Dogs International (TDI) 199
"third ear" 99
Thompson, M.J. 193
Toth, Viktoria Bakai 48
trauma, adolescent *see* adolescent trauma, healing of
Trauma-Focused Cognitive Behavioral Therapy (TF-CBT) 94

Trauma Symptom Checklist for Young
  Children (TSCYC) 99
traumatized clients 93–5, 195
Tsavoussis, S. 108

United States Association for Body
  Psychotherapy (USABP) 139
U.S. Department of Justice 107
Uvnäs-Moberg, K. 7, 208

van der Kolk, B. 8, 53, 92, 136,
  180, 190
VanFleet, R. 189, 191
Van Horn, Patricia 165
Velasquez, Meyleen 48

Walker, J.D. 136
Webb, N.B. 191

Weber, R. 3, 6
Weiss, S.J. 79
Westland, G. 80, 121, 139
Whelley, Joanne 91
White, H. 65
Whitfield, C. 136
Wieder, Serena 77
Wilson, P. 79
Winnicott, Donald 165
Wolfelt, A. 180
Wood, K. 135
Woods, Danielle 178
Worden, J. 178, 179

Young, C. 53

Zagoory, O. 167
Zur, O. 20, 139